THE Ultimate Basket Book

THE Ultimate
Basket Book

A Cornucopia of Popular Designs to Make

Lyn Siler

LARK
BOOKS

A Division of Sterling Publishing Co., Inc.
New York

Dedication

TO ALL THE BASKETMAKERS
OF YESTERYEAR WHO SO
GENEROUSLY LEFT US HEIR TO
A WEALTH OF BASKETMAKING
STANDARDS, WHICH WE WHO
LOVE THE CRAFT MAY STRIVE
TO ACHIEVE.

EDITOR
Rebecca Guthrie

ART DIRECTOR
Chris Bryant

COVER DESIGNER
Barbara Zaretsky

ASSOCIATE EDITOR
Susan Kieffer

ASSOCIATE ART DIRECTOR
Shannon Yokeley

ART PRODUCTION ASSISTANT
Jeff Hamilton

EDITORIAL ASSISTANCE
Delores Gosnell

EDITORIAL INTERNS
Megan Taylor Cox
Sue Stigleman

ILLUSTRATOR
Carolyn Kemp

PHOTOGRAPHY
Keith Wright

Library of Congress Cataloging-in-Publication Data

Siler, Lyn.
  The ultimate basket book : a cornucopia of popular
designs to make / Lyn Siler.— 1st ed.
      p. cm.
  Includes index.
   ISBN 1-57990-789-X (pbk.)
   1. Basket making. I. Title.
TT879.B3S57 2006
746.41'2—dc22   2005035464

10 9 8 7 6 5 4 3 2 1

First Edition

Published by Lark Books, A Division of
Sterling Publishing Co., Inc.
387 Park Avenue South, New York, N.Y. 10016

Text © 2006, Lyn Siler
Photography © 2006, Lark Books unless otherwise specified
Illustrations © 2006, Carolyn Kemp

Distributed in Canada by Sterling Publishing,
c/o Canadian Manda Group, 165 Dufferin Street
Toronto, Ontario, Canada M6K 3H6

Distributed in the United Kingdom by GMC Distribution Services,
Castle Place, 166 High Street, Lewes, East Sussex, England BN7 1XU

Distributed in Australia by Capricorn Link (Australia) Pty Ltd.,
P.O. Box 704, Windsor, NSW 2756 Australia

If you have questions or comments about this book, please contact:
Lark Books, 67 Broadway, Asheville, NC 28801. Telephone: (828) 253-0467

Manufactured in China

ISBN 13: 978-1-57990-789-1
ISBN 10: 1-57990-789-X

For information about custom editions, special sales, premium and corporate purchases, please contact Sterling Special Sales Department at 800-805-5489 or specialsales@sterlingpub.com.

Contents

Introduction

Did you ever hear anyone say, "I just don't like baskets?" *Never*!

Did you ever hear anyone say, "I don't want any baskets in my home?" *Never*!

I have traveled the world over and have never heard either of those remarks. Everybody likes baskets. They evoke thoughts of home and tradition, as well as feelings of contentment and warmth, in much the same way a well-worn quilt does. And I believe that the appeal of baskets is on the upswing, both as functional items for storage and as decorative accents. In earlier days, baskets really were used in and around the home. They held things—potatoes,

eggs, kindling, berries, flowers, and wool. They were handmade and were passed down from generation to generation, making them even more valuable. Then came the love affair with non-degradable, plastic containers: bags, trays, drawers, and baskets. Thankfully, that trend is waning; handmade baskets have quietly made their way back into our homes and workplaces, to hold the bits and pieces of our everyday lives. And they hold all these things much more charmingly than plastic ever could. My home is filled with baskets brimming with skeins of wool, mail, hand towels, and CDs.

The world marketplace today offers inexpensive baskets you can buy. Or you can join those of us who touch a piece of reed, oak, ash, or willow and feel obligated to weave those materials and create a handmade basket. Basketmaking is rewarding and creative, and once you learn the basics, is a very accessible craft.

In this collection, I have attempted to present you with as many different techniques as possible, using a variety of natural materials. For every pattern, there are

hundreds of variations; feel free to use the pattern as a guide to create your own unique variation.

You'll find many traditional designs, such as a market basket and a melon basket, as well as contemporary adaptations of historic designs… and some brand new designs, too.

I have also tried to classify the skill level of the baskets to make sure you're appropriately challenged— a very difficult thing to do, I might add. It's so hard to say what someone else can and can't do. If you're a relative beginner, but know in your heart and mind that you can do a twill weave, then go for it. Ignore the difficulty level and twill your heart out. You may be the one person in a hundred with a natural penchant for twills. Rib work might be effortless for you, while flat-splint work might prove to be a challenge. We all have our specialties. Try it all. Learn all the techniques and methods from anyone, anywhere you can, and then settle on the ones that capture your heart and make the hours fly. Above all, like my favorite t-shirt says, "do what you love… love what you do." Do this and your work can't be anything less than satisfying perfection.

Basketmaking Basics

Tools

Some tools are essential for basketmaking, while others are optional. The tape measure, awl, clothespins, and pencil are absolute necessities and are readily available. The newer tools on the scene, such as the spoke weight and flex-grip scissors, become essential once you've used them.

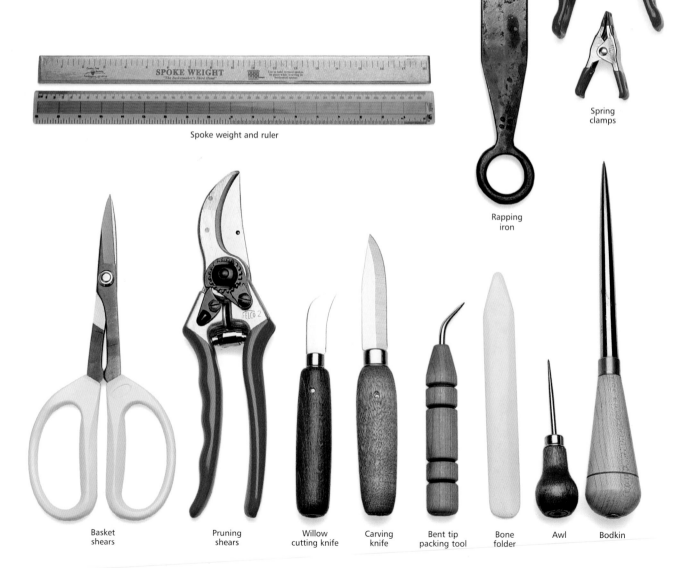

Spoke weight and ruler

Spring clamps

Rapping iron

Basket shears

Pruning shears

Willow cutting knife

Carving knife

Bent tip packing tool

Bone folder

Awl

Bodkin

Materials

Basketry materials have changed very little over the years. They're available in a variety of sizes and can be found in craft and hobby stores, most weaving supply stores, or through mail-order suppliers who advertise in craft and home-decorating magazines. The most frequently used types are shown here.

Sea grass

Willow

A variety of reeds

Size Chart of Materials

ROUND REED (in millimeters)

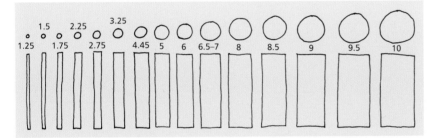

1.5   2.25   3.25
1.25   1.75   2.75   4.45   5   6   6.5–7   8   8.5   9   9.5   10

HALF-ROUND REED

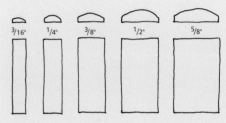

#0 #1 #2 #3 #4 #5 #6 #7 #8 #9 #10 #11 #12 #13 #14

REED SPLINE

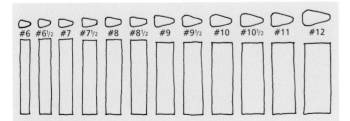

#6 #6½ #7 #7½ #8 #8½ #9 #9½ #10 #10½ #11 #12

SEA GRASS

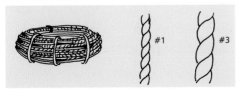

#1   #3

FLAT OVAL REED

3/16"   1/4"   3/8"   1/2"   5/8"

FLAT REED

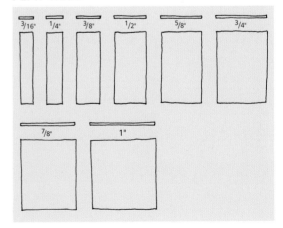

3/16"   1/4"   3/8"   1/2"   5/8"   3/4"

7/8"   1"

Basket Handles

HERB AND KEY BASKET FRAMES

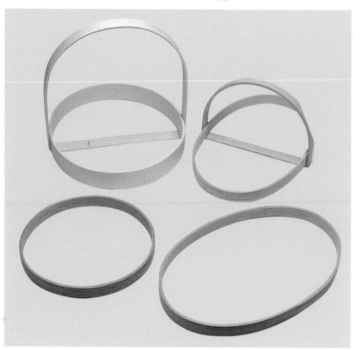

D HANDLES

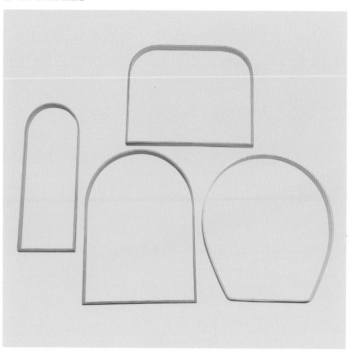

PUSH-IN AND SWING HANDLES

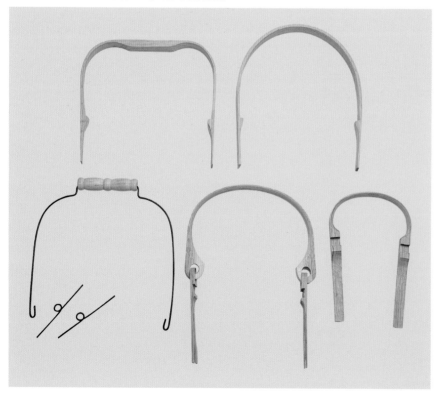

Basket Feet

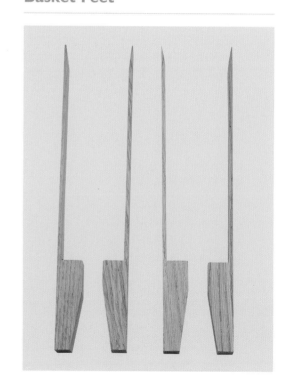

Weaving Variations

Regardless of the materials being used, weaving is the interlacing of one set of elements with another—the weft with the warp. The warp is the stationary set of elements. When you're working with flat splints, the warp consists of stakes and the weft is made up of weavers. With round reed, the warp consists of the spokes, with the weft again being the weavers. In basketry, weaving takes a number of common forms, including the following. It's a matter of semantics, it seems, as most of us recognize a process when it is illustrated or demonstrated, by whatever term we use for that process.

Plain Weave

Plain weave is the simplest and most common of all weaves, done with rigid stakes or spokes and weavers. Each weaver (weft) moves over and under the warp (stake) in opposite order, each round. Variations are achieved by changing the number of overs and unders (figure 1).

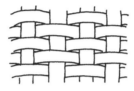
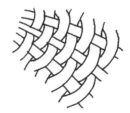

FIGURE 1

Randing

Randing is another term for plain weave, usually referring to round reed or willow. It is a simple over and under weave, done with an even number of stakes (figure 2).

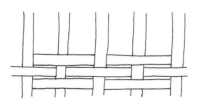

FIGURE 2

Chase Weave

Chase weave is the use of two weavers over an even number of spokes, or one folded in half, producing two ends (figure 3).

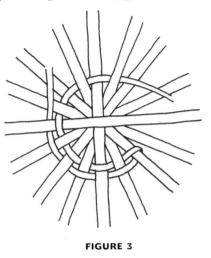

FIGURE 3

Plaiting

This is the general term used in basketry for the interlacing of two flat elements of equal width, whether vertically, horizontally, or diagonally.

Diagonal Plaiting

This is plain weaving with two like elements interwoven at right angles (figure 4).

FIGURE 4

Start-Stop Weaving

Weaving around a base one row at a time, starting and stopping at each row, is known as start-stop weaving. Using flat reed, begin the weaver on the outside of the basket, on the outside of a stake. Weave around the basket and end by weaving over the starting point, cutting the weaver behind the fourth stake.

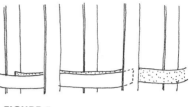

FIGURE 5

Continuous Weaving

To weave continuously means to work with one weaver round after round, weaving over the starting point indefinitely. How you add a new weaver depends on the material you're using. If you're working with flat reed, a new weaver must be added, slipping the new one under the fourth stake from the end of the old weaver. Weave with both old and new until the old one runs out, then continue with the new one. If you're working with round reed, whether weaving a start-stop row or weaving continuously, a new weaver is added. The weaver can be ended after an over or under stroke (figure 6). Some instructions also call for the new weaver to simply be laid beside the old one.

There are several methods of continuous weaving. One element will weave around an odd number of stakes (or spokes) in an alternate over/under pattern (figure 7). In order to successfully work an over/under weave around an even number of stakes (spokes), you must use chase-weave (see figure 3, page 11), working with first one weaver and then the other. Or you can use Indian weave, by weaving one round, tracing the original path for two or four stakes and then weaving over two stakes, which puts the weaver in the alternate over/under pattern (figure 8).

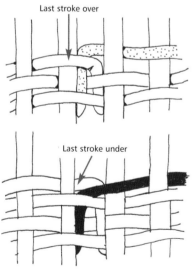

Last stroke over

Last stroke under

FIGURE 6

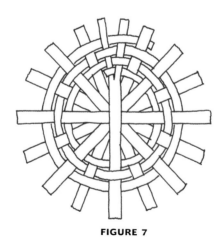

FIGURE 7

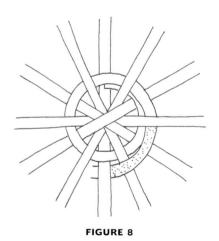

FIGURE 8

Twill Weaving

With flat reed, to twill means that a weft element is taken over two or more warp elements and under one or more. It can be accomplished by working continuous or individual start-stop rows. The illustration shows how to add a new weaver in a continuous twill weave (figure 9). The figure shows the beginning and end of a 2/2 twill start-stop row.

FIGURE 9

Continuous Twill Weaving

When you're working a continuous twill weave, the total number of stakes (or spokes) is critical. For example, working an over two, under one twill continuously requires a total number of stakes that is divisible by three, plus or minus one. If the number is minus one, the design will spiral to the right; if it is plus one, the design will spiral to the left. An over three, under two twill must have a total number of stakes that is divisible by five, plus one or plus four.

It is possible to work a continuous chase twill weave. Working in an over three, under two pattern, the total number of stakes must be divisible by five plus three. For example, 12 stakes x 12 stakes is a total of 48 stakes, which is 45 (which is divisible by five), plus three. An over two, under one pattern may be worked over a total number of stakes that is divisible by three, plus one. Continuous twill weaves may be worked over odd numbers as well, in the same formulas that were used for continuous chase weaves (figure 10).

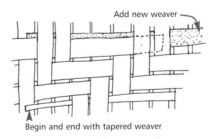

Add new weaver

Begin and end with tapered weaver

FIGURE 10. Continuous twill weave

Coiling

Coiling is an extremely tight and rigid method of basket construction, using a rigid core that is wrapped and stitched with a softer, more flexible material. Rows of the wrapped core are stacked (coiled) rather than woven (figure 11).

FIGURE 11

Three-Rod Wale

Also known as triple weave, three-rod wale is worked with three weaving elements and started behind three consecutive spokes. Each time, the farthest left weaver is taken over the two spokes to the right, behind the next and out to the front. In the illustration, the arrow shows the future path of weaver A, which is the farthest left. Next, weaver B will move over two spokes to the right, behind the third stake, and out to the front. Just be sure each time to use the farthest left weaver (figure 12).

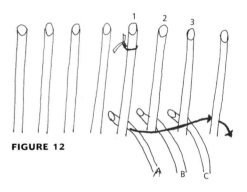

FIGURE 12

Four-Rod Wale

Four-rod wale is worked exactly like three-rod wale, except with four weavers instead of three. Of course, a five-rod wale would simply be worked with five weavers. With any of the wales, the important thing to know is that each weaver is started behind four consecutive spokes (or stakes), and each weaver is taken in its turn to the right, over three (in the case of four-rod) spokes, behind the next and out to the front again (figures 15–18).

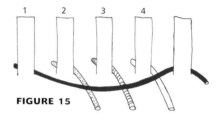

FIGURE 15

Three-Rod Coil

Also known as triple weave, three-rod coil is a single row of three-rod wale that ends with a step-up and a lock. It is woven around to the three spokes prior to the starting spokes, and then steps-up and locks (figure 13). To step-up, move the right-most weaver in front of two spokes, behind one and out to the front. Repeat with each of the three weavers. To lock them in place, push the ends, starting with the right weaver first, under the weavers already in place, coming out to the front of the basket. The weaver will end under its own starting place (figure 14).

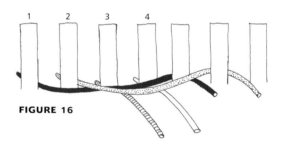

FIGURE 16

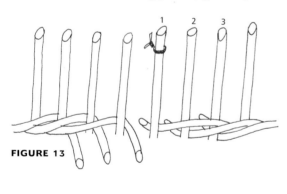

FIGURE 13

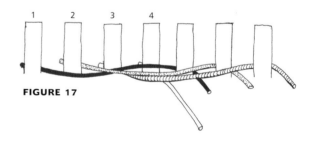

FIGURE 17

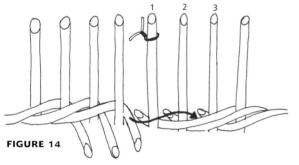

FIGURE 14

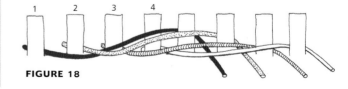

FIGURE 18

Four-Rod Step-Up

A step-up is needed if you are going to work a coil and do not want the pattern to spiral. It is a way of repositioning the weavers without continuing the waling. Instead of moving the leftmost weaver, the farthest right moves each stroke in its turn (figure 19). The farthest right weaver moves over three stakes, behind the fourth and is out to the front. The next weaver, which is now the farthest right weaver, has been moved (figure 20). The third moves and all four weavers are in place (figure 21). The step-up is complete (figure 22). If you are interested in working a four-rod arrow, the weavers are now in the correct position to begin.

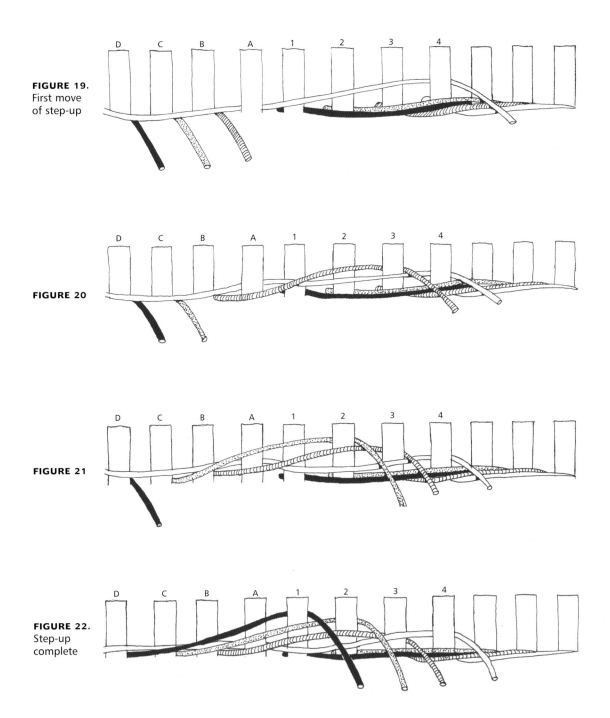

FIGURE 19.
First move
of step-up

FIGURE 20

FIGURE 21

FIGURE 22.
Step-up
complete

Four-Rod Arrow

A four-rod arrow consists of one row of four-rod wale, a step-up, one row of reverse four-rod wale, and a step-up and lock

To work a four-rod reverse row, move the left-most weaver, each in its turn, over three stakes while also moving it under the ends of the other three spokes. It continues over the next three stakes, behind the fourth and out to the front. Figures 23 through 26 show each weaver completing the stroke, each one in its turn.

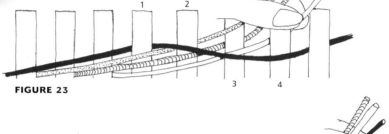

FIGURE 23

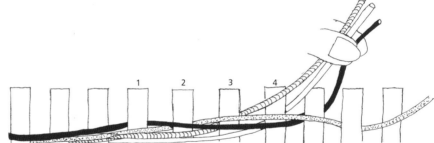

FIGURE 24

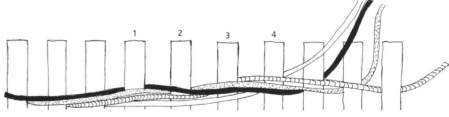

FIGURE 25

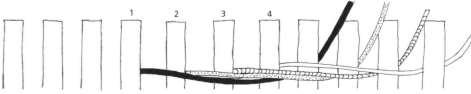

FIGURE 26

Twining

Note: For simplicity, the terms spoke and stakes are both used, but also note that twining, as well as waling, can be done when using either spokes or stakes. In basketry, twining is usually done with round reed, worked over or around either flat or round reed. Twining is often used as a locking row around flat bases to hold the stakes in place. To do this, begin by either (a) folding a round reed off center, so both weavers don't end at the same time, or (b) starting two pieces behind consecutive stakes. Twine around the corners of bases. Always weave around the corner with the bottom weaver first, and then take the top one under. In twining around an upright handle, pretend it is lying flat and weave as you normally would. To lock a row of twining, push the ends under the row that is already in place. To end twining after several rows, push the ends into the weaving beside two consecutive spokes or stakes (figures 27 through 33).

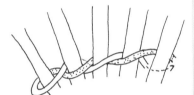

FIGURE 27. Twining

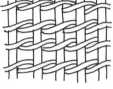

FIGURE 28. Twining with one weaver

FIGURE 29. Twining with two weavers

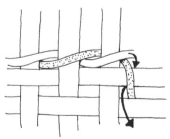

FIGURE 30. Twining around corner

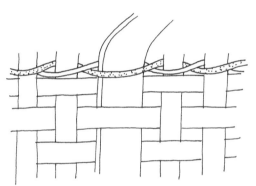

FIGURE 31. Twining around D handle

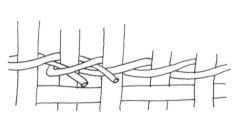

FIGURE 32. Ending twining after one row

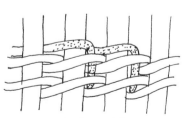

FIGURE 33. Ending twining after multiple rows

Decorative Twining Arrow

1. Work one row of plain twining (figure 34).

2. Work a step-up. Move the farthest right weaver over one stake to the right, behind the next and out to the front (figure 35). Move the other weaver over one stake to the right, behind the next one and out to the front.

3. Work one row of reverse twining. The left weaver moves next over stake #2, under the right weaver, behind stake #3 and out to the front. Next, the left weaver moves over spoke #3, under the right weaver, behind stake #4 and out to the front. Repeat with each left weaver (figure 36).

4. As in figure 37, end the row of reverse twining, taking the ends of both the weavers behind the beginning spokes and going under the weaving already in place (figure 38). To add a weaver when twining around flat or round reed, push the old end into the twined area beside a spoke after an over stroke. Push the end of the new weaver into the weaving beside the spoke before and continue with it (figure 39).

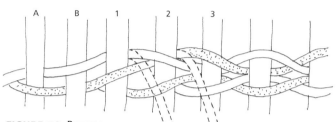

FIGURE 36. Reverse twining starting arrow

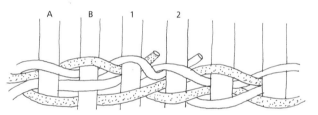

FIGURE 37. Reverse twining ending arrow

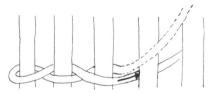

FIGURE 38. Reverse twining single row

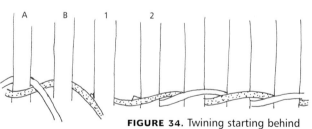

FIGURE 34. Twining starting behind 1 and 2 and ending behind A and B

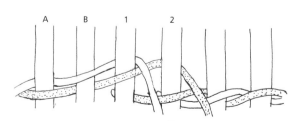

FIGURE 35. Step-up

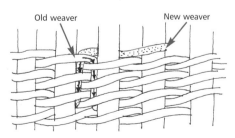

FIGURE 39. Adding weaver to twining

Weaving Techniques

If you are learning to make baskets on your own, eventually you would discover most of these techniques. These are important, tried and true techniques that will save you valuable time. The trial and error method could render some less than great baskets.

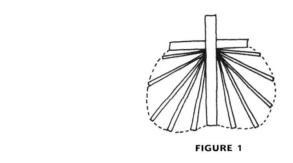

FIGURE 1

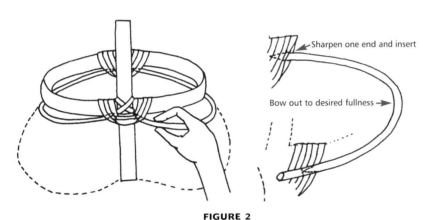

←Sharpen one end and insert

Bow out to desired fullness→

FIGURE 2

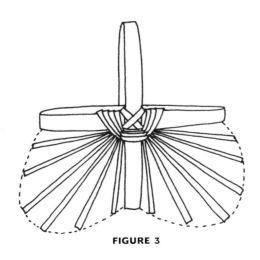

FIGURE 3

How to Measure Your Own Rib Lengths

If you're going to be a basketmaker, you must learn to create your own rib lengths. Granted, it takes some practice, but you can learn to do it by sight if you want to. Here's how:

1. Get a mental picture of the shape you want, visualizing the size of the hoops, the height of the handle, the depth of the basket, and other details. Sketch it on paper and refer to the sketch often (figure 1).

2. Join the hoops and construct the ears, based on the specific projects.

3. Sharpen one end of a piece of reed (the size you think you need) and push the sharpened end into the ear. Then hold the piece around to the other ear, allowing it to protrude to the correct fullness. Allow about $1/2$ inch to be pushed into the other ear, mark, and cut. Sharpen the other end (figure 2).

4. Cut another rib for the other side, just like the first one. Repeat this procedure for each rib. Really look at your basket, and make adjustments if the shape isn't looking like you want it to. Stand away from it so you can study it objectively; sometimes we're too close to really see the shape (figure 3).

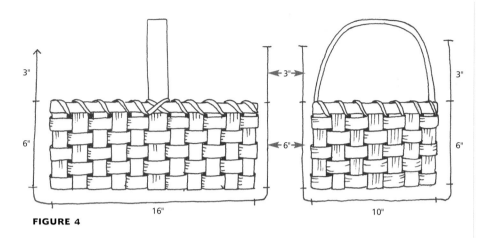

FIGURE 4

How to Measure Your Own Staked Baskets

This is a simple mathematical process. Determine the size basket you want; for example, let's make a 10 x 16 x 6-inch basket. To get a length measurement, add the base length (16 inches) and each side depth (6 inches on each side or 12 inches), and then add 6 inches (3 inches on each side) to tuck in at the top: 16 + 12 (2 sides) + 6 (tucking) = 34 inches.

To get the width measurement, add the base width (10 inches) and each side depth (6 inches) with the same 6 inches for tucking: 10 + 12 (two sides) + 6 = 28 inches.

The only thing left to determine is what size reed to use, and therefore, how many of each to cut. Draw off the area and use a ruler to figure out how many pieces of each to use. Don't forget to add spaces between stakes (figure 4).

How to Measure Spokes for a Round Basket

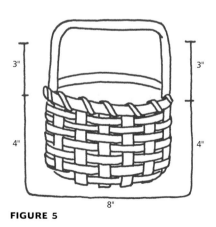

FIGURE 5

Simple! Determine the diameter of the base, 8 inches in this case. Add to that the height you want, 4 inches in this case, and then add the 6 inches for tucking in: 8 + 8 (4 inches for each side) + 6 = 22 inches. How many stakes to be cut will be determined by the size reed you use and how close together you want the spokes. You can use more stakes and start weaving closer in to the center if you taper the center, as in the drawing (figure 5).

How to Identify the Wrong Side of the Reed

There are exceptional cases in which you can hardly identify the wrong and right side of reed, but normally when it's bent over your finger, the wrong side splinters and looks very hairy, while the right side remains smooth (figure 6).

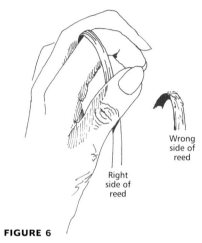

FIGURE 6

Where to Start Weaving on a Staked or Spoked Basket

Always begin the first row by wrapping the weaver around the stake that originates from underneath the woven mat or base. These stakes are anchored by a horizontal stake; the top ones are not and will not stay in place if you begin weaving around them. If you've twined around the base of a basket, this doesn't apply because all the stakes are anchored (figure 7).

FIGURE 7

Avoiding a Build-Up From Overlapping

To avoid creating a build-up from repeatedly starting and stopping (and consequently overlapping) in the same spot, move the basket a quarter turn after every row. That way you won't have to search for the ending on the last row and will know right away where to begin the next.

Losing a Lasher

To lose a lasher means to put it somewhere it can't be seen. Usually, the best way is to push it up between the two rim pieces, over the woven basket side, and back down on the other side. Cut it flush with the rim edge and it will never be seen.

Where to Begin Lashing the Rim

If you place your splices on each rim (inner and outer) near (not at the same spot, but near) the joint of the rim filler, and begin lashing just past all those joints, any fullness you might have in the rim pieces will be worked out at the end (figure 8).

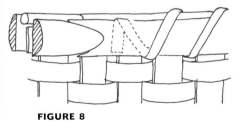

FIGURE 8

Scarfing or Beveling the Ends of the Rim Pieces

Anyone can see that two pieces of flat oval overlaid are going to be thicker than the rest of the reed. If some of the oval side is shaved away and the two overlapped areas are scarfed to fit together, you should have a joint the same thickness as the rest of the rim. This is one of the small details that contribute to a well-made basket (figure 9)

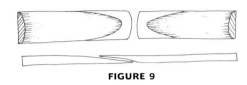

FIGURE 9

Placement of Hoops for Ribbed Baskets

Always put the handle on the outside of the rim. Think about it—if the handle hoop is on the inside of the rim hoop, the hoop can move, but where can it go if it is on the outside.

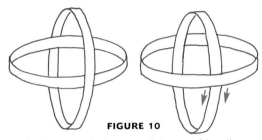

FIGURE 10

Left: rim can't slip because diameter of handle hoop decreases. Right: rim can easily slip

How to End a Row When Weaving Individual Rows

If you start the weaver on the outside of the basket (it's easier to see what is happening that way), weave all the way around, and then continue weaving over the starting point and on to the fourth stake. Cut the weaver so its end lies in the middle of the fourth stake. Even though it doesn't appear to be hidden now, it will be when that stake stands on the next row (figure 11).

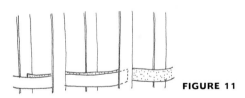

FIGURE 11

Shaping and Reshaping

In case your shaping doesn't quite work out while you're weaving the basket, it almost always can be reshaped. Rewet the basket, being very careful not to soak any machine-made hoops, and mold with your hands to reshape.

If the basket does not sit level, place a heavy object on the side that isn't sitting properly and let it dry into shape. Bricks, stones, soup cans, or other heavy objects can serve as weights (figure 12).

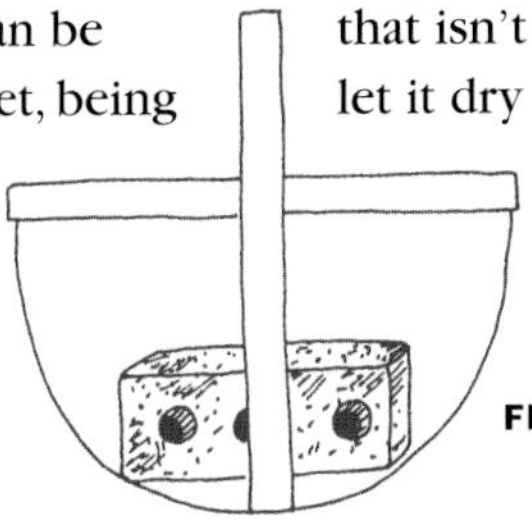

FIGURE 12

Twilling

Twill weaving is a matter of the warp passing over two or more elements of the weft. When you are taking the weaver over two stakes, stepping-up means to weave over the second stake that was covered on the row before, plus the next one that was not covered before. Dropping back is to weave over a new, uncovered stake and the first of the two that were covered by the last row (figures 13 and 14).

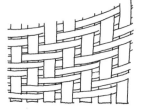

FIGURE 13

FIGURE 14

How to Add on a Weaver or Change Colors in a God's Eye

If a weaver breaks or runs out, the best way to add another is to have it end on a diagonal. Go back and start a new one by slipping the end under the old weaver and weave over the old one behind 3, then continue as usual.

If your God's Eye began with a wrap around 1, to make a complete revolution, it must return to 1. To change colors, stop the weaver at 1; tuck a new end into

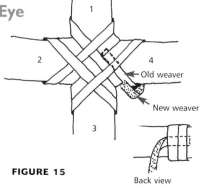

FIGURE 15

Back view

the wraps behind 1, bringing it around and over the new end, then continue as usual (figure 15).

Truing a Base

To true a base means to measure it on all sides and adjust anything that isn't correct. When it's adjusted and you're sure the measurements are correct, mark the corners in pencil on the two adjacent sides. When you begin weaving, you will be aware of any shifting because the corner marks will be out of alignment (figure 16).

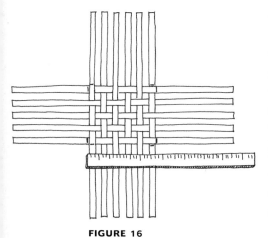

FIGURE 16

How to Replace a Broken Rib

- Remove the broken rib by pulling one piece out and then the other.
- Insert an awl into the weaving to hold the weavers in place until you replace the rib.
- Cut another rib of equal size and length; soak it until it's very flexible.
- Bend the rib severely enough so that both ends can be started into the weaving at once.
- Gradually work the two ends of the new rib into the weaving while allowing the new rib to form itself to the curve of the original rib (figure 17).

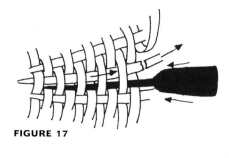

FIGURE 17

How to Replace a Broken Stake

If a stake breaks (or is too short), simply cut a length of reed similar in size and slide it into the weaving on top of the broken stake down to the base of the basket. The new piece should be exposed to the outside of the basket (figure 18).

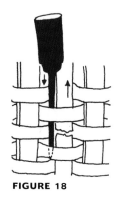

FIGURE 18

Basket Projects

Wine Basket

Cleverly designed to hold two bottles of wine in separate compartments, the Wine Basket has filled-in spaces on the base so it is safe to carry even expensive wines. Color it, add decorative strips, or just leave it plain.

DIMENSIONS
APPROXIMATELY
4¹/₂ X 9 X 14 INCHES

BASKETMAKER
JIMMIE KENT

SKILL LEVEL: **Easy**

Materials

4¹/₂ x 14-inch basket handle

¹/₂-inch flat reed (stakes)

³/₈-inch flat reed (weavers)

³/₁₆-inch flat reed (lashing and divider)

¹/₂-inch flat-oval reed (rim)

#6 round reed (rim)

Cutting the Stakes and Weaving the Bottom

Begin by marking a center on the bottom (topside) of the handle. From the ¹/₂-inch flat reed, cut eight strips that are 27 inches long and five strips that are 34 inches long. From the ³/₈-inch flat reed, cut four strips that are 15 inches long. Mark the centers of all the pieces on the wrong (rough) side. Soak them all in cool water for 2 to 3 minutes.

Begin by laying three of the 34-inch strips horizontally on the table in front of you, wrong sides up, making the two outside pieces fit the width of the handle (about 4¹/₂ inches). Place the handle on top of the three strips, aligned with the center marks of all the strips (figure 1).

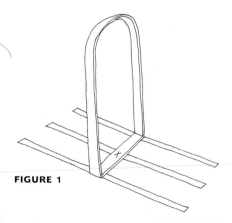

FIGURE 1

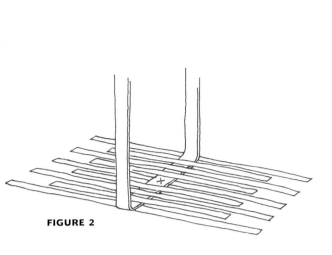

FIGURE 2

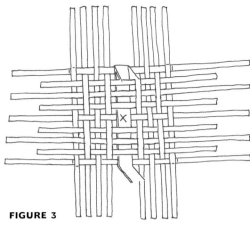

FIGURE 3

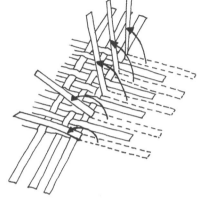

FIGURE 4

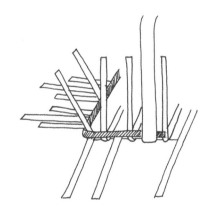

FIGURE 5

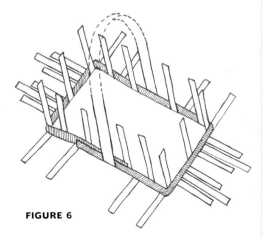

FIGURE 6

Align the center of the middle stake with the center mark on the handle bottom. Place the other 34-inch strips on top of the handle, spacing them evenly. Then lay the 15-inch strips on either side of the two longer strips with the center marks aligned. While weaving the bottom, treat the long strip and the short strip on either side as one stake (figure 2).

Weave the bottom with the 27-inch pieces in a basic over and under pattern. The first row, closest to the handle, should weave under the first stake, over the next 3, under 1, over 3, and under 1. The next row is woven opposite the first (over the first stake, under 3, etc.). Repeat these two pattern rows with all the remaining 27-inch strips, four rows on each side of the handle (figure 3). When all the rows are woven, measure and true the base to approximately $4\frac{1}{2}$ x 9 inches.

Upsetting the Stakes and Weaving the Sides

Upsett the stakes by bending each stake over upon itself toward the woven base, forming a permanent crease at the base of the stake (figure 4). The stakes will not remain upright until two rows of weaving are done.

Begin weaving with a soaked piece of $\frac{3}{8}$-inch flat reed by placing the end on the outside of the stake to the right or left of the handle, depending on which direction you prefer to weave. The wrong side of the reed should be toward the inside of the basket.

By beginning at this point, you will be making the stakes that originate from underneath the woven mat stand up first. A horizontal stake anchors them (figure 5). For a while, ignore the short filler strips. Leave them lying down and only deal with the long stakes.

When you have woven all the way around the basket, end by going over the first four stakes you wove. Cut the weaver behind the fourth stake. Both ends will be hidden either behind a stake or a weaver (figure 6).

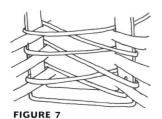

FIGURE 7

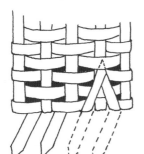

FIGURE 8

Weaving the Divider

Once the first two rows are woven, begin the divider (a long piece of soaked, 3/16-inch flat reed) by tucking one end under a 3/8-inch weaver as it goes around the handle on the inside of the basket. It then begins a figure eight pattern by moving to the other side of the handle and around the outside. The divider is hidden on the outside of the handle underneath the 3/8-inch weavers.

Continue the figure eight all the way up as you weave the sides of the basket and finish it by securing the end under the last row of weaving, just as you began. Be sure the divider strip is securely fastened, even if you must make a complete turn around the last weaver (figure 7).

After you have woven four rows around the basket, you can point the ends of the four filler strips and tuck them under the fourth row of weaving. Allow the ends to lean inward to form a point, under row four (figure 8). Weave a total of 16 rows (if you use all 3/8-inch flat reed).

Finishing the Top and Lashing

Finish the tops of the stakes by cutting the inside stakes flush with the last row of weaving and pointing the outside stakes to a length that can be tucked into the weaving inside the basket, thereby hiding all the ends (figure 9). Dampen the ends before bending them if they are dry.

After finishing the stakes, place a soaked piece of 1/2-inch flat-oval reed around the inside top of the basket, covering the top row of weaving. Bevel the ends for an inch or two with a knife or shaper and allow them to overlap as far as they are beveled (figure 10).

Hold the flat-oval reed in place with clothespins. Next, follow the same procedures with the flat-oval reed on the outside of the basket. Hold both pieces in place with the same clothespins (figure 11). Then place

the #6 round reed between and on top of the two pieces of 1/2-inch flat-oval reed, still using the same clothespins to secure all the reeds. Cut the piece of #6 round reed 1 to 2 inches too long, so that it can be cut to fit later.

Begin lashing with the soaked 3/16-inch flat reed by bringing the end up between the two pieces of flat-oval reed and moving over and under the rim pieces, from one hole to the next (figure 12). When you have lashed all the way around the basket, end the weaver by the same means you began. Bring the end of the lashing weaver up between the two rim pieces and cut off flush with the top. Make the ends of the #6 round butt together. If you wish, you can begin another piece of weaver and lash in the opposite direction, forming an X on the rim and the handle.

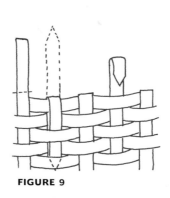

FIGURE 9

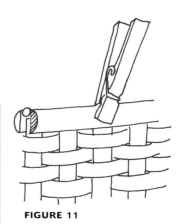

FIGURE 11

FIGURE 10

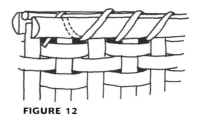

FIGURE 12

Materials

- 10 x 14-inch D handle
- 3/4-inch flat reed (stakes)
- 1/2-inch flat reed (weavers)
- 1/2-inch colored flat reed, long enough to go around the basket two times
- 1/4-inch colored flat reed, long enough to go around the basket one time
- 5/8-inch flat-oval reed (rim)
- #6 round reed or sea grass (rim filler)
- 1/4-inch flat reed (lashing and base filler)

* Measurements for a shallower version are given in parentheses throughout the instructions.

Two-Pie Basket

SKILL LEVEL: **Easy**

A great beginner basket that looks more advanced with its strips of color, it can also be made in a shallower version. The "D" handle is easy to make because it is incorporated into the basket from the beginning.

DIMENSIONS
**APPROXIMATELY
10 X 18 X 14 INCHES**

BASKETMAKER
JIMMIE KENT

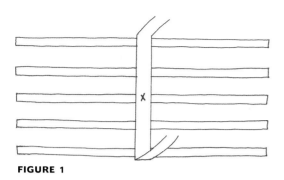

FIGURE 1

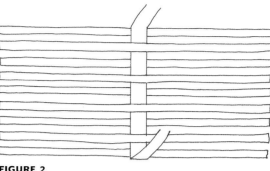

FIGURE 2

Cutting the Stakes and Weaving the Base

From the ¾-inch flat reed, cut nine pieces that are 36 inches (29 inches) long and 14 pieces that are 27 inches (20 inches) long. On the wrong (rougher) side, make a pencil mark at the halfway point on all the pieces. Soak all 23 pieces in cool water for a couple of minutes. Make a pencil mark on the handle at its center point as well.

Lay five of the 36-inch pieces horizontally on a table in front of you, wrong side up, with the center marks aligned. Then place the D handle across them on top of the center marks, making sure the center stake is in line with the center mark on the handle (figure 1).

Next, lay the other four 36-inch stakes across the D handle, in the same direction as the first five, in the spaces between the first five (figure 2).

If all this is too much to hold in place, lay a heavy book on one end of the stakes while you weave in some of the vertical stakes.

Weave the fourteen 27-inch stakes, in a plain over-under pattern (figure 3). There will be seven on each side of the handle. Although the illustration shows only one side of the handle woven, the other side should be exactly the same.

Upsetting the Stakes and Weaving the Sides

Upsett all the stakes by turning them over upon themselves (figure 4). They won't stay upright, but the crease in the stake must be made.

Begin weaving by standing the stake just past the handle (it originates from underneath the woven base) and placing the end of the weaver on top of it (figure 5). Continue to weave in the over and under pattern all the way around the basket.

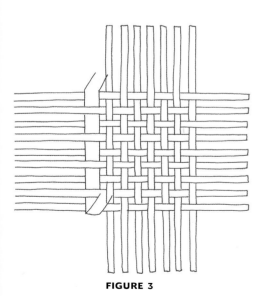

FIGURE 3

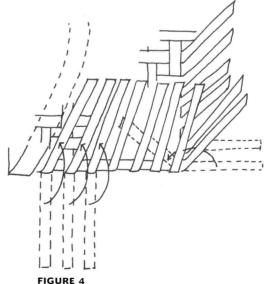

FIGURE 4

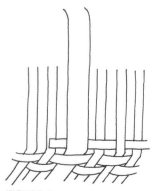

FIGURE 5

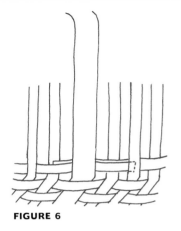

FIGURE 6

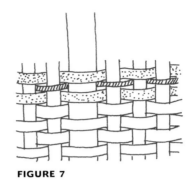

FIGURE 7

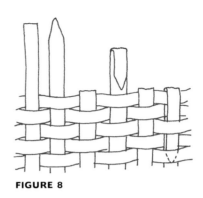

FIGURE 8

When the weaver reaches its starting point, overlap four stakes (right over the beginning of the weaver) and cut it on top of the fourth stake (figure 6).

Treat the handle as another stake. Also note that the corners are not squared, but rather rounded gently.

Weave four rows, one at a time, in this manner:

Row 5: woven the same, but with the 1/2-inch colored reed

Row 6: woven the same, but with the 1/4-inch colored reed

Row 7: woven the same, but with the 1/2-inch colored reed (figure 7)

Rows 8–12: woven in natural, as the first four rows

Finishing and Applying the Rim

Cut off the inside stakes even with the top of the weaving, and shape the outside stakes to a point so they can be inserted into the weaving on the inside of the basket. You want to have enough length to push the end of the stake down to the third weaver or farther (figure 8).

When all the outside stakes are inserted, wrap a soaked piece of the 5/8-inch flat-oval reed all the way around the outside top edge of the basket, overlapping the ends about 2 inches. Shave some of the thickness off the bottom piece. Hold this reed in place with clothespins. Then wrap another piece of the 5/8-inch

flat oval reed around the inside top edge of the basket, overlapping the ends as before. Hold the two pieces with the same clothespins. Insert the piece of #6 round reed or sea grass on top of the rim, between the two pieces of flat-oval reed, letting the ends overlap for the moment.

With a long strip of 1/4-inch flat reed, begin to lash all the rim pieces together (figure 9). Use the awl to open up the space for lashing, just underneath the rim, if necessary. Lose the end of the lasher in the rim.

Fill the open spaces in the bottom with soaked 1/4-inch flat reed (figure 10). Simply weave opposite each row of stakes, turning around the outside stakes and weaving back the other way. Overlap the ends, as you normally would end a start-stop row.

If you choose to make the shallow version, you can weave two rows of natural, the three rows of color, and two more rows of natural, or you might want to use 1/4-inch flat for all three rows of color (figure 11). Rely on your own imagination to decide what colors to use and where to use them.

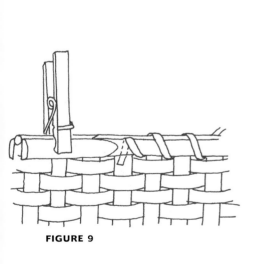

FIGURE 9

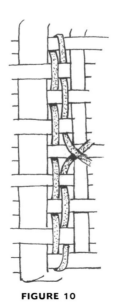

FIGURE 10

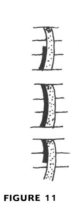

FIGURE 11

Hearth Basket

Materials

- 12 x 14-inch D handle
- ⁵⁄₈-inch flat reed (weavers & stakes)
- #6 round reed (rim)
- ³⁄₁₆-inch flat reed (lashing)
- #2 round reed (twining)
- ¹⁄₂-inch half-round reed (optional runners)

SKILL LEVEL: **Easy**

This basket design has been used for years to carry wood and to sit near or on the hearth. It also makes an ideal carrier or magazine basket. Whatever its use, it is a lovely, serviceable design.

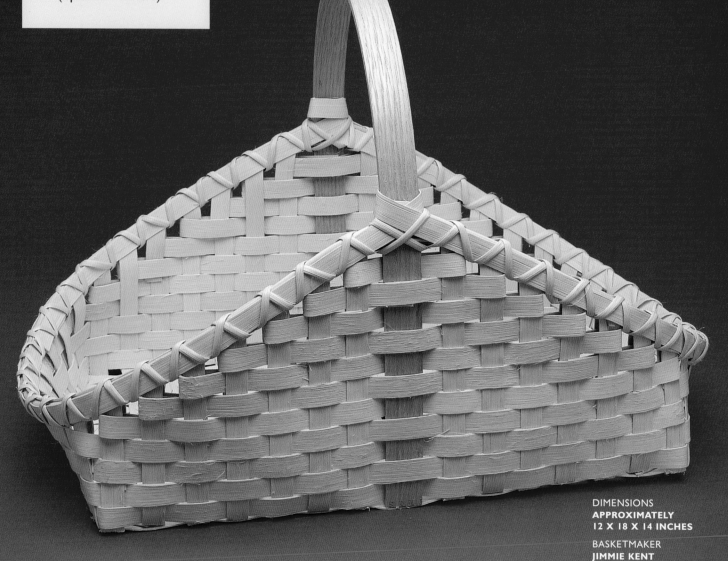

DIMENSIONS
**APPROXIMATELY
12 X 18 X 14 INCHES**

BASKETMAKER
JIMMIE KENT

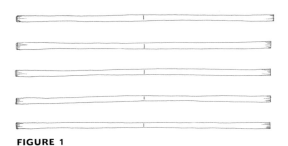

FIGURE 1

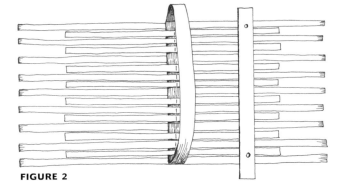

FIGURE 2

Preparing the Materials

Use a pencil to mark the halfway point on the bottom of the D handle. Select several of the heaviest strips of ⅝-inch flat reed. From these strips, cut nine pieces that are 30 inches long and eight pieces that are 25 inches long (to be used as fillers). Then cut the following:

4 pieces, 33 inches
4 pieces, 30 inches
4 pieces, 28 inches
2 pieces, 26 inches

Determine the right and wrong side of the reed; the wrong side is the rougher side. Measure and mark the halfway point on the wrong side of all these pieces. Place all the strips of reed in a container filled with warm water to soak a couple of minutes.

Weaving the Bottom of the Basket

On a table in front of you, place five of the 30-inch stakes horizontally, wrong side up. Place them so the outermost two are 12 inches apart, measuring from the outside edges (figure 1).

Next, place the D handle on top (vertically) of the five strips, making sure it is exactly on the halfway mark on the reed. Note: If your handle happens to be a little wider or a little narrower than 12 inches, simply adjust the five stakes by sliding them apart or pushing them in enough so that the outermost two are even with the outside edges of the handle.

Now, place the last four 30-inch stakes on top of the handle (horizontally, like the first five), in the spaces between the first five, wrong

side up. Also, place the 25-inch pieces on each side of the four 30-inch pieces. Note: It is awkward to hold all these pieces in place until 2 or 3 rows are woven. A spoke weight or large book on one end of the horizontal stakes will help hold them in place (figure 2).

The 25-inch filler pieces will be treated as one with the 30-inch pieces. Begin weaving across the base vertically with the longest (33 inch) stakes. Weave one on each side of the handle (figure 3). Continue to weave stakes in, alternating overs and unders in descending order, until all 14 pieces are in place (figure 4). The left side of the base (not shown) is identical to the right.

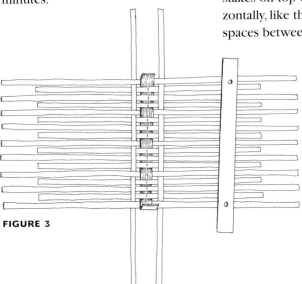

FIGURE 3

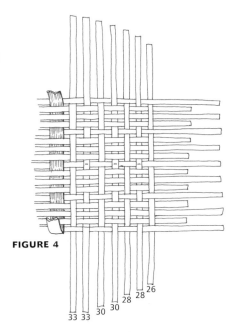

FIGURE 4

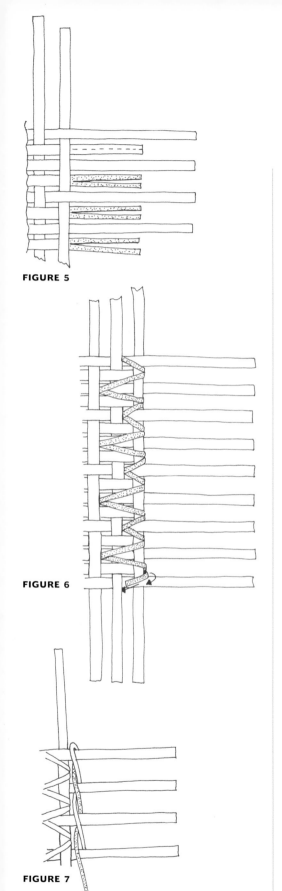

FIGURE 5

FIGURE 6

FIGURE 7

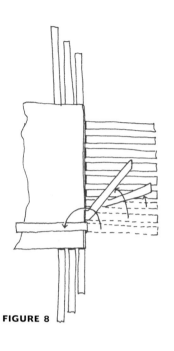

FIGURE 8

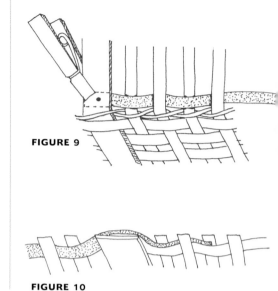

FIGURE 9

FIGURE 10

Cut all the filler pieces down the center of the stake to the edge of the woven base (figure 5). Rewet the filler pieces if necessary. Bend them over and tuck them under the first available (vertically) woven stake. Half the split goes under a stake to the right and the other half to the left (figure 6). Measure and true the base to 12 x 18 inches. Mark the comers with a pencil once the base is trued.

With a long soaked #2 round reed weaver, twine around the base (figure 7). Begin by folding the weaver in half. Place the fold around any stake and twine around one row. End the twining by pushing the end under itself where it began.

Weaving the Sides

Rewet the weavers if they are dry. To upsett the sides, bend each stake, vertical and horizontal, all the way over (to the inside) upon itself, forming a permanent crease at the base. Use ruler or piece of heavy cardboard as a guide for upsetting the sides (figure 8).

Row 1: With a long, wet strip of $\frac{5}{8}$-inch flat reed, begin weaving by placing the end of the strip on the inside of the handle and weaving over and under each stake. Weave all the way around the basket, over 1, under 1, etc (figure 9). Treat the handle as another stake. When you return to the starting point, allow the two ends to overlap four stakes before cutting. Make sure both ends are hidden (figure 10). Each row is woven separately. Cut the weaver at an appropriate place.

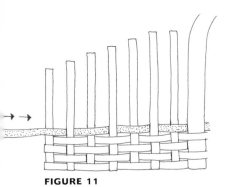

FIGURE 11

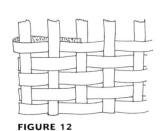

FIGURE 12

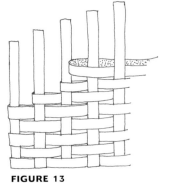

FIGURE 13

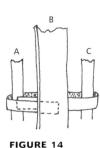

FIGURE 14

Row 2: Begin another long weaver, on the opposite side of the basket, and weave over alternate stakes—in other words, "overs" of the last row will be "unders" on this row. Repeat the ending procedure.

Rows 3 and 4: Repeat rows 1 and 2, beginning the weavers at different spots than you started rows 1 and 2.

Row 5: From now on, you will work with the long sides of the basket one side at a time (figure 11). Begin on either side with a new weaver, leaving about 4 inches free at the ends. When the row is all woven, wrap the 4 inches around the first and last stakes of the row, hiding the ends behind the third stake (figure 12).

Continue this procedure for five more rows, dropping in one stake every row (figure 13).

In the top row, the weaver begins on top of A and ends behind B (figure 14). Weave the other side the same.

Finishing the Stakes

Soak a long piece of #2 round reed. Fold it nearly in half, loop the fold around a stake and twine around the basket for three rows (figure 15). End the twining by pushing the ends under the twining where it began. Next, rewet the ends of the stakes if necessary, and after they have been pointed, bend them to the inside and tuck them behind the first available row of weaving (figure 16).

Cut the edges of the stakes that extend beyond the twining parallel with the twining (figure 17).

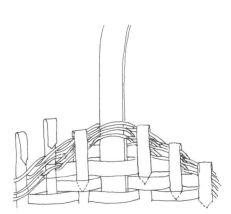

FIGURE 16

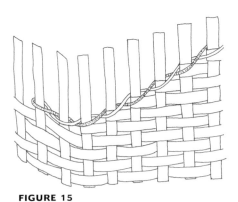

FIGURE 15

FIGURE 17. Dashed line indicates where to cut

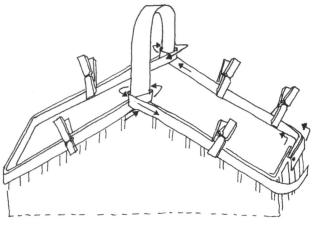

FIGURE 18

Applying the Rim

Wrap a long, soaked piece of ⅝-inch flat reed all the way around the inside top edge of the basket, making a complete turn around the handle. Hold this strip in place with clothespins every 2 or 3 inches (figure 18). The wrong side of the reed should be against the basket. Overlap the ends about 2 inches and cut off the rest.

Now, wrap another strip of ⅝-inch reed around the outside top edge, making the same complete turn around the handle. Hold this strip in place with the same clothespins.

Place a piece of #6 round reed between the two pieces of flat reed. You will need two separate pieces, so the ends will butt against the handle on both sides (figure 19). All three pieces are now held together with the clothespins.

Using a long piece of soaked ³⁄₁₆-inch flat reed, flat-oval reed, or cane, lash all three of the pieces together (figure 20). Begin the lashing on the right-hand side of the handle so if there is any excess in the round reed, the lashing will ease it out the other end. Tuck the ends behind a stake so they are secure and won't

pull out. You can square the corners by rewetting and pinching them or they can be left rounded, whichever you prefer.

The runners on the bottom of the basket are optional. Historically, they were used to give the basket a replaceable sitting surface and to keep the bottom from wearing. Measure the distance across the basket from edge to edge. Cut the ½-inch half round reed accordingly. Cut away half the thickness from the ends of the reed so they can be pushed under the outermost stakes (figure 21).

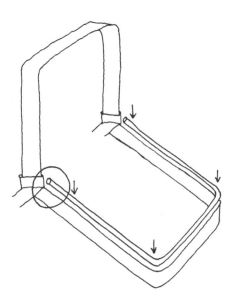

FIGURE 19. Round reed fits between flat reeds

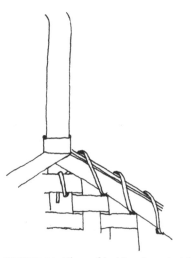

FIGURE 20. View of lashing from inside

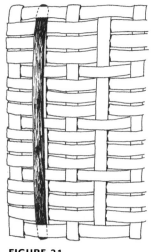

FIGURE 21

Market Basket

SKILL LEVEL: **Easy**

A great shopper, the market is a true beginner's basket, with its flat bottom and splint weave. The possibilities are endless for using color, different handles, and sizes to create your own design.

DIMENSIONS
**APPROXIMATELY
8 X 12 X 12 INCHES**

BASKETMAKERS
**JIMMIE KENT
AND LYN SILER**

Materials

- ⅝-inch flat reed (stakes)
- ⅜-inch flat reed (fillers & weavers)
- 8 x 12-inch D handle
- #2 round reed (twining)
- ½-inch flat-oval reed (rim)
- Sea grass (filler)
- 3/16-inch flat-oval reed (lashing)

Note: These instructions will produce a natural colored basket. For a colorful basket, you may dye the materials as we did for the baskets on the facing page. You also may change the size of the weavers. Be creative!

Weaving the Base

From the ⅝-inch flat reed, cut seven stakes that are 32 inches long and ten stakes that are 28 inches long. From the ⅜-inch flat reed, cut six filler pieces, each 18 inches long.

Soak all the pieces until they're pliable. Mark the centers of all the pieces on the rough side.

Lay four of the 32-inch pieces vertically on a flat surface, aligning the center marks. Place the D handle across (perpendicular to) the four pieces, covering the center marks. Align the center of the handle with the center space, between the second and third stakes (figure 1).

Next, lay 3 more 32-inch pieces vertically on top of the handle. Also, lay the ⅜-inch (22 inch long) pieces on each side of the ⅝-inch pieces (figure 2).

Next, weave the 24-inch pieces vertically through the ones you have placed horizontally. Note: Treat the filler pieces as one with the ⅝-inch pieces they lie between. Place a spoke weight or heavy book across one end of the stakes while weaving the other end.

Weave the first 28-inch stake to the right of the handle, going under the first vertical piece, over the next three, under the next, etc. Continue to weave in the 28-inch pieces, alternating overs and unders every row (figure 3). Weave five pieces to the right of the handle and five pieces to the left. The first piece to the left of the handle should be woven identically to the one on the right. When all the base pieces are woven in, measure and true the base to 8 x 12 inches.

Bend all the filler (22 inch) pieces over to the inside of the base and tuck them under the third vertical "over" piece (figure 4). Cut any pieces that are too long so they will hide under the stake.

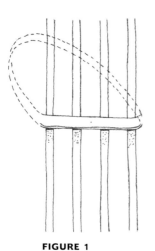

FIGURE 1

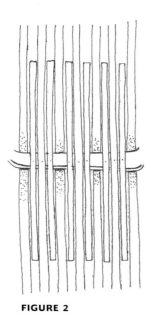

FIGURE 2

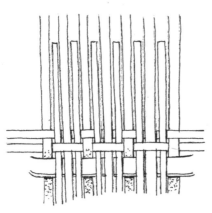

FIGURE 3

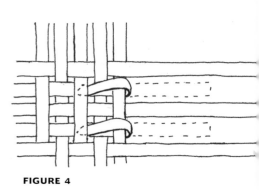

FIGURE 4

Making a Locking Row

Soak a long piece of #2 round reed until it is pliable. Fold it a little off center and begin twining (figure 5). Loop the fold around one of the stakes coming from under the woven base, taking the top weaver under the next stake each time. Try to imagine the handle as another stake and twine around it too. If you need help with twining, consult the Basketmaking Basics section on page 17.

Twine around the base, pushing the twining as close as possible against the base. Tuck the ends under the beginning and cut. If you wish, the twining row may be removed once the sides are woven or you may leave it in place.

Weaving the Sides

Rewet the stakes if they have dried. Upsett the sides by bending each stake over on itself toward the center of the basket. They will not stand, but the crease at the base of the stake is important (figure 6).

Soak a long piece of $3/8$-inch flat reed. Begin weaving start-stop rows as follows:

Making the stakes stand upright, place the end of the weaver, right side out, against the outside of a stake (figure 7). Weave over 1, under 1 around the basket. Upon returning to the starting point, weave over the beginning of the weaver to the fourth stake. Cut the weaver in the middle of the fourth stake. It will be hidden when the next row is woven and the fourth stake stands up-right. Weave 14 start-stop rows, beginning and ending each one as the first. Also, begin and end each row in a different place. Turn the basket $1/4$ turn before you begin each row. This will avoid a build-up of thickness from the overlapped areas.

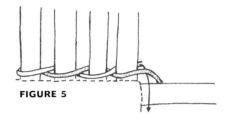

FIGURE 5

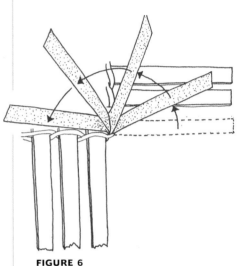

FIGURE 6

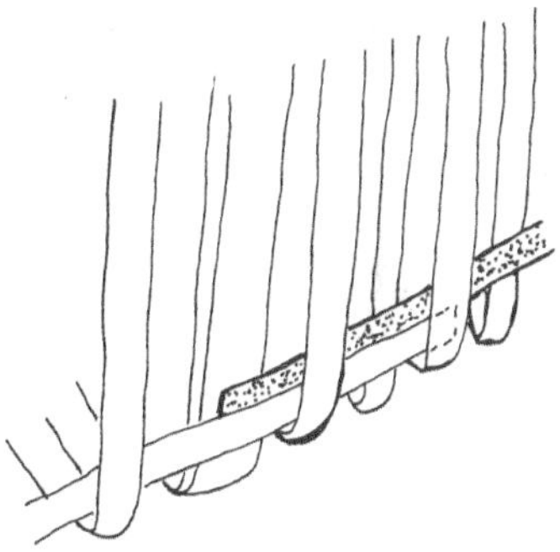

FIGURE 7

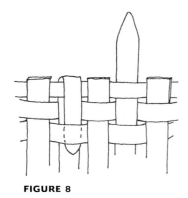

FIGURE 8

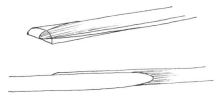

FIGURE 9

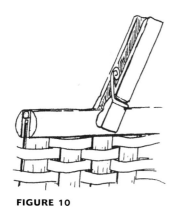

FIGURE 10

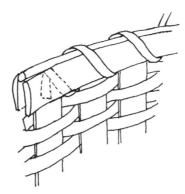

FIGURE 11

Finishing the Basket

Find the stakes that are on the inside of the top row of weaving and cut those stakes flush with the top row of weaving. Point the ones on the outside, rewet them, if necessary, bend them over to the inside and tuck them behind the first available row of weaving (figure 8).

Soak two pieces of $\frac{1}{2}$-inch flat-oval reed, both long enough to reach around the basket and overlap by 3 inches. Also soak a long piece of $\frac{3}{16}$-inch flat-oval reed and a piece of sea grass to be used as the rim filler.

Place a piece of $\frac{1}{2}$-inch flat oval around the top outside of the basket, allowing the ends to overlap. Mark the area and remove to shave the ends where they will overlap. Bevel the overlapped area so it is no thicker than a single thickness of $\frac{1}{2}$-inch flat-oval reed (figure 9). Replace it on the top of the basket and secure it with clothespins.

Repeat the above procedure with the other piece of $\frac{1}{2}$-inch flat oval on the inside of the top of the basket. When it is beveled, secure both of the rim pieces with the same clothespins. The beveled ends of both the rim pieces should be close to each other on the same side of the basket. Now place the sea grass between the two rim pieces (figure 10). Now you're ready to lash the rim to the basket.

Begin lashing just past the area where the rim pieces overlap. Push the end of the lasher up between the rim pieces and hook it over the basket wall to secure it. Lash all the rim components to the basket, going through the spaces between all the stakes (figure 11). End the lashing by hiding the ends between the rim pieces or inside the basket behind a weaver.

Large Arrows Tray

SKILL LEVEL: **Easy**   DESIGNER: **Jimmie Kent**

Here is a very simple pattern that introduces twill weave. The wooden base is a new technique that is a real time saver and sturdy too. Experiment with the colors in the arrow weave for fun.

DIMENSIONS
**APPROXIMATELY
19 X 14 INCHES**

BASKETMAKER
JIMMIE KENT

Materials

- 15½ x 10½-inch slotted oval base
- ⅝-inch flat reed for spokes, fifty 8-inch pieces
- 3/16-inch flat-oval reed (to secure spokes)
- ¼-inch flat reed
- 3/16-inch flat smoked reed or dyed a color of your choice
- ⅜-inch flat reed (rim row)
- ½-inch flat-oval reed (rims)
- Sea grass or round reed (rim filler)
- ¼-inch flat reed (lasher)
- Braided leather handles

Weaving the Basket

From the ⅝-inch flat reed, cut 50 pieces that are 8 inches long. To soften the pieces, soak them for a couple of minutes in very warm water. With the rough side of the reed up and the right side of the base up, insert the stakes into the slot in the base, placing them approximately ⅜ inches apart. The spacing is very important (figure 1).

With a long soaked piece of 3/16 inch flat reed, keep the base flat on the table and weave two rows of plain weave (over 1, under 1). Begin and end each row in the start-stop method. In order to avoid a build-up from the constant overlapping, place the beginning and endings of each row at a different spot (figure 2).

After two rows are woven, split each spoke in half lengthwise (figure 3).

The next three rows are woven with ¼-inch flat and the split stakes are still treated as one stake. Lift the basket from the flat surface and hold it close to you, with the right side next to you. You're weaving from the outside of the basket. Do not upsett the spokes, but allow the spokes to gradually round upwards (figure 4).

The arrow design begins at row six. Now you must treat the split stakes as two pieces. Continue to weave start-stop rows in an over 2, under 2 twill weave, moving the starting and stopping place of every row. For the next five rows, the over 2 weaves will step to the right one spoke each row. Next, weave four more rows, stepping the direction of the overs to the left (figure 5).

Row 15 will be just like the 5th row—you'll treat the split spokes as one, over and under the same spokes. The shaping will occur while you're weaving, as you slowly bring the sides upward.

The arrow design is complete after nine rows. Return to treating the split spoke as one again and weaving in the plain weave. Weave three rows of plain weave just as you did before the arrow.

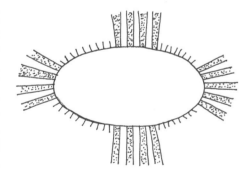

FIGURE 1

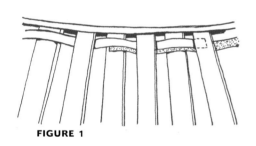

FIGURE 2. Vary the starting place on different sides of basket.

FIGURE 3

FIGURE 4

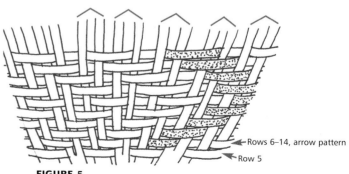

FIGURE 5

Rows 6–14, arrow pattern

Row 5

Row 15 should be woven just like the 5th row, over and under the same spokes. Rows 16 and 17 will be similar to rows 3 and 4. Row 18 is woven in start-stop plain weave with 3/8-inch flat reed and serves as the false rim row.

Finishing the Basket

Notice that half of the spokes are on the outside of the rim row, while half are on the inside. (Every spoke has two parts because they were cut in half. Treat them as two separate pieces.) Cut the ones that are on the inside flush with the top of the rim row. Cut the outside spokes to a point; after wetting them, bend them to the inside and tuck them behind a row or two of weaving.

Attaching the Handles

Attach the leather handles around the false rim, leaving the up-right part of the spoke standing (figure 6). With all the outside stakes pushed down into the weaving and the handle in place, wrap a piece of soaked 5/8-inch flat-oval reed around the inside top edge of the basket, covering only the top row of weaving. Overlap the ends about 3 inches and cut. Shave some of the thickness from the over-lapped area so it is no thicker than a single thickness. Hold the reed in

place with clothespins. Then place a second piece around the outside, covering only the top row of weaving again. Hold both pieces in place with the same clothespins. Overlap the ends and shave them as before. Position the two overlapped areas close to, but not on top of, each other. Lastly, lay a piece of sea grass between the two rim pieces allowing the ends to overlap 1 to 1 1/2 inches (figure 7).

Lashing the Rim

Lose the ends of the lasher between the rim pieces so the lasher does not pull out (figure 8). With a long soaked piece of 1/4-inch flat reed, begin to lash all of the rim pieces together just past the overlaps. If necessary, use an awl to open the space for the lasher under the rim, between the stakes.

The lasher goes up under the inside rim (wrong side up), over the wall of the basket, then down to the outside under the outside rim. Leave a tail sticking out from under the rim. It can be trimmed later.

With the other end of the lasher, go through every space under the rim, between the stakes, going around the rim every time. End the lasher as you began it, going up under the inside rim, over the wall and back down on the outside under the rim.

FIGURE 6. Inside view

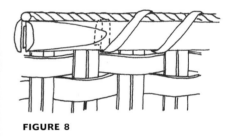

FIGURE 7. Outside view. Outer rim through handles, inner rim not through handles

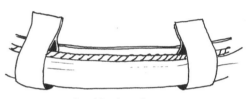

FIGURE 8

Twined Planter

SKILL LEVEL: **Easy**

This basket is a great introduction to round reed. Historically, round materials were willow, honeysuckle, die-cut hardwood, or other natural vines, all much more difficult to obtain than round reed.

DIMENSIONS
**APPROXIMATELY
10 INCHES IN DIAMETER**

BASKETMAKER
LYN SILER

Materials

- #5 round reed
- #4 round reed
- #3 round reed, natural and dyed (three shades of any color)

Preparing the Materials

From the #5 round reed, cut 20 pieces that are 39 inches long. Cut one piece that is 19 inches long. Soak all of them, along with two or three long pieces of #3 round reed.

Lay five pieces horizontally (centers marked) with the other five on top, vertically. Add the short spoke on top with the other five (figure 1).

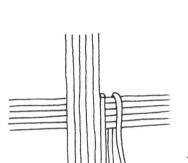

FIGURE 1

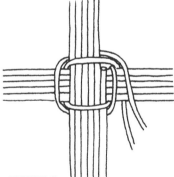

FIGURE 2

FIGURE 3

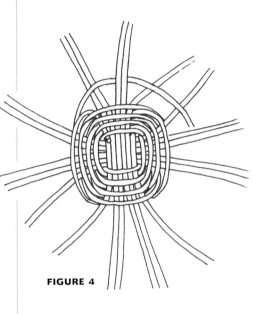

FIGURE 4

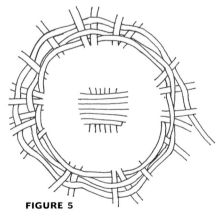

FIGURE 5

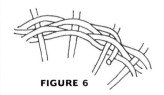

FIGURE 6

Making the Base

Begin twining around the four sections of reed by folding a soaked piece of #3 round reed in half and sliding it around one of the horizontal groups (figure 2).

Remember that in twining, the piece that was on top in the last row is under in the next row. Always pick the top piece up first and move it under the next spoke.

When one reed runs out, simply lay a new soaked piece beside the old one, allowing the two ends to overlap an inch or more. Go back later and cut them so they butt (figure 3).

Twine around the four groups four times. On the 5th row, cut one of the weavers, tuck it under the woven area discreetly, and continue with the one weaver in a simple over one-under one wicker weave, now pairing all the spokes except the odd one. Weave it as a single (figure 4).

Weave for seven rows or about 1 inch, and then split all the pairs, now weaving over and under each spoke. Continue for approximately another $1/2$ inch, and change to a soaked #4 weaver. Continue the wicker weave for the rest of the base, which should be about 7 inches in diameter (figure 5).

When the base is finished, end the weaver by tucking it into the weaving beside a spoke (figure 6).

Weaving the Basket

While you've been weaving, the edges of the base have had a tendency to curve upward. At this point turn the base over so the center is convex (giving the basket a "ring" to sit on). Resoak the spokes. Bend them upward, in the same direction as the curve of the base, to create the sides of the basket. Make sure the center of the base (inside the basket) is raised (figure 7).

Start two new pieces of #4 round reed at the base ending point. Working from the outside of the basket, begin twining around each spoke (figure 8). Twine for about 2 inches. Keep an eye on the shape your basket is assuming-the sides should rise straight up. After 2 inches, end the two pieces of #4 reed by tucking them down into the weaving beside a spoke, above the starting point.

Soak the colored #3 reed. Above the previous endings, begin three pieces of your colored reed, one of each shade, behind three consecutive spokes, and begin a three-rod wale (figure 9).

The reed to the far left moves to the right, over two spokes behind the 3rd and to the outside. Continue with your second new piece (now the farthest to the left). Work the three-rod wale for 1 1/2 to 2 inches. End the three pieces just as you began, letting them lie inside, behind three consecutive spokes, above the starting point.

Making the Border

Return to the #4 reed and resume twining for about 2 more inches. Resoak the ends of the spokes well. Pack all the weaving down as tightly as you can.

Make the border by bringing a spoke over to the right, behind two spokes, in front of the next two, and resting behind the 5th spoke (figure 10). Follow the same procedure with the spoke to the right and with each one thereafter. The last spoke will be a little difficult, but try to ignore everything that is woven and follow the same pattern.

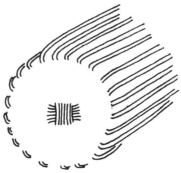

FIGURE 7

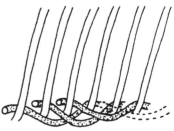

FIGURE 9

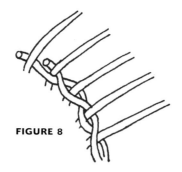

FIGURE 8

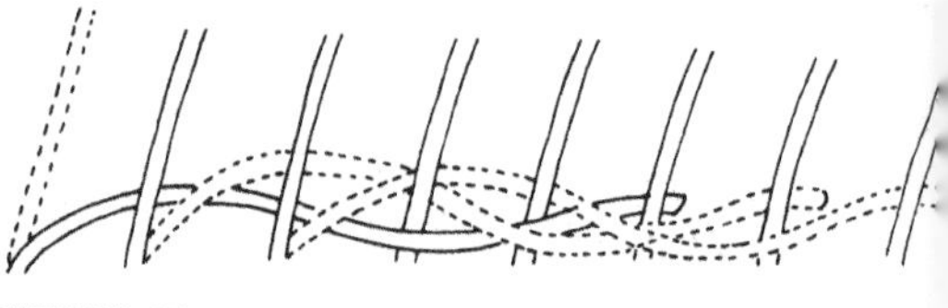

FIGURE 10

Weed Basket

SKILL LEVEL
Easy
DESIGNERS
**Judy Wobbleton
and Lyn Siler**

It may be little, but this twined basket can hold any number of small objects, from weeds, to candles, to toothbrushes, and its design is a popular one with everyone who sees it.

DIMENSIONS
**APPROXIMATELY
5 X 6¹/₂ INCHES**

BASKETMAKER
JUDY WOBBLETON

Materials

- ½-inch flat reed (stakes)
- #2 round reed (twining)
- ¼-inch flat reed, natural (weavers)
- ¼-inch flat reed, colored (weavers) (optional)
- 10-inch sea grass (rim filler)

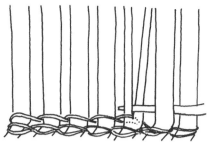

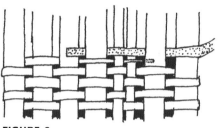

FIGURE 4. Inside view of back

Back   Front

FIGURE 5

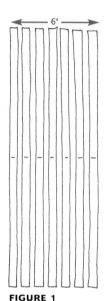

FIGURE 1

FIGURE 2

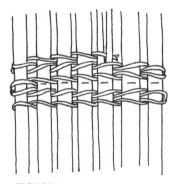

FIGURE 3

FIGURE 6

Weaving the Basket

Cut seven pieces of ½-inch flat reed, each 18 inches long. Soak them for a couple of minutes. Mark the centers on the wrong side. Lay the seven soaked pieces vertically on a surface in front of you, leaving ¼ to ⅜ inches between the stakes. Lay them wrong side up (figure 1).

Soak a long piece of #2 round reed. Begin twining on the left side, a little below the centerline. In twining, one end of the reed goes over a stake while the other end goes under. The two pieces are opposite on the next stake (figure 2).

Twine back and forth, turning at the end and reversing direction. Twine for four rows, ending at the 5th stake, which should be cut in half lengthwise down to the twining (figure 3). The side with the split stake will be the back of the basket.

Fold the two sides of the basket up, letting the twining become the bottom. For about 3 inches, taper one end of a soaked ¼-inch flat reed (natural) to approximately ⅛ inch in width and begin weaving around the basket by inserting the narrow end into the split stake (figure 4). Continue around the basket, bringing the two sides together enough so that there isn't a hole on the ends. Here are two rows of weaving in place, with the sides upright and the twining in the bottom (figure 5).

Weave continuously for 16 rows; continuous weaving is possible because of the odd number of stakes. You must control the shape of the basket—do not allow it to pull in too quickly. Pressing on the ends (seams) will cause your basket to become round. The top opening should be round and about 4 inches in diameter.

After 16 rows, again taper the end of the weaver and let it end at the split stake (figure 6).

Soak the colored reed for a couple of minutes. Wipe the whole length of it with a cloth or paper towel to be sure that no dye will run onto the natural reed. Begin weaving with the new piece, going over the two parts of the split stake, treating them as one again (figure 7). Here's what the basket should look like at this point (figure 8). Weave three rows, each row individually, with the colored reed and then change back to the natural reed for four rows, continuing to weave one row at a time. Continue to treat the split stake as one.

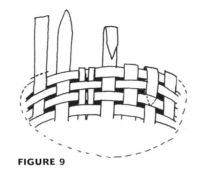

FIGURE 9

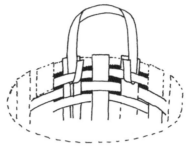

FIGURE 10

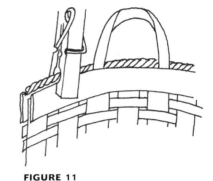

FIGURE 11

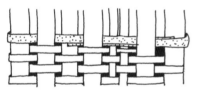

FIGURE 7

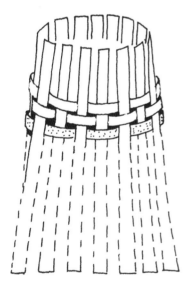

FIGURE 8

Finishing the Stakes and Applying the Rim

Finish the stakes by cutting the ones on the inside flush with the top row of weaving. Point all the outside stakes and tuck them into the weaving on the inside of the basket (figure 9). Insert a piece of ¼-inch flat reed, natural or colored, looping the ends under the second weaver and twisting it at the top (figure 10).

Next, place a piece of soaked ½-inch flat reed around the outside top, covering the top two rows of ¼-inch weaving and overlapping the ends 1 to 2 inches. Hold this reed in place with clothespins (figure 11). Do the same thing on the inside, creating a two-piece rim. Lay a piece of sea grass on top of and between the two rim pieces. Overlap the ends a little for the moment.

Begin lashing just past the spliced area of the rim by pushing one end of the soaked lasher down between the rim pieces (called losing the lasher) and lash over all the rim pieces, going into each space between the stakes (figure 12). When you have lashed to within 1 inch of the splice, cut the sea grass so that the ends butt together and then finish by losing the lasher again.

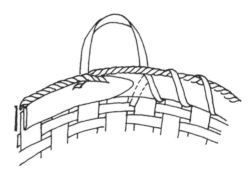

FIGURE 12

Bean Pot

SKILL LEVEL: **Easy**

This design is a reproduction of an old basket made in Pennsylvania, of rye straw. It is a popular beginner's basket, and looks particularly good either hanging on a hearth by its wire handle or decorating a tabletop.

DIMENSIONS
**APPROXIMATELY
9 X 7 INCHES**

BASKETMAKER
JUDY WOBBLETON

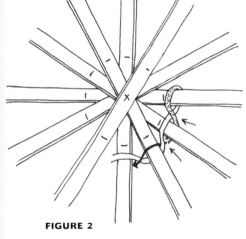

FIGURE 1

FIGURE 2

Twining the Base

From the $^1/2$-inch flat reed, cut 12 pieces that are 27 inches long. Soak all the pieces until they are pliable. Use a pencil to mark the centers of all the pieces on the wrong side. Also pencil-mark $1^1/2$ inches on each side of the center mark of six pieces.

Lay the six pieces with the $1^1/2$-inch marks like spokes in a wheel (figure 1). Soak a long piece of #2 round reed until it is pliable. Fold it a little off center and begin twining by looping the fold around one of the bottom spokes and taking the top piece under the next spoke (figure 2).

Add on to the ends of each piece if necessary by tucking the old end beside a spoke and adding a new one beside the spoke before (figure 3).

Materials

$^1/2$-inch flat reed (spokes)

#2 round reed (twining)

$^1/4$-inch flat-oval reed (weavers & lashing)

$^3/8$-inch flat reed (one piece for false weaver)

$^1/2$-inch flat-oval reed (rim)

#2 or #3 sea grass (rim filler)

Bean pot handle with eyelets

When the diameter of the twined area is about 6 inches, or when there is ample room for a new spoke, lay the other six spokes in the spaces between the existing spokes as you come to them (figure 4). Continue twining around all 12 spokes. When the diameter of the whole base is 7 to $7^1/2$ inches, end the twining by tucking the ends of the reed into the twined area beside a spoke (figure 5).

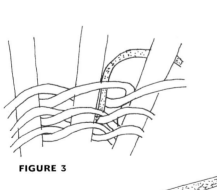

FIGURE 3

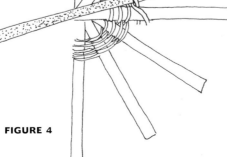

FIGURE 4

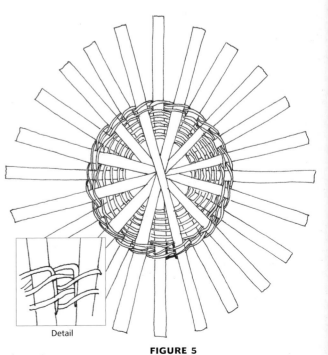

Detail

FIGURE 5

Bean Pot 49

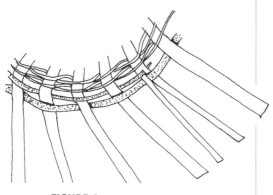

FIGURE 6

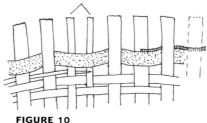

FIGURE 10

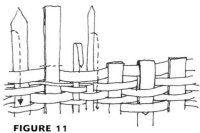

FIGURE 11

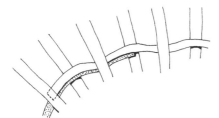

FIGURE 7

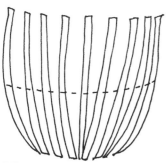

FIGURE 8

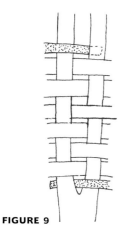

FIGURE 9

Weaving the Sides

Soak a long piece of ¼-inch flat-oval reed and taper one end for about 4 inches, so that the first inch is only about ⅛-inch wide. Cut one spoke in half lengthwise. Upsett all of the spokes by bending them over toward the center of the base.

Begin weaving with the tapered weaver by pushing the tapered end between the two pieces you created when you cut the spoke. Weave over and under the spokes around the base and continue another round when the starting point is reached (figure 6).

By cutting the spoke in half, you have created an odd number of spokes, so a continuous weave can be done.

Do not make the spokes stand straight, but rather let them lean outward to increase the diameter of the basket. Add on to the weaver when one runs out (figure 7). Slip the new weaver behind a spoke with the old one and continue with both until the old one runs out. After 10 to 12 rows of weaving are complete, the diameter of the basket should be approximately 10 to 11 inches at its widest point. From this point on, apply more tension on the weaver and press in on the spokes to make the diameter decrease to about 9 inches (after approximately 27 rows) at the top opening of the basket.

The shape of the basket should be coming together (figure 8). To end the weaving, taper the weaver for about 4 inches, again making the last inch no wider than ⅛-inch. End the weaver directly above the beginning point (figure 9).

Finishing the Basket

Soak the piece of ⅜-inch flat reed. Locate the two pieces you cut in half. Bring them together as closely as possible and weave over them as one spoke. Weave one start-stop row with the ⅜-inch flat reed, overlapping the ends for 4 spokes (figure 10).

Cut all the spokes that are on the inside of the basket flush with the top row of weaving. Point and tuck all the spokes that are on the outside of the basket. Tuck the spokes behind the first available row of weaving on the inside of the basket (figure 11).

Applying the Rim and Handle

Soak a piece of ¹/₂-inch flat-oval reed that is long enough to reach around the top of the basket two times plus 6- to 8-inches overlap. Place the ¹/₂-inch flat-oval reed around the outside of the basket, covering only the row of ³/₈-inch flat reed. Overlap the ends 2 to 3 inches. Hold in place with clothespins. Mark the reed where the overlap occurs.

Remove the rim and with a knife or plane, bevel the ends so the over-lapped area is no thicker than a single thickness of ¹/₂-inch flat oval. Repeat the procedure on the inside of the basket (figure 12).

Reposition the two rim pieces on the basket after the ends are shaved. Place the splices (overlapped areas) near, but not exactly opposite, each other. Again, hold both pieces in place with clothespins. Locate any two spokes that are directly across from each other. Curve the eyelets to fit the shape of the rim. Push the ends under a bent and tucked spoke. Make sure the eyelet is directly above the center spoke (figure 13).

Lay a piece of sea grass on top of and between the two rim pieces. Let the ends overlap for the moment. They can be cut later as the rim is lashed. Starting just past the two overlapped areas, lash the rim pieces together (figure 14). Push one end of a soaked ¹/₄-inch flat-oval reed up between the two rim pieces. Hook it over the basket wall to secure it, and take the lasher into every space between the spokes. When the starting point is reached,

either end the lasher or reverse directions to X lash. End the same way you began, by hooking the lasher over the wall, or hide the end behind a weaver inside the basket.

With needle-nose pliers, bend the ends of the handle and slip them through the eyelets (figure 15). Tighten the ends of the handle around the eyelets so it can't slip out.

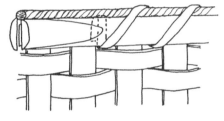

FIGURE 14

FIGURE 12

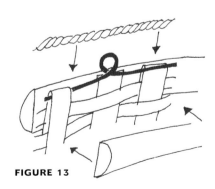

FIGURE 13

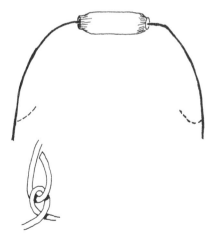

FIGURE 15

Melon Basket

A melon shape, with its perfectly round bottom, is probably one of the oldest of all ribbed baskets. It's an excellent beginner basket. Natural materials such as honeysuckle, grapevine, or wisteria make wonderful melon baskets.

DIMENSIONS
APPROXIMATELY
8 INCHES IN DIAMETER

BASKETMAKERS
CAROLYN AND JASON KEMP

SKILL LEVEL: **Easy**

Materials

#6 round reed

Two 8-inch round hoops (frame)

Waxed strips

3/8-inch flat-oval reed, 3/8-inch oval, or #6 round reed (ribs)

1/4-inch flat reed (weavers)

Preliminary Step

From the #6 round reed, cut the following pieces:

- Primary ribs: 6 pieces, 13 1/2 inches long

- Secondary ribs: 4 pieces, 12 inches long

Keep the primary and secondary ribs separate. Soak all the pieces for about 15 minutes or until they are pliable. Remove them from the water and clip them around the 8-inch hoops (figure 1). Allow them to dry in place before beginning to make the basket.

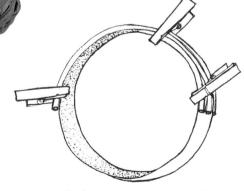

FIGURE 1. Preliminary steps to shape ribs

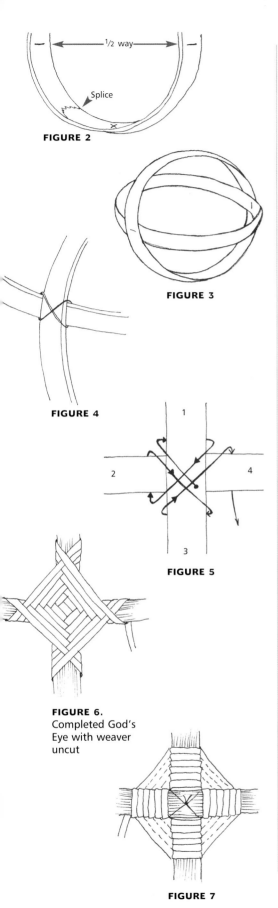

FIGURE 2

FIGURE 3

FIGURE 4

FIGURE 5

FIGURE 6.
Completed God's
Eye with weaver
uncut

FIGURE 7

Preparing the Hoops

On one of the hoops, locate the splice or seam where the hoop has been put together. Make a mark 2 inches from this splice. From this mark measure the circumference of the hoop (8-inch hoop should measure about 25½ inches). Divide the circumference in half, measure that distance from the first mark and mark again. This hoop will be your basket handle. The area between the pencil marks (containing the splice) is the bottom of the handle. On the inside of the hoop, put your name or initial (figure 2).

On the second hoop, which will be the rim of the basket, measure and mark 2 inches from the splice and again at the halfway point on the hoop. This divides the hoop into two equal parts. Now take the two hoops (handle and rim) and fit them together, sliding them until the pencil marks line up (figure 3). Make sure that the handle hoop is on the outside of the rim hoop. Using waxed string, tie the hoops securely (figure 4).

Weaving the God's Eye

Select the two thinnest, most pliable weavers for making the God's Eye, making sure that each is at least 8 feet long. Coil the strips separately and secure them with a bread tie or clothespin.

Soak both coils in warm water for 1 to 3 minutes. Remove them from the water when they're pliable and uncoil one to begin the God's Eye. Wrap the other in a towel until you are ready to begin the other side. Note: The flat reed has a right and a wrong side. The edges of the right

side are slightly rounded or beveled. The wrong side has edges that are perfectly flat and rough. Begin the God's Eye by placing the wrong side against the hoops. When weaving the basket, you need not be concerned with the right and wrong sides.

Start to weave. It may help to number the four hoop sections as shown (figure 5). The God's Eye must be very flat. Pull the weavers tight and press firmly as you make the revolutions, making sure the weaver is pressed completely flat against the hoop and the previous row. Use your thumbs to flatten the weavers as you work.

Begin with the weaver on top of the hoops at the dot. Move up and behind 1, diagonally to 2, behind 2, diagonally to 3, etc. From 4, move diagonally to 1 and repeat the entire counterclockwise revolution five more times. You will notice that the starting point (end of reed) is covered as the weaver moves from 2 to 3.

The finished God's Eye will have six revolutions, counting from the back (figure 6). The God's Eye is flat to the touch. The weavers must not overlap each other, as any overlap will make the God's Eye bulky. Look at the back of the God's Eye to be sure the wraps are equal at all four points (figure 7).

A good flat God's Eye is critical. The success of the basket depends on its construction. Don't be discouraged if your first try isn't perfect. Just take it out and try again. At the end of the sixth revolution, the weaver is behind 4. Do not cut; secure with a clothespin. Repeat the God's Eye on the other side with the other coiled weaver.

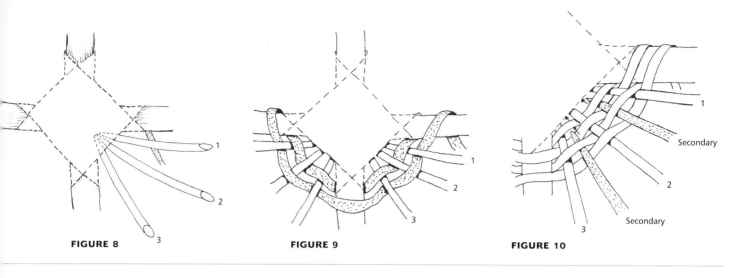

FIGURE 8

FIGURE 9

FIGURE 10

Making and Inserting the Ribs

Remove the ribs from the hoops and sharpen all the ends to a point with a knife or pencil sharpener.

Insert the primary ribs, one at a time, into the two God's Eyes. The ribs will slide in behind the eye in the pocket formed between the rim and the lowest part of the handle (figure 8).

Note: If you're using the oval or flat-oval reed, taper the ends gradually with a knife for approximately 3 inches.

Weaving the Basket

Take the clothespin off only one of the weavers. If it is dry or stiff, rewet it. Begin weaving by going over rib 1, under rib 2, over rib 3, under the lower handle, over and under the remaining ribs until you reach the rim. This first row of weaving should be snug against the God's Eye. Bring the weaver up from the back, over the rim to the front, and begin the over and under pattern in the opposite direction (figure 9).

Note: The most important part of weaving is to push the weaver snugly against the previous row. Pulling the weavers hard is unnecessary and tends to misshape the ribs. The figures show weavers loosely woven to clearly illustrate the weaving pattern. Do not weave this loosely. Also, be careful to weave under 1 rib, over 1 rib, etc. If you weave over 2 ribs at any time, the alternating over-under pattern will be disrupted.

Weave four complete rows and clamp with clothespins. These first four rows anchor the primary ribs in place. However, they may still move and slip out of place, so take care to check their position as you go along.

Adding Secondary Ribs

You should have four 12-inch ribs left to insert. Add one rib between the first and second primary ribs, pushing the points (one end and then the other) into the same space with the first ribs. Be sure to conceal each point under a weaver. Add the other secondary rib between the second and third primary ribs, concealing the points as before (figure 10).

With four rows of weaving complete on both sides and all ten ribs in place, the basic skeleton of the melon basket should be obvious (figure 11). At this point, make sure that each of the ten ribs follows the same curve and extends out the same distance as the hoops. It may be necessary to adjust the lengths of the ribs by pushing them further into the weaving or pulling them out slightly.

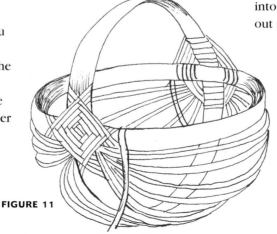

FIGURE 11

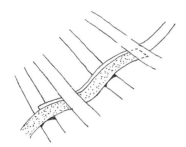

FIGURE 12. New weaver added on top of old weaver

Note: The first row of weaving, after any new ribs are added, will alter the over-under pattern. Continue to weave in the over-under pattern each rib. The weaving will correct itself on the second row and a new pattern will be established.

Splicing

When you have 2 or 3 inches of weaver left, it is time to join a new soaked weaver to it. This joining should not take place at the rim, so backtrack if necessary. Overlap the new weaver on top of the old one (figure 12). You will be weaving with two pieces of reed for 3 or 4 ribs. Hide the ends under a rib.

Finishing the Basket

Continue weaving the basket, one side at a time. Do not weave all of one side, and then the other. Instead, weave three rows on one side, then three rows on the other, to keep the basket balanced. Weave until both sides meet in the center. If there is a space that has not filled in, simply add a short weaver and fill in the space, making sure you end up with the over-under pattern on alternating rows. Push the weavers out from the center to make room for the last row if necessary.

Measurements for Other Sizes of Melon Baskets

Basket Dia.	Primary Ribs	Secondary Ribs
6"	9"	7½"
8"	12½"	12"
10"	15½"	14"
12"	19"	17½"

Melon Basket Using Vine Rattan

Soak the entire coil of vine rattan. It's almost impossible to separate when dry, but one or two pieces can be pulled out easily if it's wet.

Make your own hoops from the vine rattan by forming a circle with one piece and wrapping other pieces around it until it's as thick as you want. Construct two hoops and fit one inside the other, just as is described on page 53. Make the God's Eye with a long piece of rattan. Make the ribs by twisting 2 or 3 pieces together as one. Splice a new piece on when an old one runs (figure 13).

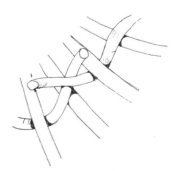

FIGURE 13. Inside view if using natural material

Potato Basket

SKILL LEVEL: **Easy**

Materials

10-inch hoop (rim)

#6 round reed

Waxed thread

1/4-inch flat reed

Historically made in the Appalachian Mountains, this basket was most certainly brought from Ireland and England. Even when using the same directions, no two ever turn out exactly alike. So, if you experiment a bit, imagine what exciting baskets you could get.

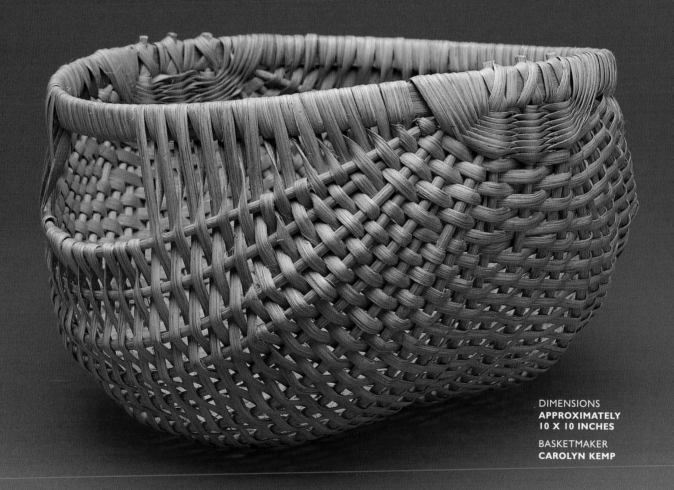

DIMENSIONS
**APPROXIMATELY
10 X 10 INCHES**

BASKETMAKER
CAROLYN KEMP

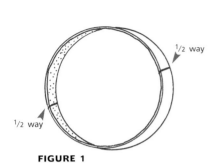

FIGURE 1

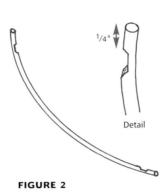

Detail

FIGURE 2

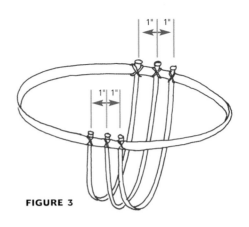

FIGURE 3

Measuring and Marking the Hoop

Measure the circumference of the 10-inch hoop with a tape, then divide the circumference in half, making pencil marks at the halfway points (figure 1). Hoops vary slightly in size, so each one needs to be measured.

Cutting the First Three Primary Ribs

From the #6 round reed, cut three ribs, each 20 inches long. Each rib will probably have a natural curve from being coiled. On the outside of the curve, cut a notch 1/4-inch from the end, and scoop out an area about half the thickness of the rib and as long as the width of the hoop, being careful not to cut off the 1/4-inch rib end (figure 2).

Securing the First Three Primary Ribs

On the two pencil marks you made, fit one of your three ribs on the inside of the hoop—one end of the rib on one mark, the other end on the opposite mark. Tie securely with waxed thread. With the center rib (A) in place, measure and mark 1 inch to the right and 1 inch to the left. The other two ribs (B and C) are tied to these marks, just as the first rib is tied. It is crucial to tie these ribs very securely. Trim the ends of the waxed string (figure 3).

Making the Ear

Coil two weavers separately, each being at least 8 feet long, securing with bread ties or clothespins (figure 4).

Soak the coiled weavers in water for one to two minutes. Using one of the wet weavers, begin the ear. You'll be making the ear around the three primary ribs (A, B, C) and hoop (or rim) on both sides of ribs. Begin on the right and make X's on top of the three primary ribs (figure 5).

After making X's, and using the same weaver, begin the ear by going around the rim, over C, under A, over B, then up and around the other rim. The area between the last rib and the rim must lie flat; a half twist in the weaver is necessary to make it flat (figure 6). Continue weaving the ear until you've gone around six times on both rims. Do not cut the weaver—secure it with clothespins at the rim (figure 7).

FIGURE 4

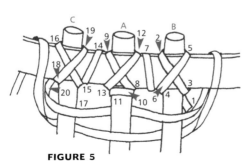

FIGURE 5

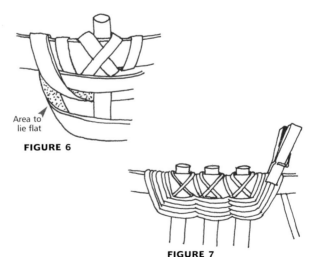

Area to lie flat

FIGURE 6

FIGURE 7

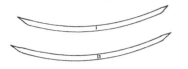

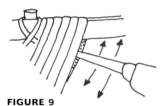

FIGURE 9

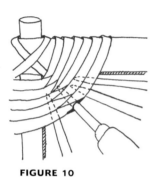

FIGURE 10

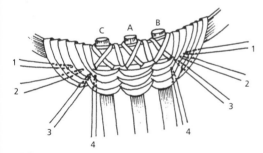

FIGURE 11

Cutting and Inserting Other Primary Ribs

Cut two of each of the following ribs, and number them as you cut them:

1: 14 inches
2: 16 inches
3: 17 inches
4: 18 inches

After cutting the eight ribs, sharpen the points on both ends with a pencil sharpener or sharp knife (figure 8).

Insert rib 1 in the first opening, just underneath the hoop, one on each side. Use an awl or some pointed tool to open it sufficiently (figure 9). Then, insert rib 2 in the same opening as 1 (below) on both sides. Insert rib 4 in the opening beside C on one side and B on the other side, using an awl to enlarge the space as above, if necessary. Lastly, insert rib 3 in the center of the lashing by making a space for the rib with an awl.

You must actually split the reed between the ribs 2 and 4 (figure 10). This is the area you made lie flat. If it doesn't lie flat, you'll have trouble making a hole in it.

After you've added all eight of the primary ribs, you have the basic skeleton of the potato basket (figure 11).

Measure the Opening for the Handle

With a tape measure, measure the distance from the edge of one ear to the edge of the other ear. Put a mark at the halfway point. For example, if the distance is 12 inches, make your mark at 6 inches. Then, from the center, measure 2 inches to the right and mark, and then measure 2 inches to the left and mark. Thus you have measured and marked off a 4-inch opening which will become your handle (figure 12).

Weaving the Basket

After all the ribs are securely in place, begin weaving using the remainder of the weaver with which you made the ear. Simply weave under one rib, over the next, etc., going around the rim and reversing the process, making sure your rows are alternating (in one row the weaver is over the rib, in the next row the weaver is under the rib, etc.). Weave five rows on the one side of the basket and secure with clothespins. Weave five rows on the other side of the basket and secure. Stop and cut the secondary ribs (figure 13).

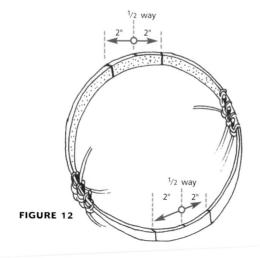

FIGURE 12

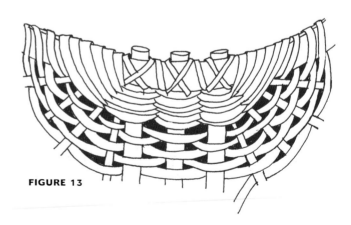

FIGURE 13

Cutting and Inserting the Secondary Ribs

Cut two of each of the following ribs:

5: 14 inches
6: 16 inches
7: 16½ inches
8: 17 inches

The secondary ribs do not go all the way into the ear. They only go into the five rows of weaving, with points hidden under a weaver.

Place the secondary rib 5 in the same space as the primary rib 1. Place the secondary rib 6 in the same space as the primary rib 2. Do the same with secondary ribs 7 and 8 (figure 14).

Once the secondary ribs are in place and secure, begin weaving again, weaving over one rib, under one rib, just as before.

Do not be alarmed if your over-under pattern is disturbed for the first row. Adding ribs always interrupts the pattern for one row. The second row corrects itself if you always weave over one and then under one.

Splicing

When you have 2 to 3 inches of weaver left, it's time to join a new soaked weaver to it. This joining should not take place at the rim, so backtrack if necessary.

Overlap the new weaver on top of the old one (figure 15). You will be weaving with two pieces of reed for three or four ribs. Hide the ends if possible under a rib.

Finishing the Basket

Continue weaving the basket. Do not weave all of one side, and then the other. Instead, weave several rows on

one side, and then several rows on the other, to keep the basket balanced.

On this particular basket, you must leave an opening in the side for a handle. On the rim you have already marked off a 4-inch space. When your weaving reaches the mark on each side, rib 1 becomes the point at which you turn and go back down rather than weaving around the hoop, thus leaving an opening between the first rib and the hoop. Continue in this manner until all the space is filled. Rib 1 will fill in before the bottom of the basket does. When you can no longer fit any more weavers in, drop down to the next rib, turn and go back, just as you turned around your hoop. Continue in this manner until all the space is filled in (figure 16).

Wrapping the Handle

This step is entirely optional. If you wish to cover your handle, insert a short weaver into the weaving behind the rim. Wrap in a continuous motion until the area is covered. Cut the weaver, leaving a 1-inch tail. Insert this end into the weaving on the back of the rim on the opposite side (figure 17).

If you don't want to weave the handle, simply continue with the weaver wrapping the handle and continue down the other side with the regular weaving (figure 18).

Try an oval potato basket using the same basic shaping procedure as the round, but making the basket sides round out and the bottom basically flat.

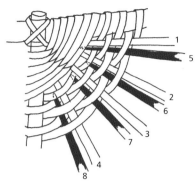

FIGURE 14

New weaver   Old weaver

FIGURE 15

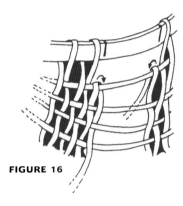

FIGURE 16

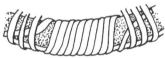

FIGURE 17

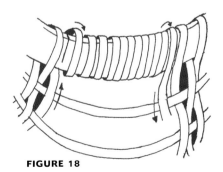

FIGURE 18

Materials

- ³⁄₈-inch flat reed (stakes)
- ³⁄₁₆-inch or ¹¹⁄₆₄-inch flat reed, 18-inches dyed (weavers)
- ¹⁄₄-inch flat-oval or half-round reed (rim)
- #7 or #8 round reed (handle)

Cherokee Comb Basket

SKILL LEVEL: Moderate

This is a very useful little wall basket and not necessarily just for holding combs. As with most baskets, it can hold anything you want. This same basket was also made by Maine Indians using brown ash.

DIMENSIONS
**APPROXIMATELY
3 X 7 X 8 INCHES**

BASKETMAKER
DIANNE KENNEDY

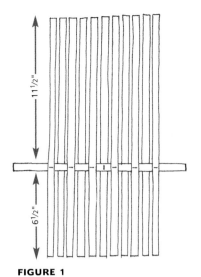

FIGURE 1

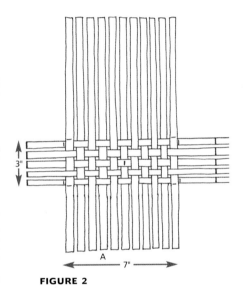

FIGURE 2

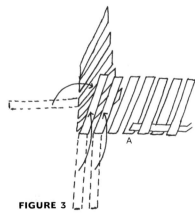

FIGURE 3

Cutting the Stakes and Weaving the Base

Cut 11 pieces of $\frac{3}{8}$-inch flat reed that are 18 inches long and five pieces of $\frac{3}{8}$-inch flat reed that are 17 inches long. On the wrong side of the reed, make a halfway mark on the 17-inch pieces. On the wrong side of the 18-inch pieces, measure and mark $11\frac{1}{2}$ inches from one end (or $6\frac{1}{2}$ inches from the other).

Lay the 18-inch pieces vertically on a surface in front of you, leaving about $\frac{1}{4}$ inch between each stake. Align the marks. Next, weave one of the 17-inch pieces over and under (horizontally) the vertical pieces, aligning the center marks. This will be the center stake (figure 1).

Weave in the other four stakes, two on each side of the center stake, alternating overs and unders. Make sure the ends are even and the marks are aligned (figure 2).

The base should be 3 x 7 inches. Measure and true the base. Mark the corners in case any slipping occurs.

Upsetting the Stakes and Weaving the Sides

Fold all the stakes over upon themselves to form a permanent crease at the base (figure 3). Soak a piece of $\frac{3}{16}$-inch reed (natural). Begin weaving by placing the weaver (wrong side against the stake) on

the outside of a stake that originates on the bottom of the woven base (stake A). Continue weaving over and under all the way around the basket. Overlap the beginning end and continue to the fourth stake. Cut the weaver so it will be hidden behind the fourth stake when it stands (figure 4).

Each row will be woven separately. Begin each row in a different spot to prevent a build-up from starting and stopping in the same place. Hold the first row in place with a clothespin or use a brake.

Weave the following rows in the following colors, or the colors of your choice (figure 5):

Rows 1–3: natural

Rows 4–6: brown

Rows 7–10: natural

Rows 11–13: brown

Rows 14–17: natural

Cutting and Tucking Stakes on Three Sides and Applying the Rim

Leave the long, back stakes standing. Cut the inside stakes on the other three sides flush with the top row of weaving. Point all the outside stakes and tuck them into the weaving inside the basket (figure 6).

Note: Cut the stakes in half so they aren't so hard to push in.

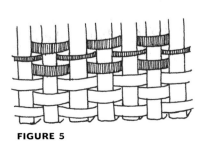

FIGURE 5

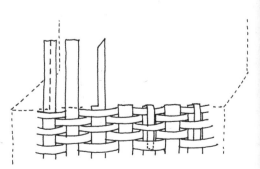

FIGURE 6. Inside view

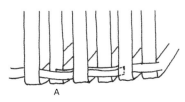

FIGURE 4

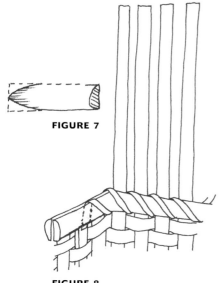

FIGURE 7

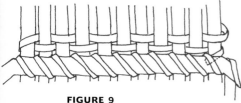

FIGURE 8

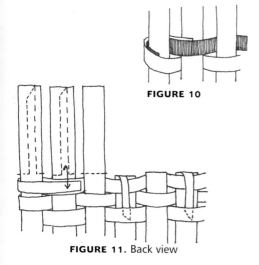

FIGURE 9

FIGURE 10

FIGURE 11. Back view

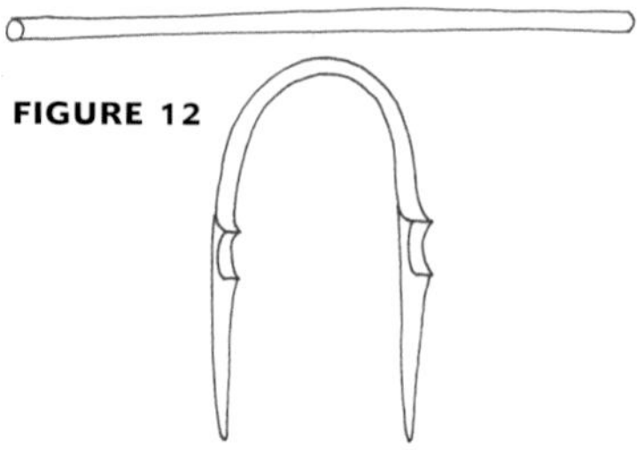

FIGURE 12

Place a piece of ¼-inch flat-oval reed around the top row of weaving on the outside. Overlap the ends about 2 inches. Shave some of the oval side off so the overlap won't be too thick (figure 7). Repeat the same procedure on the inside. Lash the rim in place with a piece of ³/₁₆-inch flat reed (figure 8).

Weaving The Back

Begin another piece of ³/₁₆-inch flat reed (natural) by pushing the end between the two rim pieces and weaving across the back. Turn around the other end and reverse directions (figure 9).

Change to a brown weaver (figure 10). Weave five rows in brown, and then change back to natural for the final seven rows. Or be creative: try changing the number of colored rows or vary the colors.

Cut the stakes so tucking in will be easier (figure 11). Bring the weaver

around the corner to the back and tuck the stake in over it.

Soak a piece of #7 or #8 round reed (cut 7-inches long), until it's pliable and bend it around to form a U. Mark off a ¼-inch space on each side and scoop out the reed about halfway through for a notch. Taper the ends so they are paper thin at the tips (figure 12).

Push the handle down into the weaving on the back of the basket, fitting the notch around the last row of weaving. Place a soaked piece of ¼-inch flat-oval reed around the top, fitting it in the notches and overlapping the ends about an inch. It will cover the last row of weaving (figure 13).

Start a new lasher by pushing the end into the weaving on the back. Lash the two rim pieces together, going over the handle to the other end (figure 14). Lose the lasher at the end of the row (figure 15).

FIGURE 13. Back view

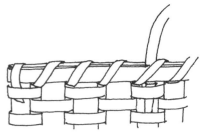

FIGURE 14. Back view

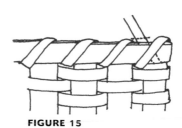

FIGURE 15

Chitimacha Style Tray

You can't go wrong by reinterpreting classic designs and helping to keep basketry traditions alive and fresh for generations to come. This is my take on an original Chitimacha design, using a twist on the structure and a playful mirror image.

DIMENSIONS
APPROXIMATELY
7 X 7 X 2 INCHES

BASKETMAKER
LYN SILER

SKILL LEVEL: **Moderate**

Materials

3/16-inch ash or flat reed
(stakes and weavers)

3/8-inch flat reed or heavier
ash (false rim row)

Long-leaf pine needles,
dyed black (rim)

Black waxed linen thread
and tapestry needle
(lashing)

Preparing the Weavers

Select the heavier pieces of 3/16-inch ash or flat reed for the stakes and the thinner pieces for weavers. Use medium- or heavy-weaver weight for weavers in ash and heavy-weaver weight for stakes. Dye 14 deep red pieces, that are each 12 inches long; dye 22 pieces dark black. Note: To get a really dark black, use three times the dye you normally would, in almost boiling water, and add a little dark brown to cut the blue in the black dye. Also cut 32 pieces of natural. Rinse thoroughly and wipe each piece before using. Use the ash almost dry. Spray it only lightly or dip your fingers in water and tap the material with them. Even reed should only be slightly dampened.

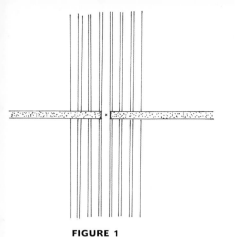

FIGURE 1

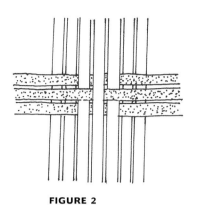

FIGURE 2

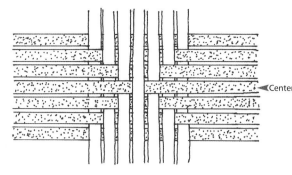

◄Center

FIGURE 3. Two sides end in under seven. Two sides end in under five.

Weaving the Base

Note: All the weaving in the base is over 4, under 4 except for the centers and they are over or under the center 1, 3, 5, or 7.

Begin by laying seven of the red stakes vertically in front of you. Mark a center.

If there is a right and wrong side, lay the right side up. Weave one red piece in horizontally, under the center red piece (figure 1). Next, weave in two more pieces of red under the center 3, top and bottom (figure 2). Then, weave in two more pieces, under the center 5, top and bottom; and then two more pieces top and bottom under all 7 (figure 3).

With all of the red pieces woven in, two of the sides end in under 7 and two end with an under 5. On the sides that end with an under 5, weave a black piece under 7. Now all the sides are woven the same.

Continue to weave in pieces of black, but now weave under the center pieces in the same order as before: 1, 3, 5, and 7. When all 22 of the black

pieces are woven in, all four sides will end with an under 1 in the center. Two sides will have five black pieces and two sides will have six.

Change to natural and continue to weave in the pattern on all four sides. The last natural piece will be woven under the center 1 on all four sides. See the graph (figure 4).

Weaving the Sides

Gently upsett the sides. Make more of a rolled upsett than a sharp defined one. With a long dampened weaver, weave the same as the second row back (over 7) in the center of the sides. Start with the weaver over the center 7, then weave under 4, over 4 to the corner. The corners will be woven under 4, over 3, under 4. Repeat on all four sides. Then overlap the ends and shave half the thickness from the top of one side and the bottom of the other to eliminate any excess thickness.

Before starting row 2 and every subsequent row, turn the basket a quarter turn.

Row 2: Centers are over 5.
Corners are over 2, under 1, over 2.

Row 3: Centers are over 3.
Corners are over 3, under 1, over 3.

Row 4: Centers are over 1.
Corners are over 3, under 3, over 3.

Row 5: Centers are under 7.
Corners are under 2, over 1, under 2.

Row 6: Centers are under 5.
Corners are under 3, over 1, under 3.

Row 7: Centers are under 3.
Corners are under 3, over 3, under 3.

Row 8: Centers are under 1.
Corners are over 2, under 1, over 2.

Pack all the rows down quite snugly as you weave in a false rim row of ³⁄₈-inch flat reed opposite the last

FIGURE 4.
Pattern graph

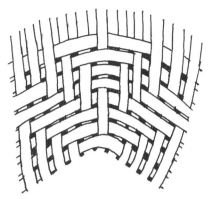

FIGURE 5. Corner view

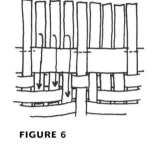

FIGURE 6

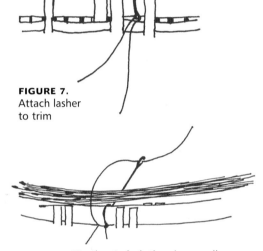

FIGURE 7. Attach lasher to trim

FIGURE 8. Starting to lash the pine needles

row of weaving (figure 5). If the over or under 1 is a problem, combine it with another group. Let the ash dry thoroughly before finishing. You may dry it in a very low heat oven or 10 seconds at a time in a microwave oven if you are in a hurry.

Finishing the Basket

Dampen only the ends of the stakes and turn the basket upside down for a few minutes to drain. Bend the ones on the inside of the weaving over the false rim to the outside and tuck them behind a row of weaving on the outside (figure 6). Cut the ones on the inside flush with the top of the last row of weaving.

Note: You usually bend stakes to the inside, but on this basket the inside is most visible.

Now the basket is ready for its rim. Soak a handful of pine needles for several minutes. Thread a long piece of thread onto the tapestry needle and tie one end of the thread onto the basket around the false rim (figure 7).

Place the pine needles around the rim, over the false rim. Put half on the inside and half on the outside. Bring the needle to the outside of the basket and go through the second space between stakes to the outside. Take the needle between the stakes or between every two stakes (figure 8).

Adjust the needles so they're staggered and don't run out all at the same time. Add in a new pine needle every time one runs out by pushing the end up into the core of needles. Keep the bundle size consistent (figure 9).

When you've gone all the way around the basket, you'll need to mesh the beginning and ending needles together, adjust the bundles, and then stitch them together (figure 10). Some of the bulk can be reduced by selectively cutting the pine needles to staggered lengths.

When you've reached the beginning stitch, make a couple of backstitches under the false rim between the stakes to secure it. Bring the tapestry needle up at an angle and through the bundle. Cut. You can cut the ends off the pine needles or leave them on.

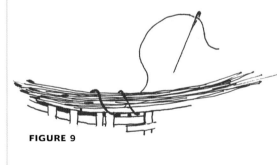

FIGURE 9

FIGURE 10. Meshing the needles

Gourd Vessel

SKILL LEVEL
Easy

DESIGNER
Judy K. Wilson

Working with gourds is easy, and this simple vessel is a perfect way to work on your coiling technique, refine your drawing skills, and expand your repertoire.

DIMENSIONS
**APPROXIMATELY
4 INCHES IN DIAMETER**

BASKETMAKER
JUDY K. WILSON

Materials

- Small gourd
- Craft knife
- Sandpaper
- Sweet grass
- Drill with small bit
- Raffia
- Sharp needle with large eye
- Beeswax
- Pencil
- Fine-tipped permanent marker

Cleaning the Gourd

If your gourds aren't already clean, scrub the outside with warm water (do not soak them). Using the craft knife, cut off the top of the gourd wherever you like. Rinse the inside with hot water until all of the debris is removed. Let the gourd dry completely and gently sand the edge of the cut until it's smooth.

Stitching the Coiled Neck

Soak 10 to12 pieces of sweet grass in warm water. Remove them from the water and wrap them in a damp towel.

The size of the holes you drill depends on the size of the gourd, the size of the needle, and the size of the core of sweet grass you use. For a small gourd, drill holes about $1/8$ inch apart, and about $1/16$ inch from the edge (figure 1).

FIGURE 1

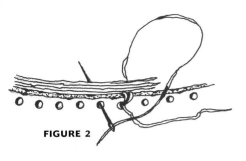

FIGURE 2

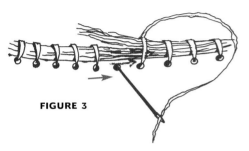

FIGURE 3

FIGURE 4

Select three or four pieces of sweet grass, holding the smaller end. Take a piece of raffia and split it lengthwise with the sharp needle, so that you get three to four strands out of each piece. It also helps if you first pull the raffia over a cake of beeswax. A needle with raffia threaded through the eye must be able to pass through the drilled hole.

Moving from the outside to the inside of the gourd, go into the first drilled hole, then go into the same hole a second time, in the same direction. Leave a 2- to 3-inch tail of raffia on the outside of the basket. The double stitch locks the raffia in place without a knot.

Lay the sweet grass with the small ends staggered on the right and the long section of sweet grass to the left. Leave about an inch of over- hang. Begin to stitch the first row in place, always going into the drilled hole from the outside of the gourd, working to the left (figure 2).

Once the first row is almost fin- ished, work the tails you left in the beginning into the coil (figure 3). When you start the second row, stitch in front of the previous stitch—not on it, but right beside it. When the grass feels thin, add another piece or two, adding the small end first. It is best to cut off the wide end at a long angle, so there is no light-colored grass mixed in. Before your raffia gets too short, add in a piece as you coil (in the back of the coiled portion) so you can switch the needle over. If desired, let the old tail hang out a little, to add to your gourd's charm.

Continue to repeat this stitching until you have the top neck as tall as you wish. Work until the last row is level and let the grass run out gradually, rather than cutting it off. To end the neck portion, run the needle down through the coils, so that the end is hidden within the grass (figure 4). You can let the tail hang down each time you add a new piece of raffia.

How to Draw the Design on the Gourd

Looking down onto the gourd top, divide the gourd into quarters, pen- ciling lightly, and marking down- ward. This will be erased later. Pencil in all designs first and then go over the lines with a fine-tipped perma- nent marker (figure 5). Feel free to use the sample patterns provided (figure 6).

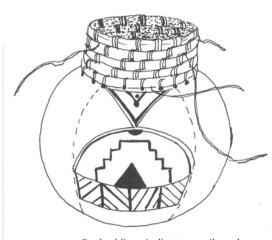

FIGURE 5. Dashed lines indicate pencil marks.

FIGURE 6. Sample patterns

Nantucket Lightship Style Basket

SKILL LEVEL: **Moderate**

Unique to its place of birth, the Nantucket Lightship Style Basket is also unique in the use of wooden molds. Originated more than 150 years ago by captains and crew while manning coastal lightships, it is among the most admired and respected basket designs.

DIMENSIONS
**VARIOUS,
DEPENDING
ON STYLE**

BASKETMAKER
JIM KENT

Materials

- Mold
- Cane (weavers)
- Flat-oval reed (ribs)
- Half-round reed (rim)
- Ear
- Base
- 1/4-inch carriage bolt and nut
- Rubber bands
- Brass or copper rivets
- Brass escutcheon pins
- Clear shellac (optional)

Note: There are wooden molds available from some basketry suppliers. But if you don't want to invest in a wooden mold, there are many suitable plastic replacements (butter tubs, plastic pails, or plastic flowerpots). The container must have a 1/4-inch hole in the bottom so the base can be bolted to the container. It should have an indentation in the bottom into which the base will be recessed, but this is not absolutely necessary. It's not hard to find a mold, as there's no one shape it must have—these baskets are made in all shapes and sizes.

The instructions for this basket will be very general because all sizes can be made; it will call for cane and reed, not handmade materials. As a general rule, the smaller the mold, the smaller the materials to be used for the ribs. For example, a 3- to 4-inch basket uses 1/4-inch binder cane, 3/16-inch or 1/4-inch flat-oval reed; a 5- to 8-inch basket uses 3/8-inch flat-oval reed; a 9 inch or larger basket uses 1/2-inch or 5/8-inch flat-oval reed.

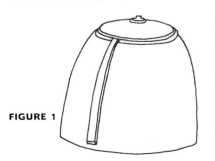

FIGURE 1

Measuring and Inserting Ribs Into the Base

Once you have found a mold and a base to fit, begin by pushing a piece of reed into the groove of the base to determine its depth. With the base on the mold, measure the distance from the base to the bottom of the mold. Add the depth of the groove and use this measurement for the length of all the ribs (figure 1).

Begin cutting the ribs, tapering one end 1 1/2 to 2 inches (figure 2). As a general rule, taper the ribs to half their original width. Insert the ribs into the groove, spacing them about 1/8 inch apart at the insertion point (closer on very small baskets). If you find your rib material too thick, simply shave a little thickness away with a shaper or knife. You want the rib to fit snugly in the groove of the base, so be careful not to shave away too much (figure 3).

Note: You must use an uneven number of ribs so that the over-under weave will be continuous.

When you're sure you have the correct number and spacing of ribs, remove them from the base and soak them in lukewarm water until they're very pliable. When they're well-soaked, reinsert them into the groove. The soaking will have caused some swelling—force them in so when they dry and constrict, they'll still fit. With the carriage bolt, fasten the base (with ribs inserted) onto the mold, using the nut to hold it tight. While the ribs are still wet, bend them all gently and smoothly down around the mold and secure them with one or more heavy rubber bands (this may prove to be a four-hand job). On larger baskets, a tire inner tube, cut in 1- to 2-inch strips, works well. Allow the ribs to dry in position (figure 4).

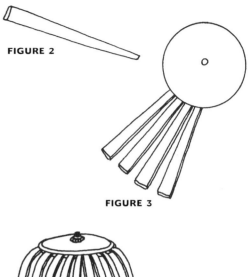

FIGURE 2

FIGURE 3

FIGURE 4

Weaving the Basket

Note: The finer the cane, the longer the weaving time, but the more exquisite the basket. A very large 12- to 14-inch basket might be woven with 3/16-inch cane, narrow or medium binder cane, down to fine-fine or superfine cane on the smallest. Some baskets are begun with a very fine cane and changed to a larger size once the weaving starts up the sides.

Taper the end of a 2-foot piece of cane the size you have chosen to use, for about 3 inches, and begin weaving by inserting the end behind a rib or in the groove with a rib. If you find your ribs are loose, allow the first row of weaving to slide into the groove with the ribs, making them fit more snugly. Weave over and under the ribs. By using the awl to lift each rib, you must

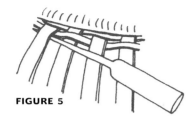

FIGURE 5

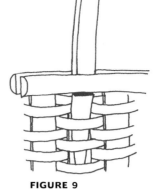

FIGURE 8

FIGURE 9

FIGURE 10

almost thread the cane under the ribs. Pull the cane tautly to get a smooth weave (figure 5).

Use relatively short pieces of cane (12 to 28 inches) because of the wear and tear each piece gets from the constant threading through such a tight space. Be sure the cane is always wet. When one piece runs out, splice a new one by letting the new end hide under a rib. Weave with both pieces until the old runs out on the inside of the basket. Old ends can be trimmed later so they are not noticeable from the inside (figure 6).

The rubber bands may be removed once the sides of the basket are well established and they won't lose their shape. Some people remove the rubber bands as soon as they begin to weave; use whichever method works best for you. Take care to pack each row as snugly against the last as possible. Continue adding weavers until the sides reach the height you desire (figure 7). Remove the basket from the mold if you haven't already done so.

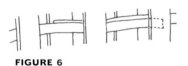

FIGURE 6

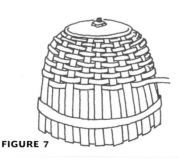

FIGURE 7

Finishing the Rim, Ear, and Handle

On the last row, taper the weaver for the last 5 inches, so it's half its width. The weaver should end at the same rib where the weaving began, so the top of the basket will be level.

Before actually applying the rim, select two ribs opposite each other (they won't be exactly opposite because of the odd number of ribs). Mark these two ribs so you can easily find them when you insert the ears.

If you plan to use a notched stationary handle or an ear to which the handle will later be attached, it should be inserted now. If you have a ready-to-use ear, insert it either on the inside or the outside of the basket, so the notch is placed where the rim will fit into it (figure 8). You can carve your own ear from any wood of your choice. Or you can use a stationary, notched handle, secured by the rim (figure 9). If

you're using ivory or porcelain knobs, they must be bolted through the handle and rim pieces (figure 10).

If you're using brass ears, insert them now (figure 11). You can make your own brass ears; just cut them with scissors from .010 or .015 gauge brass strips, obtainable from hobby shops or basketry supply shops. The handle should be attached to the brass ear (figures 12 and 13). A kerf or slit is sawn into the ends of the handles for about $\frac{3}{4}$ to 1 inch. They are then fitted down over the brass ears on both sides and secured with a rivet and washer.

Thoroughly soak (15 to 30 minutes) a piece of half-round reed that is long enough to reach around the top inside of the basket and overlap itself for about 3 inches. Use $\frac{3}{8}$-inch half-round for smaller baskets, $\frac{1}{2}$ inch for medium baskets, and $\frac{5}{8}$ inch for larger baskets.

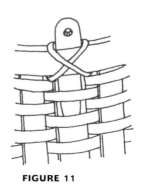

FIGURE 11

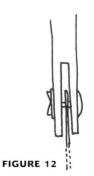

FIGURE 12

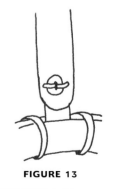

FIGURE 13

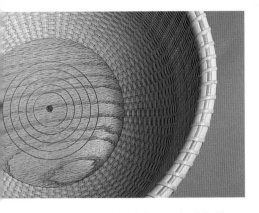

FIGURE 14

FIGURE 15

Bevel one end of the soaked half-round reed to approximately half its original thickness and fit it inside the basket, with the top of the rim even with the top of the weaving. Hold the rim in place with clothes-pins or clamps. Be sure the rim is level all the way around. When the ends meet, allow them to overlap and mark the beginning of the over-lap on both ends with pencil. Remove the rim piece and bevel the second end to fit smoothly over the first. The area of overlap should be no thicker than the rest of the rim (figure 14).

Replace the rim inside the basket, again clamping it, and nail it in four or five places with escutcheon pins, being sure to nail through a rib. Cut the nails off flush with the back of the rib. Note: If you are using brass ears, or an un-notched stationary

handle, be sure a nail goes through the rim and the ear of the handle.

Repeat the same procedure and apply the rim to the outside. This time, nail all the way through both rims and a rib, cutting the pins if and when they are too long (figure 15). Cut the ribs off flush with the top of the rim (figure 16).

Next, lay a soaked piece of the wider binder cane on top of the two rim pieces, cane side up, to cover the space between the two rims and the ends of the ribs. With a long, wet piece of smaller cane, begin lashing around the rim. You must force the cane to lie flat as you lash (figure 17). Begin and end the lashing either by bringing the end up between the two rim pieces and cutting it flush with the rim or by tucking it behind the weaving on the inside of the basket.

If you have used a notched wooden ear, attach the handle by drilling a hole through the ear and the handle and inserting a brass or copper rivet. Secure the rivet with a washer in the recommended manner. If you cannot find a satisfactory rivet, a small bolt and nut will do. Even a wooden dowel can be used or any-thing that will hold the two pieces together and still allow the handle to swing from side to side.

Most Nantucket baskets are painted or sprayed with clear shellac or, more recently, with polyurethane, which adds stability and gives the basket a more finished appearance.

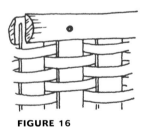

FIGURE 16

FIGURE 17

Miniature Three Diamonds

SKILL LEVEL: **Moderate**

A little gem, this basket is naturally prized for the fine, intricate diamond pattern and very narrow ash material. It certainly can be made from reed in a larger version.

DIMENSIONS
**APPROXIMATELY
4½ X 4 INCHES**

BAKETMAKER
LYN SILER

Materials

⅛-inch ash heavy weight
(dyed stakes)

3/32-inch or ⅛-inch ash
medium weight
(weavers)

¼-inch ash heavy weight
(false rim)

Long-leaf pine needles
(dyed)

Waxed linen (lashing)

Tapestry needle

Note: The ash stakes are very fragile and require being damp at all times. Not soaking wet, but dampened with a slight spray or wet sponge. Treat them gently to avoid damage.

Weaving the Base

From the ⅛-inch stake material, cut 22 pieces that are 13 inches long and one piece that is 5 inches long. Lay 11 pieces horizontally (with a center marked) and weave the other 11 pieces in a 3/3 twill (figure 1). If there is a right and wrong side, lay the right side up. The illustration shows how the first 6 rows are woven to the right of the center. Repeat the rows from the beginning to the right and in reverse to the left (the first row to the left will be a repeat of the sixth stake).

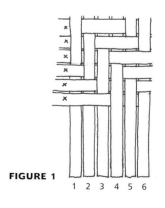

FIGURE 1
1 2 3 4 5 6

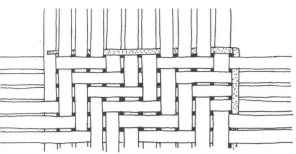

FIGURE 2. Starting tapered weaver mitering corner

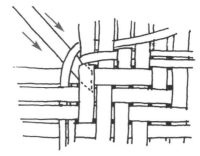

FIGURE 3. Adding short stake in corner

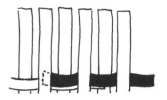

FIGURE 4. Starting new weaver

Weaving the Sides

Taper the end of a $^3/_{32}$-inch weaver to $^1/_{16}$ inch, far enough to reach around the base one time. Begin the tapered end just to the right of a corner and weave opposite the base weaving all the way around, mitering the corners. Do not cut the weaver (figure 2).

When you have woven the locking row, continue with the same weaver to weave the first row of over 2, under 2. When you have reached the starting point, insert the short stake (to create an odd number of stakes and enable you to do a continuous weave) in a corner, hiding the end under the base weaving (figure 3). This extra stake will throw off the weaving pattern so the over-twos will step over one stake each row.

Continue to weave with the base lying flat on a table surface, over 2, under 2 for six or seven rows. As you weave the rounds, pinch the corners and spread (starburst) the stakes from the center of the side to the left and right, filling in the corners with stakes and forming small peaks on the corners to serve as feet. When a weaver runs out, add one by letting the old end stop on the outside. Place the new weaver so the end is hidden behind a stake

and weave with both the old and the new one together until the old one runs out (figure 4).

Mark side 1 (the side with the added stake in the left corner).

Mark side 2 (rotate the basket 90 degrees).

Mark side 3 (straight across from side 1).

Mark side 4 (straight across from side 2).

On side 1, just after the added stake, change to over 1, under 1 (plain weave).

The first row of plain weave will be easy. The second row will be more difficult. Spread the stakes to allow more room, as you need it. After the second row of plain weave, lift the base off the surface. Just lifting it off the table will make the sides automatically start to go upright.

Note: If you have too much trouble getting the weaving in, put the base back on a flat surface for another row or two.

Once you lift it from the table, watch the shape that is emerging. Make sure all the sides are leaning evenly. Adjust the stakes and pack the rows down tightly as you go. The secret of successful shaping is to keep the stakes evenly spaced.

If you feel the spaces are getting wider, check to see if the sides are leaning outward more. Likewise, if the spaces are getting tighter, the sides are probably going in too fast. Weave five or six rows of plain weave or until the weaving fits in quite easily.

Locate and mark the center stake on all four sides or as close to the center as you can get. To do this you must locate the stake on which the next row of weaving will be an over. Even if it isn't the very center one, use the next one over, or the one that looks the closest to being the center of that side. Mark the stake and designate the next row as the first row of the pattern. The center stake is an

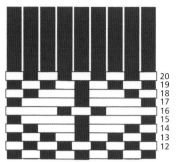

FIGURE 5. Pattern graph

20
19
18
17
16
15
14
13
12

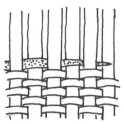

FIGURE 6. Ending weaver by tapering

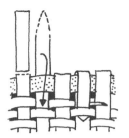

FIGURE 7. Cutting and tucking false rim

over on the first (12th row) pattern row. Even though it is the first pattern row, it is still just plain weave. Consult the graph (figure 5).

Row 13 is also plain weave. Row 14 begins the pattern changes. Looking at the graph, weave the next 25 rows. Remember that like a quatrefoil, the same things happen on sides 1 and 3 and 2 and 4 within the same row. Watch to see when a new row begins with side 1. It's rather difficult to do, as you tend to become absorbed in the pattern, but don't forget to check on your shaping.

Note: Remember that everything is plain weave except the center diamond. Keep in mind that whatever you do to side 1, you will do also to side 3 (likewise with sides 2 and 4).

After all the pattern rows are done, weave four or five rows (or as many as you want) of plain weave and taper the end of the weaver so it runs out above the starting point on side one (figure 6).

Finishing the Basket

Weave in one row of ¼-inch flat heavy weight material as a false rim. Pack all the rows down as snugly as possible. Let the basket dry before finishing the rim. If you are in a hurry, use a hair dryer, a warm oven, or even 10 to 15 seconds at a time in the microwave. If not, just let it dry in a warm place overnight or longer if possible.

When it is dry, pack the rows down again, and point the stakes that are on the outside of the false rim row. Bend them to the inside and push them behind a row or two of the weaving. Cut every other stake flush with the top of the false rim row (figure 7).

Hold 10 to 15 (or as many as you think you need) soaked pine needles on top of the rim, half on the inside and half on the outside. Thread the tapestry needle with a long piece of waxed linen (approximately 2 yards). Tie one end onto the basket around

the false rim. Take the tapestry needle from the outside to the inside around the pine needles (figure 8). Stagger the ends of the pine needles both inside and outside so they don't all run out at the same time. Continue to lash everything together, taking the needle from the outside to the inside. Keep a close eye on the inside to make sure the false rim row is being covered. There is a natural tendency for the needles to roll up. If the rim row shows when you are finished, a spot of black permanent marker or black dye works wonders.

Keep adding needles as one is running out by pushing the new end into the center of the bundle. Always keep the bundle approximately the same size. When you are nearing the end, you must mesh the beginning ends with the ending ends (figure 9). Cut some off prematurely just to keep the bundle the same size. What looks like a mess will eventually all work together to be a smooth ending.

End the waxed linen by back stitching a couple of spaces and bringing the tapestry needle up through the rim at a long angle. Cut it off and you're finished!

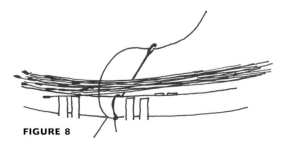

FIGURE 8

FIGURE 9

Choctaw Pouch

Versions of this basket appear in the work of several Indian tribes. A bit difficult at first, but once the diagonal technique registers, it's a snap.

DIMENSIONS ·
**APPROXIMATELY
12 X 9 X 16 INCHES**

BASKETMAKER
CAROLYN KEMP

SKILL LEVEL: **Moderate**

Materials

1/2-inch flat reed
(stakes and weavers)

1/2-inch flat-oval reed (rim)

1/4-inch flat reed (lashing
and handle wrap)

#5 round reed or
sea grass (rim filler)

3/8-inch flat reed,
30 inches (handle)

Cutting the Weavers
and Weaving the Base

From the 1/2-inch flat reed, cut 23 pieces that are 28 inches long. Dye 11 strips in the color of your choice. Rinse thoroughly and wipe off any excess dye that might bleed. Soak the remaining 12 strips. Mark a halfway point on the wrong side of the natural strips (figure 1).

On the wrong side of the colored strips, mark at 7 1/2 inches from one end and make another mark 14 inches from the other end (this is the center). Begin twill weaving the 11 colored pieces at the center mark on the natural stakes, moving to the left (figure 2 on page 60). Be sure the first stake weaves under 2, over 2, etc.

Note: The base is shown very loosely woven for clarity only. In reality, the stakes should be flush against each other.

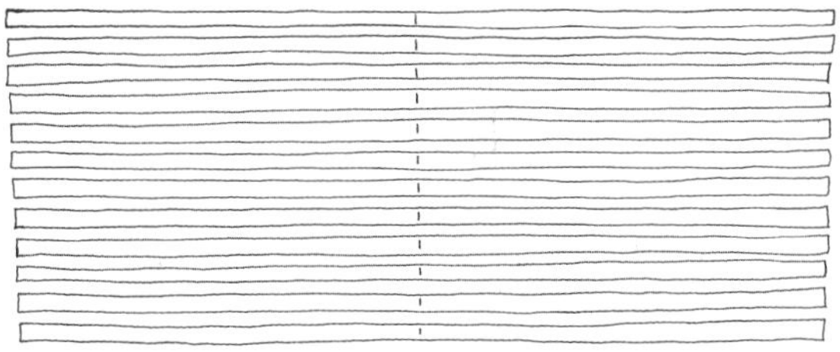

FIGURE 1

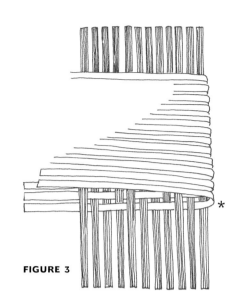

Natural

Colored

Plain / Natural

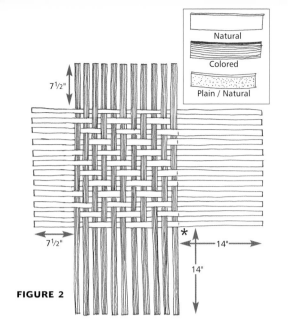

7½"

7½"

14"

14"

FIGURE 2

*

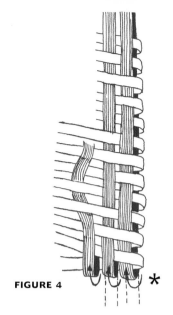

FIGURE 3

*

FIGURE 4

*

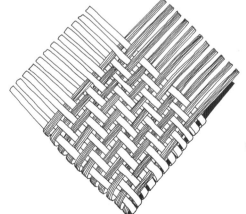

Weaving the Basket

Roll the natural stakes over the woven area—do not crease them (figure 3). They won't be easy to hold in place, but use a weight on the very ends if you need to. Just don't fold them flatly.

Begin twill weaving the colored stakes into the natural ones (figure 4). Be sure to follow the illustration. Make a mental note of the asterisk at the lower right corner; this will become the point at the bottom of the basket.

Continue weaving all the colored stakes into the natural ones, stepping up one stake each row. When you finish weaving all the colored stakes into the natural ones, your square is complete (figure 5).

Forming the Basket

You'll need to work on the shape of the basket at this point (figure 6). The drawing on the left is the shape you have now. Hold the basket on the sides at points A and C and, pressing on both sides, force D and B outward. The vertical diamond should become a horizontal diamond. The side you rolled and did not crease as you began to weave is now the front of the basket and the asterisk is the point. Notice that the colored weavers are horizontal on the front and vertical in the back (figure 7).

Now, weave one row at a time, the natural soaked strips around the top (vertical ends) in a regular over-under pattern, overlapping the ends

FIGURE 5 *

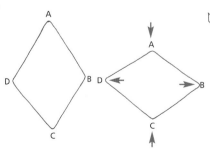

A

B

D

C

D

A

B

C

FIGURE 6. Top view

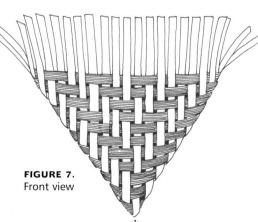

FIGURE 7.
Front view

*

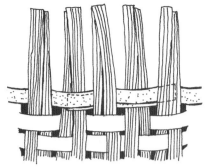

FIGURE 8

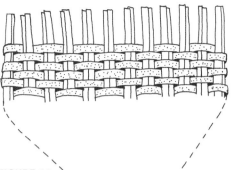

FIGURE 11

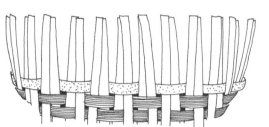

FIGURE 9

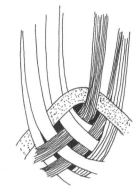

FIGURE 10

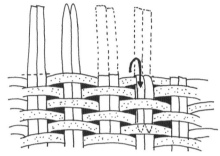

FIGURE 12

(figures 8 and 9). Notice that you're bringing two stakes together and treating them as one, except at both corners. Here, you weave over or under (whatever the weaving pattern dictates) a single colored stake (figure 10).

Weave over and under for six rows (figure 11).

Finishing the Basket

Cut off the inside stakes even with the top of the weaving and shape the outside stakes to a point so they can be tucked into the weaving on the inside of the basket (figure 12). Rewet the outside stakes, if necessary.

Place a soaked piece of $1/2$-inch flat reed around the rim, covering the top or last row of weaving on the inside and the outside, placing the overlaps near each other, with a piece of #5 round reed or sea grass in between. Hold all the pieces together with clothespins (figure 13). Begin lashing, losing the lasher inside the rim pieces (figure 14). Lash in only one direction or in both directions, forming an X.

Making the Handle

Cut a piece of $3/8$-inch flat reed that is 29-inches long. Push the ends through an opening on the sides of the basket (under the rim) and bring the ends back up about $2 1/2$ inches to form a loop (figure 15). Wrap the entire handle by sticking the end of a soaked piece of $1/4$-inch flat reed between the overlapped pieces. Wrap tightly all the way across and finish in the same manner.

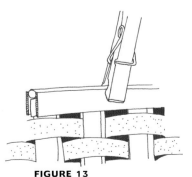

FIGURE 13

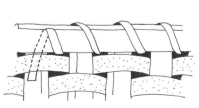

FIGURE 14

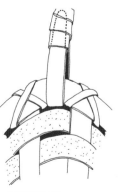

FIGURE 15

Double-Wall Basket

DESIGNER: **Kathy Tessler**   SKILL LEVEL: **Moderate**

Kathy Tessler, a self-taught basket artist and workshop instructor from Michigan, has taken the mystery out of double-wall construction. The neat thing is that the first wall is there to act as a mold for the second one.

DIMENSIONS
**APPROXIMATELY
5½ X 5½ INCHES**

BASKETMAKER
KATHY TESSLER

Materials

1/4-inch flat reed, natural and dyed in three colors (spokes)

1/4-inch flat reed, dyed (weavers and inside wall)

1 1/64-inch flat-oval reed, natural (weavers and outside wall)

1/4-inch flat reed (rim rows)

3/8-inch flat-oval reed (rim)

1/8-inch ash or cane (lasher)

Miniature sea grass (rim)

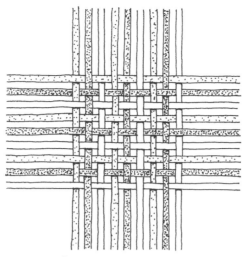

FIGURE 2. Base

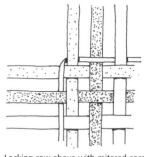

Locking row above with mitered corner

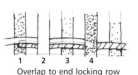

Overlap to end locking row

FIGURE 3

Cuts

- 1/4-inch flat in natural, 18 spokes at 15 inches

- 1/4-inch flat in color A (black plum), six spokes at 15 inches

- 1/4-inch flat in color B (slate blue), six spokes at 15 inches

- 1/4-inch flat in color C (dark green), six spokes at 15 inches

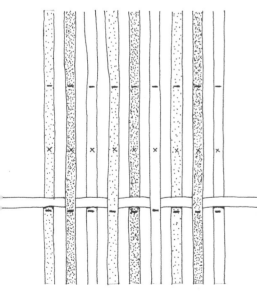

- Plum

- Blue

- Green

FIGURE 1

This basket uses double-wall, double-base construction techniques. Because of this, the good side of the reed will show on both the inside and outside of the basket. You need to be very careful when starting a weaver. Remember that the rough side of the reed will be facing you for the inside wall.

Mark the centers on all spokes on the rough side. The base is woven with dyed 1/4-inch spokes.

Lay out all vertical spokes in the following order: plum, blue, green, plum, blue, green, plum, blue, and green (figure 1).

Place marks 1 3/4-inches above and below the center marks on the vertical spokes. These marks set the outer dimensions of the base. Allow a 3/16-inch space between the spokes. Hold them in place with a spoke weight.

The first horizontal spoke is green. Position it just above the marks 1 3/4-inches below the center marks on the vertical spokes.

Continue to add spokes in the following order, working up from the first horizontal spoke: green, blue, plum, green, blue, plum, green, blue, and plum.

Adjust the base to measure 3 1/2 x 3 1/2 inches at this point. Mark the corners when everything is measured (figure 2).

Cut a piece of 1/4-inch blue flat reed that is long enough to go around the base one time with a 3-inch overlap. Weave a locking row opposite the base weaving to hold the base in place, mitering (folding) the reed at a right angle, with the weaver at the corners. When you have woven all the way around the basket, overlap the beginning for four spokes, ending the weaver behind a stake (figure 3).

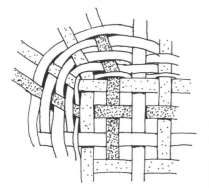

FIGURE 4. Starburst

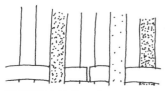

FIGURE 5. Butt ends

FIGURE 6. Tucking inside stakes to outside, outside view

Weaving the Sides

The inside wall is woven with ¼-inch dyed reed in start/stop rows.

The sides of the inner basket are woven first and will serve as the mold for the outer wall of the basket. Be very careful to position your weavers with the right side of the reed facing the inside of the basket.

Weave the first four rows from the outside of the basket with the base held flat to the table, shaping the corners into peaks. Spread the stakes toward the corners until the empty space at the corner is all filled in and the stakes are starburst (figure 4). The base corners slowly rise up off the table if you tighten the weaver around the corners. After weaving four rows with the base on the table, pick the basket up and continue to weave with the basket rolling on its side on the table or your lap for shaping.

Keep the weavers snug at the corners. Remember, you're weaving on the outside of the basket with the good sides of the weavers on the inside. Turn the base as you weave so that you're always pulling the weavers toward you, rather than trying to push them away from you. Keep rows tight together as you go—it is difficult to tighten later.

The rim will cover the top row of weaving. Cut the ends of this row to butt together; this decreases bulk inside the rim (figure 5).

Point and tuck the inside spokes to the outside of the basket and push them behind the first available row of weaving (figure 6). Cut off the outside spokes flush with the top row of weaving.

Outer Base

The outer base begins by sliding a natural spoke between the two intersecting center spokes of the inner basket. This connects the two baskets at the center of the base (figure 7).

Complete the base in a single layer with the rest of the spokes, plain weaving them as in the inner base. Spokes will be placed directly above corresponding spokes. Twist-tie the two bases together at the corners to prevent shifting of the bases as you weave the outer wall (figure 8).

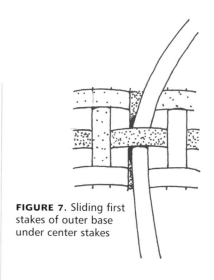

FIGURE 7. Sliding first stakes of outer base under center stakes

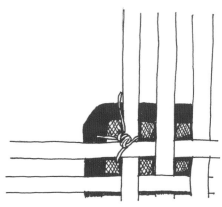

FIGURE 8. Center base on top of inner base, twist-tied together

FIGURE 9. Funky overlap

Outer Wall

The outer wall is woven in continuous weave with $^{11}/_{64}$-inch flat-oval reed.

Note: For the outer wall of the basket, use the funky overlap to create a smooth outer surface (figure 9). Begin rows of weaving by slipping the end of the reed under three spokes just to secure them. Do not weave the new ends with the old weaver. End the rows by cutting and hiding the end of the weaver under one spoke. When done correctly, no double layers of reed are seen on the outside of the basket (figure 10).

Taper the beginning end of one weaver. Place the tapered end behind a spoke and weave over one, under one around the basket. Clothespin the corner spokes together to help shape the outer basket.

When you reach the beginning point of weaving, weave under two and continue weaving. The under two will travel around the basket, shifting one spoke to the right each time you weave around the basket. This is how you can weave continuously with an even number of spokes. Taper the end of the weaver to level the basket.

Weave one row of $^3/_8$-inch flat reed, making the ends only butt instead of overlap.

Tuck the outside spokes between the walls of the basket. Cut off spokes that are between the walls of the basket.

Applying the Rim

Place the soaked rim pieces in place over the false rim. Clip on the rim pieces one at a time and mark the overlaps. Allow for a 3 to 4-spoke overlap. Make sure the overlaps are pointed to the right (if you lash to the right). You'll start the lasher just past both of the overlaps.

Remove the rim pieces and bevel the overlaps so the overlapped area is no thicker than a single rim piece (figure 11). Taper the rim filler overlap. Replace and clip the inner and outer rims securely in place (figure 12). Make sure the overlaps are pointing to the right, as you'll start lashing just to the right of the overlaps and move to the right around the rim.

Start the lasher by pushing the end up under the inside rim piece, over the false rim and under the rim filler, to the outside of the basket. With the remaining long end, take the lasher into every space under the rim between spokes. End the lasher as it began, going under the inside rim, up over the wall, and to the outside. Cut the end of the lasher flush with the bottom edge of the rim.

The basket can be stained with natural spray stain.

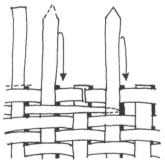

FIGURE 10. View from outside

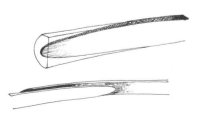

FIGURE 11

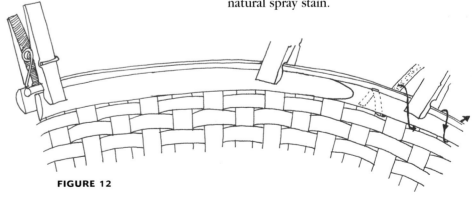

FIGURE 12

Hatteras Purse

SKILL LEVEL: **Moderate**   DESIGNER: **Judy Wobbleton**

This beautifully shaped, simple purse is charming and easy—a delightful combination. The wooden base makes it oval from the beginning. Enjoy making and carrying your Hatteras Purse.

DIMENSIONS
**APPROXIMATELY
5 X 10 X 7½ INCHES**

BASKETMAKER
JUDDY WOBBLETON

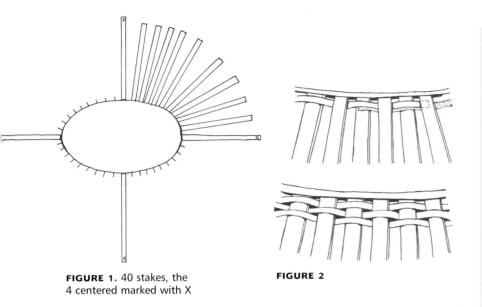

FIGURE 1. 40 stakes, the 4 centered marked with X

FIGURE 2

Materials

⅜-inch flat reed
(stakes and rim row)

4¼ x 9-inch slotted
oval base

¹¹/₆₄-inch flat-oval reed
(weavers and lasher)

¼-inch flat-oval reed
(weavers)

32-inch leather purse
handle

½-inch flat-oval reed (rim)

Sea grass (rim filler)

Preparation

For the stakes, cut 40 pieces of ⅜-inch flat reed that are 10 inches long. Soak them until they're pliable.

Inserting the Stakes Into the Base

Insert the soaked stakes into the slot in the base, wrong side up. Place one stake at the center point on each side of the base (one at each of the pointed ends and one on each long side). Mark an X with pencil on the extended tip of each of these four stakes. Evenly insert the remaining 36 stakes into the base, nine in each quarter (figure 1).

Weaving the Sides of the Basket

Weave the first two rows of the sides with the base still on a flat surface, using a soaked piece of ¹¹/₆₄-inch flat-oval reed. Make sure the first row is woven by starting one end of the weaver on top (outside) of the center stake of one of the long sides of the basket.

Weave over and under all the way around the base. Using the start-stop method, continue to weave over the beginning of the weaver to the fourth stake before cutting it to hide it (figure 2). If the reed is thick, shave the top of one end and the bottom of the other where they're overlapped to avoid any unnecessary build-up at that point (figure 3).

Gently pull the sides of the basket up as you weave the next five rows, still using ¹¹/₆₄-inch flat-oval reed. The sides should lean out for 7 to 10 rows at the beginning; then very gradually the diameter should decrease (figure 4).

Weave 18 rows of ¼-inch flat-oval reed, starting and stopping at a different place each row to avoid any build-up from the double thickness. It's helpful to turn the basket a quarter turn each row.

Watch the shape of your basket as you weave. Concentrate on keeping the center stakes (marked with the X) in the center of each side as you weave and make sure the diameter decreases. The circumference at the 18th row should be approximately 26 inches.

FIGURE 3

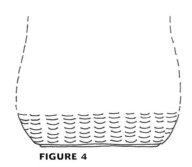

FIGURE 4

Applying the Handle

Weave the 19th row with $1/4$-inch flat-oval reed and attach the handle. Insert the weaver through the leather handle loop so it is positioned on the center stake on each short end of the basket (figure 5).

Weave four more rows with $1/4$-inch flat-oval reed. Weave one row of $3/8$-inch flat reed for the false rim row.

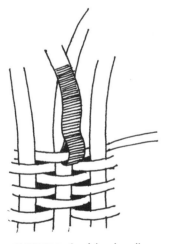

FIGURE 5. Applying handle

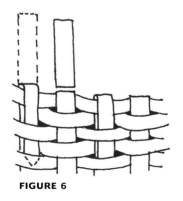

FIGURE 6

Finishing the Basket

Dampen the ends of the stakes by spraying or dipping the ends into water.

Cut all the stakes that are on the inside of the false rim flush with the top of that row. The stakes on the outside should be pointed. Bend them over the false rim row and to the inside of the basket, pushing them behind the first available row of weaving on the inside (figure 6).

Measure the basket circumference and add 3 to 4 inches for overlap. Cut two pieces of $1/2$-inch flat-oval reed that length and soak them until they're pliable. Place one piece on the inside of the basket with the overlap pointing in the direction you'll be lashing. Place the other piece on the outside, again making sure the overlap is pointing in the direction you'll be lashing. Position the overlaps near but not on top of each other. Hold both pieces in place with clothespins or clamps.

Place a piece of sea grass between the two rim pieces, letting the ends overlap 2 to 3 inches.

Soak a long piece of $11/64$-inch flat-oval reed until it is pliable. Start the lashing just to the right of the two overlapped areas by taking one end of the $11/64$-inch reed, wrong side up, under the inside rim from bottom to top, over the wall of the basket and under the sea grass (figure 7). Take it down under the outside rim to the outside of the basket (you can cut the end flush with the bottom of the rim later). With the end secured, begin lashing with the other end, going into every space between stakes under the rim. Keep the oval or right side up as you lash. End the lasher just as it began by hooking it over the wall of the basket under the rim pieces. Use the awl to open up a space to push the end under the rims and the sea grass.

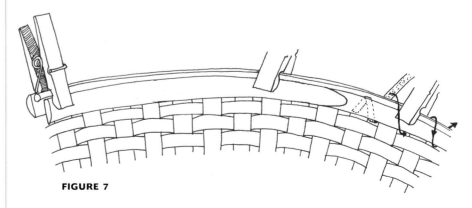

FIGURE 7

Willow Field Basket

SKILL LEVEL: **Moderate**   DESIGNER: **Bonnie Gale**

You can make this sturdy basket from willow or round reed. Large enough to hold children's toys, dried flowers, or lots of magazines, it is functional as well as decorative.

DIMENSIONS
**APPROXIMATELY
19 X 14 INCHES**

BASKETMAKER
BONNIE GALE

Materials

- One pound of 4-foot willow (French randing and bottom foot weavers)
- One pound of 5-foot willow (base weaving, bottom, and top waling)
- Two pounds of 6-foot willow (bottom sticks, stakes, and two roped handles)
- Knife
- Large awl or bodkin
- Rapping iron
- Pruning shears
- Grease horn
- Weights
- Ruler
- Damp towels

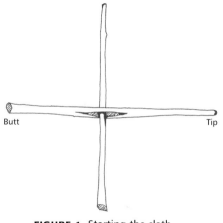

FIGURE 1. Starting the slath

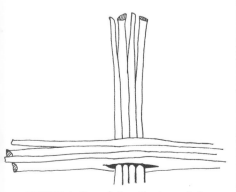

FIGURE 2. Completing the base slath

Soaking the Willow

6-foot willow, soak for 5 days

5-foot willow, soak for 4 days

4-foot willow, soak for 3 days

The willow should mellow under cover the night before use.

Grading the Base

From the bundle of 6-foot rods, choose the eight very thickest rods for the base sticks. Choose six thick, long rods for the two roped handles (you need four, but two rods are spares), and 32 medium-thick rods for the stakes. Label and reserve under cover.

Making the Slath

Cut the eight reserved rods at 15 inches from the butt end. Insert the knife into the center of one of the four thickest sticks; turn the knife in the rod to open up the slit and insert a thinner rod through it (figure 1). Split the other three thickest sticks and place them on the solid stick, making sure that the butts and tips of the sticks are alternated and the concave shape of the sticks is facing down. The convex side is the top of the base or the inside of the basket. With all of the split stakes on the one

solid rod, push the other three thinner sticks through the splits, again alternating butts and tips (figure 2). You have just made a 4 x 4 slath.

Pairing the Base

Grade 30 of the thin 5-footers. Take the thinnest pair of rods and shave the butt end down for about 6 inches. Insert the shaved ends into the horizontal pocket of the slath, with the shaved sides outermost (figure 3). Then start a pairing weave with the two rods by taking the top shaved rod to the right over the top of the four sticks of the slath, and then down in the back of the slath. Make sure that all four quadrants are equal in length. Both weavers are now in the rear of the slath.

For the pairing weave, take the left weaver (in the back) behind the slath, in front of the slath to the right, and then down behind the slath again. This motion of behind/in-front/behind is repeated in turn with each of the two weavers, as the base is turned clockwise. Make sure that the shaved sides of the rods are turned to the inside of the base so they aren't visible (figure 4). The left weaver becomes the right one and the old right becomes the new left weaver. This motion is

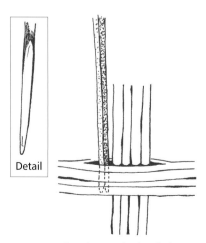

FIGURE 3. Starting to tie the slath

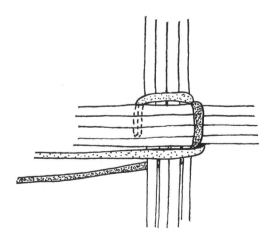

FIGURE 4. Pairing around the 4x4 Slath

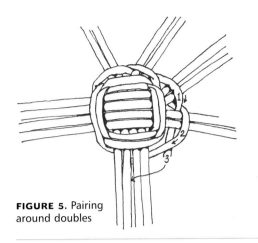

FIGURE 5. Pairing around doubles

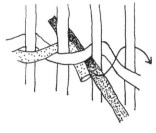

FIGURE 6. Pairing joins

completed for the entire base. For two rounds, the base is woven as a 4 x 4 slath. Separate the four sticks into pairs for two rows (figure 5). Then weave around the sticks singly. Add tips to tips and butts to butts (figure 6). As you weave, make sure to spread the butt joins around and work a convex or domed shape to the base.

Finishing the Base

When there's a diameter of 13 inches, weave out to a pair of tips, as measured across the underside of the base. Weave the tips of the rods individually in and out of the last row of pairing to complete. Trim the ends of the rod joins on both sides of the base.

Staking Up and Upsetting

Slype the 32 six-foot stakes by making a sloping cut using the curved knife (on the butt end of the rods on the belly side). Willow rods have a natural inside curve or belly (the outside curve is called the back).

With the concave side of the base towards you, push the slyped rods into the base so the cuts are facing you. Push the slyped rod down beside each side of each bottom stick and insert the rods for approximately three inches. Continue around the base until all the stakes have been inserted (figure 7).

Turn the base over and bring all the stakes up to a 90° angle with the base. Push a knife or bodkin into the junction of the stake and base. If the stake cracks, remove it and re-slype it, if enough rod thickness remains. Then reinsert the stake into the base. Bring up the pricked-up stakes and tie them with a rubber band (figure 8). It's helpful to use the flat side of a rapping iron to push the stakes into the base, as necessary.

To upsett or bottom wale, take 12 thin, 5-foot rods and start a three-rod wale, with tips on two opposite sides of the base. Trim the six longest rods to the same length and add three tips on opposite sides of the base. The tips are added to three consecutive stakes, so the tips come to the front on the right side of the stakes (figure 9).

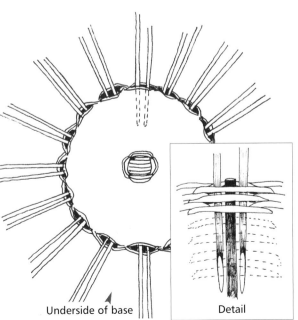

Underside of base

Detail

FIGURE 7. Staking up

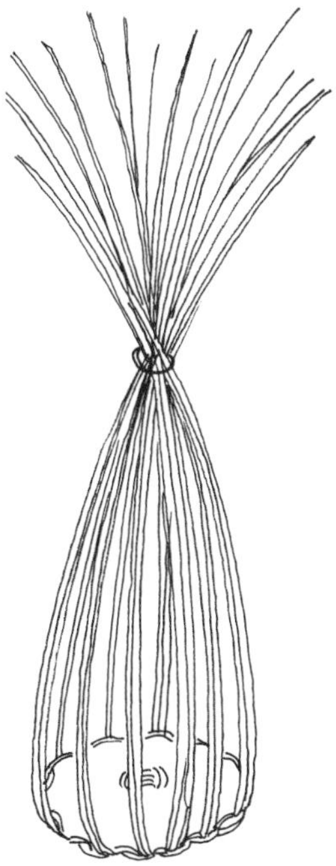

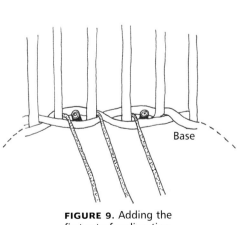

FIGURE 8. The staked up basket

Base

FIGURE 9. Adding the first set of waling tips

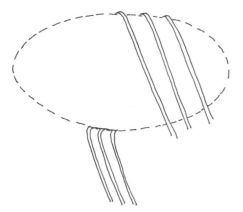

FIGURE 10. Showing the additional set of walers

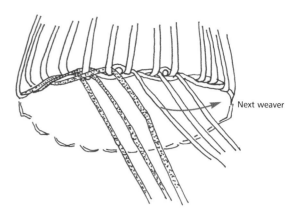

Next weaver

FIGURE 11. Junction of the two waling sets

To three-rod wale, take the left hand waling rod in front of two stakes, then behind the next stake (to the right) and out to the front of the base. Add a second set of three tips to the opposite side of the base; these two sets will chase each other around but never overtake each other (figures 10 and 11). The weaving sequence is repeated to the butts of the rods where new butts are added in the same manner as the pairing joins in the base. Weave the new rods out to the tips.

When the waling is completed (with the tips left on the outside of the basket), place several stabilizing weights inside the basket.

French Randing on the Siding

Grade the bundle of 4-foot rods by height into two sets of 32 rods (one set thicker and longer than the other). It is important to remove the very thick rods. Randing rods must be thinner in diameter at the base than the stake diameter.

After shaping the basket (still tied) and rapping (beating down) the waling, take the longest set of French randing rods and insert into the siding. To insert a weaver, place the butt end of the rod an inch into the basket, then kink the rod in the front of the next stake to the right, weave to the inside of the next stake to the right and bring the rod

to the outside, in front of the next stake to the right. This sequence of in-front/behind/in-front (after the rod has been placed to the inside of the basket) is repeated with the other rods, but the new weavers are added to the left of the existing weavers (figure 12). To add the last two rods of the set, lift up the first two weavers that were added initially and weave the last two rods underneath the first weavers (figure 13). When all 32 randers have been inserted, rap the weaving down.

Continue to weave the set of rods just added by starting anywhere on the basket and taking a rod in-front/behind/in-front, making sure that

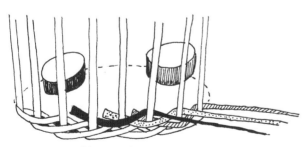

FIGURE 12. Adding the first set of French randing weavers

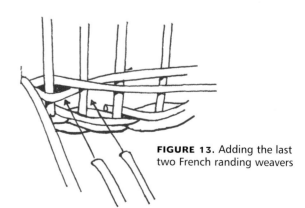

FIGURE 13. Adding the last two French randing weavers

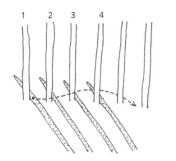

FIGURE 14. Starting the top waling

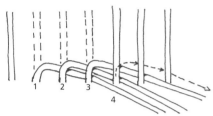

FIGURE 15. Starting the four-behind-two border

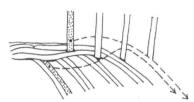

FIGURE 16. The border in progress

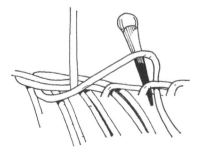

FIGURE 17. Ending the border

the next weaver is taken from the left. Single or multiple rows of weaving can be accomplished at a time. The basket has an inside dimension of 18 inches and a height of 10 inches prior to the border, so keep measuring in order to achieve this shape.

When the first set is woven out to the tips (there will be one tip coming out to the front by each stake), add the second set of 32 rods in the same manner as the first, making sure to rap down after the new rods have been added. Continue with the second set in the same manner as before and end with tips.

Top Waling

The top four-rod waling is made with eight medium 5-foot rods. Add four tips to four consecutive stakes (figure 14). Take the left of the group in front of two stakes, behind two stakes, and out to the front. Repeat with the next weaver from the left and continue, adding butts to butts and working back to tips. Rap down and measure the height of the basket (10 inches) to make sure it's level.

Four-Behind-Two Rod Border

Starting anywhere on the basket, kink (turn over) four stakes ¼ inch above the level of the waling. From the left, take each of these stakes behind two upright stakes, to the

right, and out to the front of the basket. You now have four stakes turned down horizontally in the front of the basket (figure 15).

The border now has two steps. First, take the left horizontal in front of two upright stakes to the right (actually in front of three stakes but one is already turned down), behind the next stake, and out to the front. Then take the left upright stake down behind and beside the horizontal rod to make a pair. This two-part process is completed with every turned down stake, so the remaining three horizontal rods will gain an upright to become pairs. Try to keep the pairs flat and the two rods side by side, or the border won't be level. When you have four pairs, the two-part weaving method is the same, but the right of the pair will be used as the weaver and the left of the pair will be left behind and trimmed off at the end of the border (figure 16). To complete the border, the weaving is the same, but some stakes and weavers have already been used. Weave the last rods through the beginning of the border (figure 17). When the border is completed, trim the whole basket.

Removable Foot

Invert the basket and insert the slyped cut off ends of the 32 stake from the border to the base. Insert one rod into each stake (figure 18).

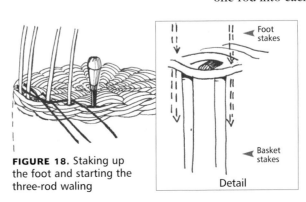

FIGURE 18. Staking up the foot and starting the three-rod waling

Foot stakes

Basket stakes

Detail

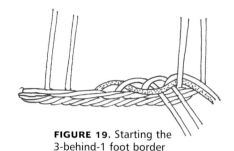

FIGURE 19. Starting the 3-behind-1 foot border

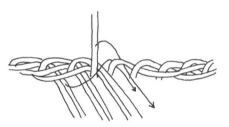

FIGURE 20. Bending down the last upright on the foot border

FIGURE 21. Finishing the foot border

Using six thin 4-foot rods, start a three-rod wale with tips, add butts to butts, and finish with tips (figure 19). Rap it down and make a 3 behind 1 border. Kink three stakes of the foot and take each behind one stake and out to the front. Take the left horizontal in front of one upright, then behind the next stake and out to the right. Take the left upright stake behind and down to make a pair (figure 20). Weave these three pairs around to the right. Weave through the end of the border and trim the foot (figure 21).

Roped Handles

Decide on the location of the handles—anywhere except where waling rods have been joined. Insert one of the thick slyped 6-foot rods down into the basket beside a stake, using a greased bodkin. Carefully work the rod into an arc for the handle bow and take the rod from the outside to the inside of the bas-

ket where you want the handle to be located. Pull the rod through and then rope it, cranking the rod around in increasingly larger circles in order to break down the fibers. Twist the rod back up and make tight turns in the roped handles. Reform the bow and start on the right inside side, twisting the rod up and making three turns along the handle bow, ending by coming to the inside of the basket (figure 22).

Take the roped rod under the top waling from the inside to the outside of the basket and then follow the turns back to the other side, ending under the waling. Then take the second 6-foot rod on the other side of the existing handle, rope the whole length and then take the rod along the existing pattern, back and forth (figure 23). The tip of this rod should end on the other side of the handle. Weave the two tips away along the bottom of the top waling rods. Repeat for the second handle.

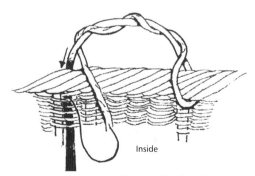

FIGURE 22. Inserting the first handle rod

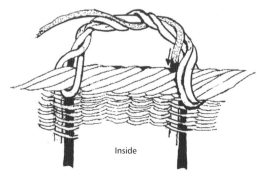

FIGURE 23. Inserting the second handle rod

Wool Drying Basket

SKILL LEVEL: **Moderate**

Historically, the Wool Drying Basket was used for drying fleece by the fireside. In addition to its elevated design, it was probably woven in a plain weave so that air could circulate through the wool. Today, it would be perfect for holding knitting or sewing supplies beside a favorite chair.

DIMENSIONS
**APPROXIMATELY
11 X 11 X 12 INCHES**

BASKETMAKER
JUDY WOBBLETON

Preparing Materials and Weaving the Base

From the ⅝-inch flat reed, cut 34 pieces, each 34-inches long. Mark the centers (on the wrong side) of some of the pieces. Note: You can align a few center marks and then align the ends of the stakes. Soak all the pieces until they're pliable.

Lay 17 stakes, horizontally, on a flat surface in front of you, wrong sides up (figure 1).

Weave the center stake across the center marks (figure 2). From the top the pattern is: over 2, under 2, over 2, under 2, etc., and ending over 1. From this point, follow the Pattern Chart, weaving eight stakes to the right of A and eight stakes to the left (figure 3).

Materials

⅝-inch flat reed (stakes and weavers)

⅝-inch flat-oval reed (rim)

#12 spline or #12 round reed or 2 bushel basket handles (handles)

#7 round reed (rim filler)

4 feet (optional)

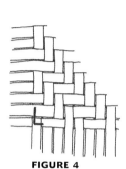

FIGURE 3

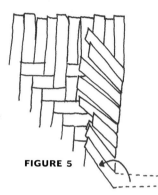

FIGURE 4   **FIGURE 5**

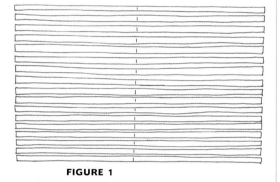

FIGURE 1

FIGURE 2

Pattern Chart

O = Over, **U** = Under

LEFT OF A

O1, U2, O2 ending O2

U2, O2, U2 ending U1

U1, O2, U2 ending U2

O2, U2, O2 ending O1

RIGHT OF A

U1, O2, U2 ending U2

U2, O2, U2 ending U1

O1, U2, O2 ending O2

O2, U2, O2 ending O1

Repeat the pattern twice on both sides. Pack the stakes tightly together. Measure and true the base to 11-inches square, marking the corners (figure 4).

Weaving the Sides

Upsett all the stakes by bending each one over upon itself toward the base to form a permanent crease at the base of the stakes (figure 5).

Begin weaving with a long, soaked piece of ⅝-inch flat-oval reed by going around any two stakes. Hold the weaver in place with clothespins or a brake (figure 6). Continue under 2, over 2 all the way around the basket. End the row by overlapping the beginning end for six stakes to secure the weaver and hide the end (figure 7).

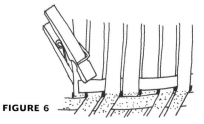

FIGURE 6

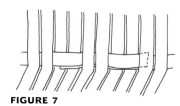

FIGURE 7

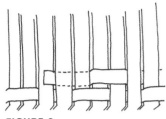

FIGURE 8

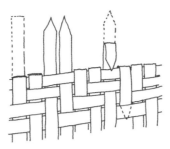

FIGURE 9

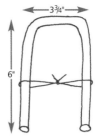

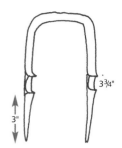

FIGURE 10   **FIGURE 11**

Start another row (on a different side) by going over the second of the stakes that was outside on the first row and continuing over 2, under 2 around the basket again. You have stepped-up one stake (figure 8).

Weave in the same manner for twelve rows. Do not square the corners; let them round and the top will be round or oval. Pack all the rows down as snugly as possible.

Point all the outside stakes and cut the inside ones flush with the top row of weaving (figure 9). Tuck the pointed ones into the weaving inside the basket.

Finishing

If you have bushel basket handles, insert them into two opposite sides, centering them in the weaving. If you're making your own handles, refer to the handle directions in the Hannah's Marriage Basket on page 141. Pay attention to the dimensions of your handles (figures 10 and 11). Insert the handle (figure 12).

Soak enough ⅝-inch flat-oval reed to go around the top of the basket two times, plus 6 to 8 inches for overlap. Bevel, or scarf, the ends of the two pieces (figure 13). Place one piece on the inside and one on the outside. Hold them in place with clothespins or cable clips. Next, fit a piece of #7 round reed around the top of the basket above the two rim pieces. Scarf the ends of it as well.

Begin a lasher by pushing one end down between the two rim pieces. Wrap around the round reed as many times as needed to reach the second stake (figure 14). Take the lasher straight down into the space between the stakes, under the rim, to emerge on the other side and wrap again around the round reed. End the lashing by losing it between the rim pieces. Scarf the other end of the round reed so the two ends fit together smoothly and can be wrapped.

Insert the feet (figure 15). They usually fit snugly, but in case they don't, nail them to a weaver or the rim, if they reach. Place two on one side, with the end stakes, and two on the opposite side with the same stakes.

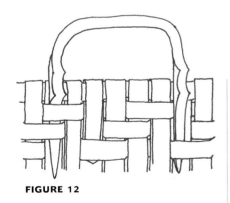

FIGURE 12

FIGURE 13

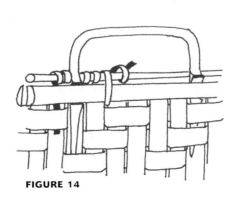

FIGURE 14

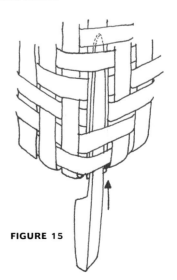

FIGURE 15

Krista's Oval Basket

SKILL LEVEL: **Moderate**

DESIGNERS: **Lyn Siler
and Judy Wobbleton**

Materials

3/4-inch flat reed (stakes)

1/4-inch flat-oval reed (weavers)

1/4-inch flat reed (lashing)

Sea grass (weaving)

10-inch oak push-in handle (open notch)

1/2-inch flat-oval reed (rim)

Originally designed for my daughter Krista, this multi-purpose oval basket features rows of seagrass woven into its construction. Try experimenting with various lengths and widths of reed.

DIMENSIONS
**APPROXIMATELY
6 X 14 X 14 INCHES**

BASKETMAKER
JUDY WOBBLETON

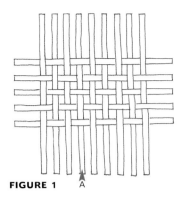

FIGURE 1   A

Measure, Cut, and Weave the Bottom of the Basket

Cut five pieces of $3/4$-inch flat reed, each 33-inches long. Cut nine pieces of $3/4$-inch flat reed, each 28-inches long. With a pencil, mark the centers of all the pieces on the wrong side. Soak the pieces in warm water for a few minutes.

Remove them from the water and place the five longer pieces horizontally on a table with the center marks aligned, about $1/2$-inch apart. Next, begin to weave the shorter pieces over and under, vertically. Place the first short piece directly over (and under) the center marks on the longer pieces—this is the center stake. Continue weaving the other pieces (four on each side), alternating the over-under pattern. After all the pieces are woven, you should have a mat (figure 1).

Measure and true the base to approximately 6 x 11 inches, and mark the corner so you'll know if any slipping occurs.

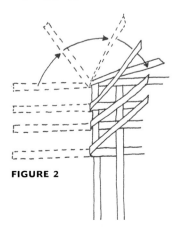

FIGURE 2

Upsetting the Sides and Beginning to Weave

Upsett the sides by bending each stake all the way over upon itself, creating a permanent crease at the base of the stake. The stakes will not stand upright by themselves, but the crease is necessary (figure 2).

Note: The sides of this basket do not stand straight up. You must try to weave around the stakes and still allow them to lean outward a little. Check the shape after each row to be sure you're not pulling too tightly, especially around the corners.

Soak a long piece of $1/4$-inch flat-oval reed for a few minutes. Begin weaving around the sides by placing the flat side of the reed against a stake that originates from underneath the woven area. In figure 1, A is one of the stakes that originates from underneath. Use clothespins to hold the weaver in place when you begin to weave (figure 3).

Weave all around the basket, over one stake, under the next, etc. When you reach the starting point, remove the clothespin and fit the weaver in with the piece already there for three more stakes. Cut the weaver so it will be hidden behind the third stake after the starting point (figure 4).

Begin the next row and every subsequent row in a different place so as not to create a build-up from always starting and stopping in the same spot. Make sure the sides are rounded as you weave, not standing straight

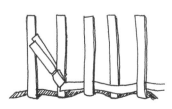

FIGURE 3

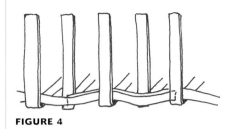

FIGURE 4

FIGURE 5

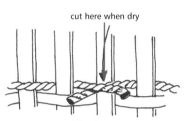

cut here when dry

FIGURE 6. Inside view

up (figure 5). Continue to weave one row at a time for six rows.

Change to sea grass on the seventh row. Soak the sea grass for a few minutes, and begin to weave as before, except the rows of sea grass should begin and end inside the basket. Since they are too thick to overlap, the ends are left free for about an inch inside the basket. When they're dry, clip the ends so they butt (figure 6). Weave four rows of sea grass, then six rows of $1/4$-inch flat-oval reed. Repeat the pattern two more times, ending with eight rows of $1/4$-inch flat-oval reed, instead of six. The rim will cover the top two rows. After the second section of sea grass, begin to tighten on the weaver as you go, gradually bringing the sides of the basket in.

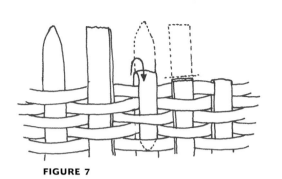

FIGURE 7

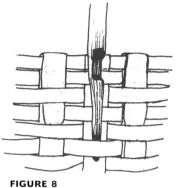

FIGURE 8

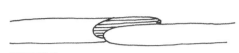

FIGURE 9

Finishing the Stakes and Inserting the Handle

When all the rows are woven, finish the stakes by cutting the inside ones flush with the top row of weaving. Then, point the outside stakes, rewet them, and tuck them inside the basket into the weaving (figure 7). Push the ends of the handle down into the weaving of one row only on the inside of the basket, making the notch fall on the false rim row (figure 8).

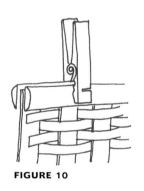

FIGURE 10

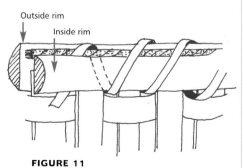

FIGURE 11

Applying the Rim

Wet a piece of the 1/2-inch flat-oval reed and a very long piece of 1/4-inch flat reed. Place the 1/2-inch flat-oval reed on the inside of the basket, covering the top two rows of weaving, allowing it to fit into the notches you made in the round reed. Hold it in place with clothespins. Allow the ends to overlap for about 2 inches. Scarf the ends with your knife so the overlapping area is not too thick (figure 9).

Repeat the same procedure by placing another piece of 1/2-inch flat-oval reed on the outside of the basket. Treat the ends the same way as before and hold both pieces together with the same clothespins (figure 10).

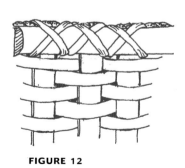

FIGURE 12

Lashing the Rim

Before beginning to lash the rim, place a piece of sea grass on top of and between the two rim pieces. It should lie on the inside of the handle. Soak a long piece of 1/4-inch flat reed. From the inside of the basket, bring one end of the lashing up between the inside rim and the basket, over the sea grass, and down the other side between the basket and the outside rim (figure 11). Next, push the lashing through the first available space between the stakes, from front to back. Continue lashing all the way around with the lashing moving diagonally from one space to the next. Lash in the opposite direction, if you wish, to create an X pattern (figure 12).

Topsail Treasure Pine Needle Tray

SKILL LEVEL: **Moderate**   DESIGNER: **Dianne Masi**

A shell picked up on Topsail Island in North Carolina was the inspiration for this pine needle tray basket. Many people find coiling with pine needles a particularly satisfying kind of basketmaking.

Materials

Artificial sinew

Darning needle and thread

Center start

3 ounces dyed pine needles (ends trimmed)

3 ounces natural pine needles (ends trimmed)

Piece of drinking straw for gauge

DIMENSIONS
**APPROXIMATELY
8 X 7 X 2 INCHES**

BASKETMAKER
DIANNE MASI

Starting the Basket

Cut a piece of sinew about an arms length and split it down. Some sinew splits down five times, others split down only three times. Use the thickness that you like. Thread the needle and tie the loose end onto your center start by knotting it so that it won't pull loose. Make sure the knot is on the edge of the center start so the pine needle coil can cover it (figure 1).

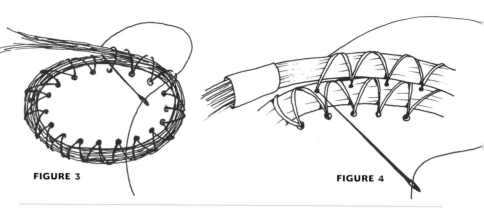

FIGURE 3

FIGURE 4

Take approximately six dyed pine needles in your left hand and place the ends over the knotted sinew on the edge of the center start. The right side of the center start should be facing you. Holding the threaded needle in your right hand with the thread behind the needle, place the needle through the same hole as the knot. Pull snug. Now stitch two stitches in the next hole to the left of the center start. This forms one slanted stitch and one bar stitch, also known as the wheat stitch. Continue the wheat stitch in three more holes (figure 2).

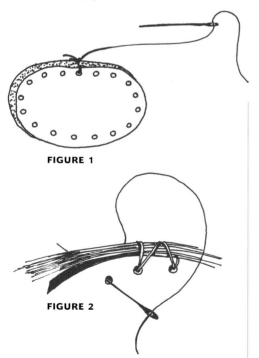

FIGURE 1

FIGURE 2

Start adding pine needles by inserting them one-at-a-time into the center of the coil, until you feel it catch under the last stitch. Add two or three pine needles, stitch two or three wheat stitches, and repeat until you have gotten back to the beginning. In the first hole where you tied on, place one stitch while covering the ends of the pine needles with the working coil. To finish this first wheat stitch so it looks like one complete V shape, take a half stitch in the top third of the first bar stitch (figure 3).

Rows 2 through 9: Put the gauge on to the ends of the pine needles so that your coil will be a consistent shape. Continue with the wheat stitch for seven rows of colored needles and then change to natural needles. When changing from one color to another color, start about halfway around the coil to insert your new color in the center of the coil. The old color will gradually run out and the new color will take its place.

Every stitch or two, add two pine needles to the gauge until it is full, but not so tight that the gauge can't easily be moved. Don't forget to add needles as you go along. You'll probably only be able to do two or three

wheat stitches before you have to add pine needles.

For rows 2 through 9 you will be doing the wheat stitch. To do this stitch, insert the sewing needle into the top $1/3$ of the coil on the right side of the bar and come out on the left side of the bar stitch in the back of the coil (to make the slanted stitch). The bar stitch is formed by placing the needle in the exact same place (figure 4).

Starting and Stopping Threads

There are many ways to start and stop threads in a coil. Some coilers like little knots that pop through the coil and hide in the middle. Some tie one thread to another and hide it by coiling over the knot and ends. Others like to run their needle and thread through the coil for an inch or two. I prefer what I call an over-locking stitch. This is not an original idea. I picked it up somewhere in my readings and it works well for me.

To end a thread when it's about 4 to 5 inches long, backstitch to the right over the stitch you have just completed. To do this, angle your needle toward your left hand and insert it

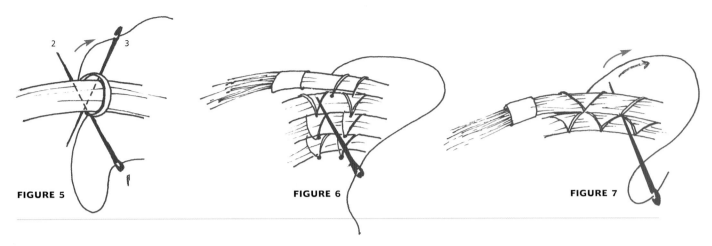

FIGURE 5   **FIGURE 6**   **FIGURE 7**

into the coil. Do this twice and cut off your thread close to the coil.

Starting a new thread works the same way (figure 5). Go in on the right side of a stitch (1) about an inch to the right of where you left off, come out on the left side of the stitch (2), and loop over that stitch and insert the needle back in and pull through to lock over (3). Do this three times to get back to where you ended the previous thread.

Shaping the Sides

At the beginning of the next row, start to pull the coil toward you while you're stitching. The needle will shift as you stitch, being put in at the bottom third of the coil and coming out on the top of the previous coil instead of top third of coil. This shift in stitching will allow the sinew to hold the coil up and develop the sides. Once this first side coil is complete, keep stitching front to back to stack you coils. Shaping your sides depends on how you stack the coils. If you slant them outwards, the sides will flair. If stacked exactly on top of each other, your sides will be straight up and down. If slanted in, then the sides will pull inward. On the sides of this

basket you'll switch to the diamond stitch and coil eight rows of natural needles, and then change to your colored needles on the last row.

Diamond Stitch

As you're starting to form the sides, you'll want to change from the wheat stitch to the diamond stitch. The diamond stitch is a two-part stitch, which is very effective on the sides of the basket.

To begin the diamond stitch, while center starting to pull the sides, do a single whipstitch (or overcast stitch) in the straight bar portion of the wheat stitch (figure 6). If the stitches seem to be too far apart, add a stitch in the slanted portion of the wheat stitch also. Continue the whipstitch around one complete row, then reverse direction and whipstitch in the exact same spots, except in reverse. This will form a V design.

To develop the diamond design, on the next row, place your whipstitch where the V's meet (figure 7). Again overcast using the whipstitch all around this coil until you complete the row and then reverse directions again to form the V shape. Your

beautiful diamond design immerges! Continue eight rows up in natural needles, with the last two rows being pulled in toward the center from the curve. Halfway through the last natural row, start to change back to your original color to accent around the top.

Ending the Top Row

Stop adding pine needles about 4 to 5 inches before the end of the last row. You can randomly clip the longest needles to eliminate some of the length. If I feel the coil might thin out too quickly, I take a couple of the clipped pieces and reinsert them into my coil. As you come around the last row, check how the coil will be ending by bending it into place to see if the coil ends in the correct spot. Take off the gauge about 3 inches from the end and continue to whipstitch to the end of the row. By this time you should only have a few scraggly pieces hanging out from under your last stitch. If you have more than this, randomly clip some of the center pine needles to thin the coil before stitching to end of row. Now reverse to complete your diamond design and end your thread.

Twill Weave Market Basket

SKILL LEVEL: **Moderate**

Historically, any square or rectangular basket with a flat bottom is broadly classified as a market basket, and there are endless design possibilities. Included here are instructions for dyeing multi-colored reed so that you can make your own colorful interpretation.

DIMENSIONS
**APPROXIMATELY
8 X 12 X 12 INCHES**

BASKETMAKERS
**LYN SILER AND
CAROLYN KEMP**

Materials

- ½-inch flat reed
  (stakes and weavers)
- 8 x 12-inch D handle
- ½-inch flat-oval reed (rim)
- #5 or #6 round reed (rim)
- ³/₁₆-inch flat reed (lashing)

Note: These instructions will produce an 8 x 12-inch twill woven basket that uses an 8 x 12-inch D handle. If you choose not to use the D handle, you can substitute a push-in U handle or swing handles. Instructions for both these alternatives are given at the end. If you want a square rather than rectangular basket, cut all the stakes the same length and use the same number of stakes vertically and horizontally.

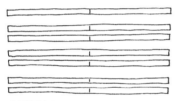

FIGURE 1

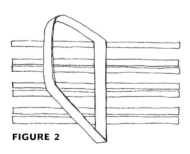

FIGURE 2

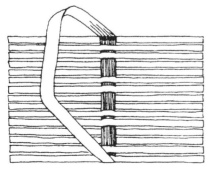

FIGURE 3

Preparing the Materials

From the ½-inch flat reed, measure and cut the following stakes:

- 15 pieces, 32 inches long
- 20 pieces, 28 inches long

Using the pencil, mark the center on the wrong side of the reed. When bent in half, the wrong side splinters and the right side doesn't. Place all 35 pieces in water for a minute or two to make them pliable.

Placement of Stakes

Lay seven of the 32-inch stakes down horizontally in front of you, with the wrong side up, in three groups of two and one by itself (figure 1). Place the D handle perpendicularly across the seven stakes along the center mark (figure 2).

Place the remaining eight 32-inch stakes on top of the D handle in pairs, in the same direction as the original seven, filling in the spaces between the first seven (figure 3). Spread apart or push in all 15 stakes, making the bottom of the basket the exact width of the D handle.

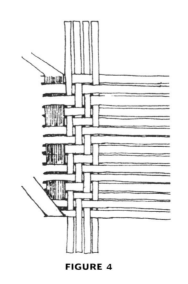

FIGURE 4

Note: This is going to be difficult to hold in place for a while. A large book placed on one end of the stakes will help.

Weaving the Bottom of the Basket

With the fifteen 32-inch stakes in place, begin weaving across with the 28-inch stakes. The following guide will tell you exactly how to weave, so you'll have the twill pattern on the bottom as well as on the sides.

Pattern Chart

O = Over, **U** = Under

LEFT SIDE OF HANDLE

Row 1: U2, O2, U2, O2, etc … ending O1

Row 2: U1, O2, U2, O2, etc … ending O2

Row 3: O2, U2, O2, U2, etc … ending U1

Row 4: O1, U2, O2, U2, etc … ending U2

RIGHT SIDE OF HANDLE

Row 1: O2, U2, O2, etc… ending U1

Row 2: U1, O2, U2, O2, etc … ending O2

Row 3: U2, O2, U2, O2, etc … ending O1

Row 4: O1, U2, O2, U2, etc … ending U2

Note: The pattern reads from the top. These four rows will be repeated once and you will end with Row 2 (on both sides of the handle), with ten rows on each side. Double-check the first four rows of weaving (figure 4).

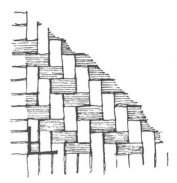

FIGURE 5

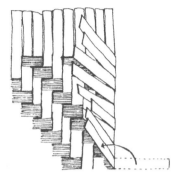

FIGURE 6

Upsetting the Sides

When all 20 of the 28-inch stakes are woven in, measure and true the base of the basket, making sure it is 8 x 12 inches. Mark the corners with a pencil when you're sure of the measurements. If you're going to have problems keeping the base square, it will be with the corners. If you mark the exact angle, at least you'll be aware if any slipping occurs (figure 5).

Upsett the sides of the basket by turning all the stakes all the way over upon themselves, to cause a permanent crease at the base of the stake. The stakes will not stand upright until you have woven several rows, but the crease is necessary (figure 6).

Starting to Weave the Basket Sides

With a soaked piece of $1/2$-inch flat reed at least 45-inches long, begin weaving at the point shown (figure 7). Continue around the basket, weaving over two stakes and under two stakes. Be sure the right side of the weaver is on the outside of the basket. Use clothespins frequently to hold the stakes upright. You'll soon realize that you're not picking up all the stakes—only in the third row of weaving will you make all the stakes stand upright.

Move clothespins on the second row of weaving when they are in your way and replace them as needed. When you've woven all the way around the basket and have returned to the starting point, allow the ends of the weavers to overlap to the fourth stake. Check to be sure the ends of the weavers are going to be hidden behind a stake before cutting them. Begin weaving the next row, and every row thereafter, in a different place to avoid a build-up.

Begin weaving the second row by inserting the end of the weaver between two of the stakes that were covered by the weaver on the previous row (figure 8). This is called stepping-up a stake. You're weaving over one of the same stakes you wove over in the previous row, plus a new one. Treat the

handle as a stake. The twill pattern will be established after four rows of weaving (figure 9).

Note: Always remember to begin each row at a new place and to keep the right side of the weaver on the outside of the basket.

Continue weaving until the basket is 6- to 7-inches deep. Keep pushing the weaver down snugly.

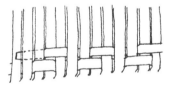

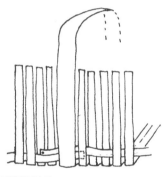

FIGURE 7

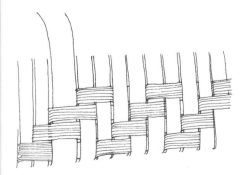

FIGURE 8

FIGURE 9

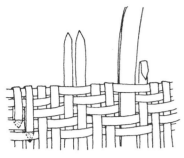

FIGURE 10

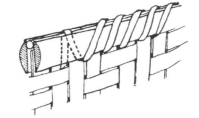

FIGURE 11

Finishing the Basket

When you've finished weaving all 12 rows (or more if you prefer), you'll find that some of the stakes are in front of a weaver and some are behind it. Wet the top part of the stakes again. With scissors or wire cutters, cut off the inside stakes so they're even with the last row of weaving. Then shape the outside stakes to a point, checking each of them to be sure they will reach inside at least to the first row of weaving. Now, bend the pointed stakes over and insert them into the weaving inside the basket (figure 10).

Note: You may need to use an awl to help get the stakes into the weaving.

Applying the Basket Rim

With all the outside stakes pushed down into the weaving (if you are not using a D handle, insert a U handle now), wrap a piece of $^1/_2$-inch flat-oval reed all the way around the outside top edge of the basket. The flat or wrong side of the reed should be against the basket. Overlap the ends about 2 inches and cut off the rest.

Shave half the thickness from each end of the overlap so it is no thicker than a single thickness of flat oval. Hold the reed in place with clothespins, pinching the corners with your fingers as you go around.

Take a second piece of wet $^1/_2$-inch flat-oval reed and wrap it all the way around the inside top edge of the basket, overlapping as before. Hold the two pieces with the same clothespins. Finally, place a piece of #5 or #6 round reed between the two pieces of flat-oval reed butting the ends.

Lashing the Rim

With a long strip of the $^3/_{16}$-inch flat reed, begin to lash all the rim pieces together (figure 11). Use your awl to open the space for lashing, just underneath the rim (below the top

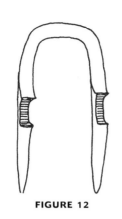

FIGURE 12

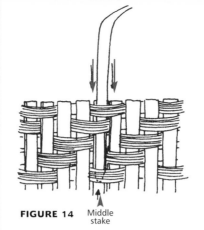

FIGURE 14 Middle stake

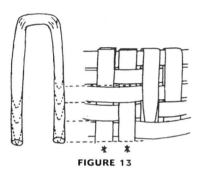

FIGURE 13

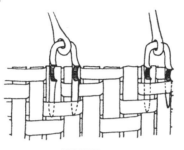

FIGURE 15

How to Dye Multi-Colored Reed

Coil strips of the reed and tie them loosely with a bread tie (figure 16). The coil was dipped into the first dye at 6:00 until it reached up to 3:00 and 9:00. It was then dipped into the second dye at 12:00 until it reached to 3:00 and 9:00, and then into the third dye at 3:00 and 9:00, causing the two colors to be separated and creating a gradual blending. Any color combinations and any number of colors may be used as long as they overlap each other for the blending process.

row of weaving). Tuck the ends of the 3/16-inch lashing between the two rim pieces.

If your basket isn't perfectly square when you finish, rewet the whole thing and square the corners by pinching them and allowing them to dry again.

There are three handle alternatives for this basket: D handle (shown in these instructions), swing handle, and a push-in square, notched U handle.

If you choose to use a swing handle, refer to the loop-making instructions in Hannah's Marriage Basket on page 141 (figure 12). In this case, because of the twill weave, the loops will need to be long enough to reach the third row of weaving, depending on where you choose to insert them. Consequently, you should decide where the loops will be placed before cutting them. For

example, one side of the loop will be behind row three, and the other behind row two (figure 13).

If you're using a push-in handle, simply find the center stake and insert the handle into the weaving before putting the rim on. It can be placed on the inside or the outside of the basket (figure 14).

If you're not using a D handle, remember to add an extra vertical (shorter) stake to replace the handle. Begin by laying the horizontal strips and weaving the extra stake in the center, replacing the D handle (figure 15). The arrow in the illustration points to the center stake. Also, to compensate for the width of the D handle, add two extra rows (one on each end) for length. This means you'll cut twenty-three 28-inch stakes. The 32-inch stakes remain the same; just be sure the distance across them is approximately 8 inches.

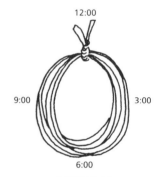

FIGURE 16

Materials

1/2-inch flat reed
   (stakes and weavers)

Williamsburg handle

1/2-inch flat-oval reed (rim)

#6 round reed (rim filler)

3/16-inch flat reed (lashing)

Williamsburg Basket

SKILL LEVEL: **Moderate**

Somewhere along the way, this basket shape became known as the Williamsburg Basket, though this one is not made exactly like the ones originally associated with the design. Regardless, it is a strong and handsome multi-purpose basket that will serve you well.

DIMENSIONS
**APPROXIMATELY
7½ X 12 X 10 INCHES**

BASKETMAKER
JENNY ANTOLINE

Weaving the Base and Upsetting the Stakes

Cut 17 pieces of $1/2$-inch flat reed, each 28-inches long. On the wrong (rougher) side, make a mark at the halfway point. Soak all the strips in warm water for a couple of minutes. Lay four stakes on a surface in front of you, aligning the center marks, wrong side up (figure 1).

Place the handle across the stakes, on the center marks (figure 2). Then lay the remaining five stakes on top of the handle in the spaces and on each end (figure 3).

FIGURE 1

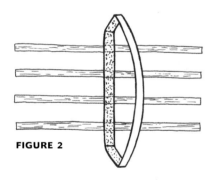

FIGURE 2

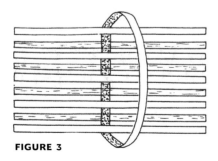

FIGURE 3

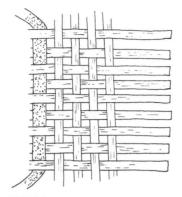

FIGURE 4

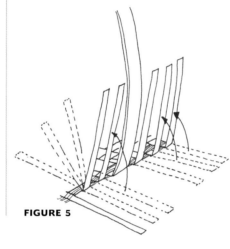

FIGURE 5

With all the nine horizontal stakes in place, begin weaving the other strips in a regular over-under basket weave (figure 4). There will be four on each side of the handle. When they're all in place, measure and true the base to $7 1/2$-inches square.

Upsett the stakes by bending them over upon themselves to form a permanent crease at the base of the stake (figure 5). They won't remain upright, but will stand as you weave around the basket.

Weaving the Basket

Soak a long piece of $1/2$-inch flat reed. When it's pliable, begin by placing one end of the weaver, wrong side against the stakes, either on the handle, or on any stake that originates beneath the woven mat (figure 6). Weave all the way around the basket, being careful not to square the corners, and end the row by overlapping the ends (figure 7). The two ends are overlapped four stakes, and each end is hidden behind a stake or a weaver.

Begin the next row and every subsequent row on a different side of the basket to avoid a build-up on one side.

Note: Turning the basket $1/4$ turn every row is a good idea. When weaving, the sides of the basket (supported by the handle) will follow the shape of the handle, but you must concentrate on making the other two sides flare out in the same fashion.

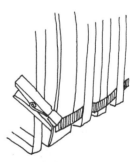

FIGURE 6

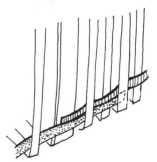

FIGURE 7

Finishing the Stakes and Applying the Rim

When you've woven as far as you want (ours is about 10 inches), find the stakes that are on the outside of the weaving. Point these with scissors or wire cutters, rewet them, and bend them to the inside. With the aid of the awl, push them into the weaving as far as they'll go. The other stakes (the ones on the inside of the weaving) are cut off flush with the top row of weaving (figure 8).

Apply a piece of wet $\frac{1}{2}$-inch flat-oval reed around the outside top of the basket, holding it in place with clothespins. Allow the ends to overlap about 3 inches. Apply a second piece of wet $\frac{1}{2}$-inch flat-oval reed to the inside top of the basket. Hold both pieces to the top row of weaving with the same clothespins. Finally, place a piece of #6 round reed between the two top pieces of flat oval, still holding all the pieces together with the same pins (figure 9). Place the shaved overlaps near, but not on top of, each other.

Then, with a long, soaked piece of $\frac{3}{16}$-inch flat reed, lash all the rim pieces together (figure 10). Lose the ends of the lashing reed into the rim anywhere it's convenient and inconspicuous. You may want to lash in the opposite direction as well, forming an X pattern (figure 11).

To make the smaller sized basket, use the same directions and the following measurements: From $\frac{3}{8}$-inch flat reed, cut 13 pieces that are 20-inches long. Weave with either $\frac{1}{4}$-inch flat reed or $\frac{3}{8}$-inch flat reed. Use $\frac{1}{2}$-inch flat-oval reed for the rim.

FIGURE 8

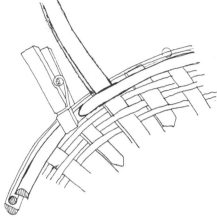

FIGURE 9

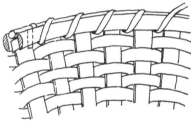

FIGURE 10

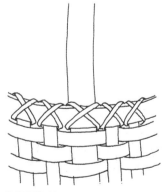

FIGURE 11

Fancy Quatrefoil

SKILL LEVEL: **Moderate**
DESIGNER: **Joel Simpson**

A tightly woven ash basket is satisfying to hold, and will last for many generations to come. Its swing handle and intricate design seem to flow effortlessly from its oak base.

DIMENSIONS
APPROXIMATELY
6^1/$_2$ X 5 X 6^1/$_2$

BASKETMAKER
JOEL SIMPSON

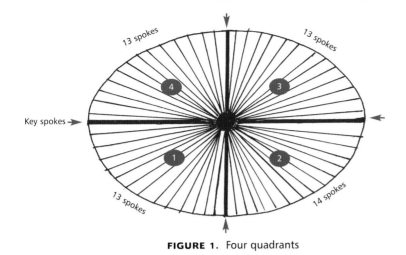

FIGURE 1. Four quadrants

13 spokes
13 spokes
Key spokes →
13 spokes
14 spokes

Materials

1/4-inch ash or oak spoke material

Oval slotted oak base

1/16-inch ash (weavers)

1/4-inch oak half round (rims)

1/16-inch ash (lasher)

6-inch oval basket mold

Handle with ears

Spoke Placement

Cut 57 spokes that are each 5 inches long from the 1/4-inch ash spoke material. Taper the spokes for 2½ inches until they're about 1/8-inch wide at the tip. The spokes are inserted into the slotted base and can be held in until the weaving starts by one of several ways: apply a drop of glue to the tips and allow them to dry overnight; wedge a 1/16-inch weaver in with the spoke; or start a weaver and weave in the spokes as you go.

The easiest spoke layout starts by inserting a spoke at the ends and sides of the oval base to create four equal spaces around the base. These four spokes are your key spokes and should be centered and at right angles to each other. They will determine where the centers of the pattern are. The four equal arcs between the key spokes are the four quadrants of the oval.

Weaving the Basket

Next, insert 13 spokes in each quadrant. One quadrant will get one extra spoke so that there will be a total of 57 spokes (4+13+13+13+1). The odd spoke lets you weave continuously,

rather than using start-stop rows. A spoke template helps the spoke spacing enormously. Taper a long 1/16-inch weaver for about eight inches and start weaving just past the quadrant with the odd spoke. Weave over 1, then under 1 around the basket for two full locking rows (figure 1).

At the first key spoke on the side of the oval, make sure the weave is over 1 and then weave under 2, over 2 for six pairs of spokes. At the key spoke on the end of the oval, you will weave under 3 with the key spoke in the center of the three. Continue over 2, under 2 until the next key spoke. Weave over 1 as you did on the opposite side and then under 2, over 2 to the next key spoke where you'll weave under 3

again. The pattern continues so that you weave an over 2, under 2 twill everywhere except at the key spokes. For each row, the weave changes at the key spokes in a regular pattern (figure 2).

The Pattern

	SIDES	ENDS
Row 1	O1	U3
Row 2	O3	U1
Row 3	U1	O3
Row 4	U3	O1

The pattern then repeats. This will give a V pattern on the sides and an inverted V pattern at the ends.

Continue weaving this regular quatrefoil pattern until you have about 25 rows. Stop weaving when you have completed an over 3 on both side keys (figure 3).

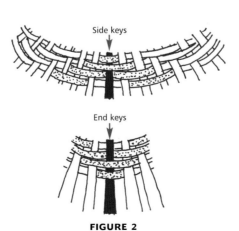

Side keys

End keys

FIGURE 2

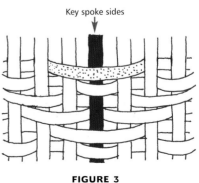

Key spoke sides

FIGURE 3

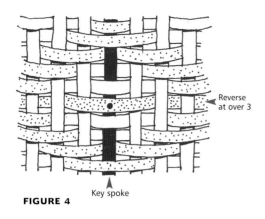

FIGURE 4

FIGURE 5

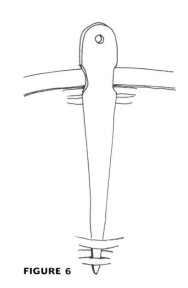

FIGURE 6

Reversing the Pattern

At this point, you want to reverse the pattern to produce a diamond shape in the weaving. This is a problem with the continuous weave. There are several ways to reverse a continuous quatrefoil—the goal is to make the transition as inconspicuous as possible.

As you weave the last row before you change the pattern, taper the weaver so the skinniest part ends in the quadrant with the extra spoke. Remember, at this point the basket should be symmetrical; that is, the weave on each side should be over 3 and under 1 on each end.

Taper the end of a new weaver and add it in the extra spoke quadrant, weaving in the opposite direction. For the pattern to reverse, you should weave under 3 at the first end, and then over 1 at the key spoke on the long side. Take time to make sure the weaving is working out correctly before you weave too far. The pattern now stair steps back the opposite way from the first half of the basket (figure 4).

There can be some difficulty in weaving in the opposite direction. To remedy that, start weaving with the top of the basket facing towards your body (rather than the bottom).

You'll continue to weave around to the right, as you were before. This can be accomplished either in your lap or by using the 45° hole on the mold stand and swinging the stand around so the post leans back away from you (figure 5).

Continue weaving to the top of the mold (about 25 more rows) and taper out the end of the weaver for a few inches. Weave in a $^1/8$-inch false weaver (O2, U2), then trim the ends of the outside spokes and bend them toward the inside of the basket. These should be trimmed so they won't protrude past the lower edge of the inside rim. Clip them in place and let them dry.

Insert the handle ears on the inside, so the tips tuck behind only one or two weavers near the bottom of the basket (figure 6).

Finishing the Rim

Measure the circumference of the rim and add 3 to 4 inches of overlap. Cut two pieces of $^1/4$-inch half round oak for the rims that length. Soak them and pre-form them if pos-

sible. Shave half the thickness from the top of one side and the bottom of the other to avoid any excess thickness. Place the rims on the basket, making sure the overlapped piece is pointing in the direction you will lash. Position the two overlaps near, but not on top of, each other and begin lashing just past both of them (figure 7).

To secure one end, take the soaked lasher up under the inside rim, over the wall of the basket and down to the outside under the outside rim. With the other end, come around the rim and go between the next two spokes and bring the weaver out on the inside. Pull very tightly. Take the lasher into every space between spokes. Make an X at the handle if you wish. End as you began by losing the lasher between the two rim pieces, going over the wall of the basket. Enjoy your heirloom.

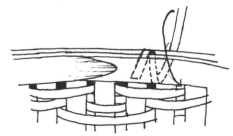

FIGURE 7. Starting to lash

Traditional Egg Basket

SKILL LEVEL: **Advanced**

Representative of early American baskets, the Appalachian egg basket is also known as a "gizzard" basket or "fanny" basket because the design keeps collected eggs from rolling around. It is a ribbed basket and, if you pay attention to details, not all that difficult to construct.

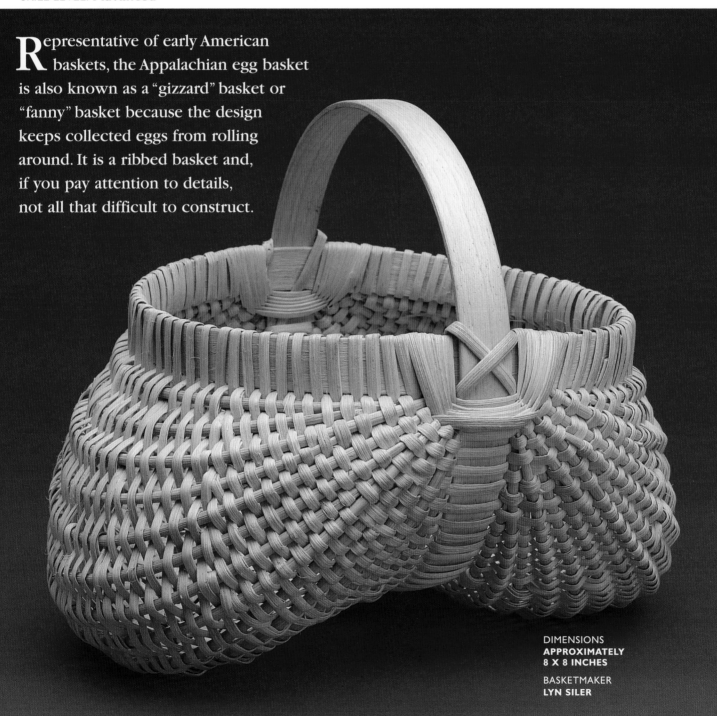

DIMENSIONS
**APPROXIMATELY
8 X 8 INCHES**

BASKETMAKER
LYN SILER

Materials

Two 8-inch round hoops

Waxed string

#6 round reed (ribs)

3/16-inch flat reed (weavers)

Measuring and Preparing the Hoops

The 8-inch egg basket requires a 12-inch exposed handle, which should be identified and marked first. Locate the splice (the point where the hoop has been joined in manufacturing) on the inside of one of the hoops. Holding the hoop with the splice in the bottom (or at 6:00), place an identifying mark on the inside of the hoop. This will be the bottom of your handle hoop. Next, on the outside of the hoop, pencil a mark at 9:00. With a tape measure on this mark, measure 12 inches around the top of the hoop and mark again on the outside. This second mark will be approximately at 3:00. The marked area will become your basket's handle (figure 1).

Next, make a mark 1/2-inch below the one at 9:00. Do the same at 3:00.

On the second, or rim, hoop, place the splice again at 6:00. On the outside of the hoop, pencil a mark across the width of the hoop at approximately 9:00. From this mark, measure the circumference of the

hoop. Divide the circumference in half and mark again on the outside of the hoop. This halfway mark should be at exactly 3:00. From these marks, measure 1/2-inch clockwise and mark again. You now have marked four points at which the two hoops will intersect.

Slide the second hoop (rim) through the first hoop (handle) at a right angle, aligning the marks (figure 2).

With a piece of waxed string, tie the two hoops together, making an X over both hoops (figure 3). Note: The handle hoop always goes on the outside of the rim hoop.

Cutting the Ribs

As you cut the ribs, number them in pencil. Place the numbers anywhere on the rib except the very end. From the #6 round reed, cut 2 each of the following lengths: #1, 14 inches; #2, 15 1/2 inches; #3, 18 inches; #4, 16 1/2 inches; #5, 14 inches. Sharpen both ends of each rib with a pencil sharpener (figure 4). The #3 rib needs to be especially sharp. Place these ribs aside.

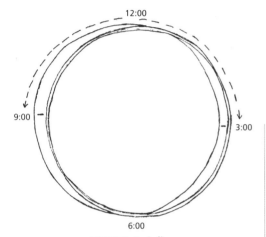

FIGURE 1. Splice

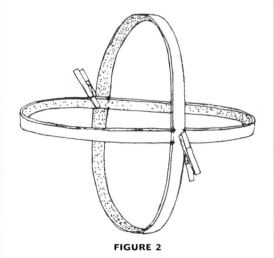

FIGURE 2

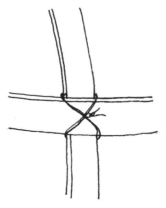

FIGURE 3

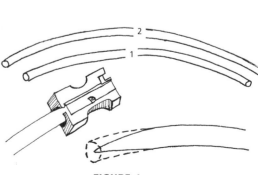

FIGURE 4

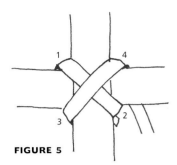

FIGURE 5

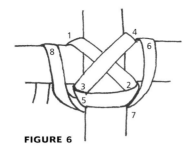

FIGURE 6

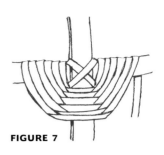

FIGURE 7

Making the Ear

Identify the wrong and right side of the weavers. The wrong side has absolutely flat edges. The edges of the right side are slightly beveled or rounded.

Select a long weaver (at least 8 feet) and soak it until it's pliable. Begin the ear by placing the end of the weaver behind the intersecting point of the hoops, wrong side of the weaver against the hoops, leaving about 1 inch free. Make an X over the intersecting hoops, starting at the dot and following the numbers in the illustration (figure 5). Be sure to take the weaver over its tail when moving from 2 to 3.

Then begin the actual ear (figure 6) Bring the weaver over the top of the handle hoop, up and around the right rim (6), down to (7) under the handle hoop and up to the left rim (8). Repeat, moving from one side to the other, keeping the wrong side of the weaver against the hoops, until you have six rows on both sides. Count the rows from the top of the rim. Note: If the loose end of the weaver is in your way after the first revolution, secure it with the weaver, and then cut it off. Make the ear as tight as possible (figure 7). Do not cut the weaver. Secure it at the rim with a clothespin. Repeat the procedure on the other side.

Inserting the Primary Ribs Into the Ear

The finished ear has four openings—one underneath each rim (2) and one on either side of the bottom or handle hoop (2). Insert an awl into each of these spaces and move it around enough to open the space even more (figure 8).

Now, insert the #1 ribs into the openings just underneath the rim, pushing and twisting at the same time until they feel secure. Insert one on each side of the basket. Insert the #2 ribs into the same space as #1, underneath #1.

Next, insert the #5 ribs into the space on either side of the handle hoop (bottom of basket). Insert the #4 in the same space as, and above, the #5.

Make a hole in the reed between the #2 and #4 ribs (figure 9). This space was formed as a flat area when you made the ear. Move the awl back and forth to open up this space. The reed will actually split. Insert the #3 rib in this opening on both sides, until all the ribs are inserted (figure 10).

With all the primary ribs in place, the basic skeleton of the basket is formed. If the shape doesn't look right, adjust the ribs now by lengthening or shortening, as needed.

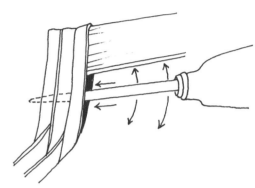

FIGURE 8

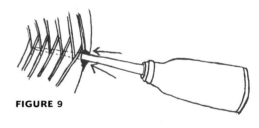

FIGURE 9

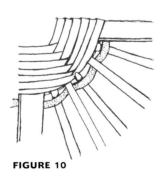

FIGURE 10

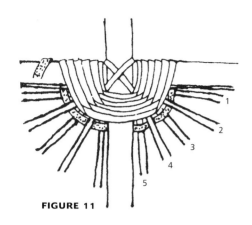

FIGURE 11

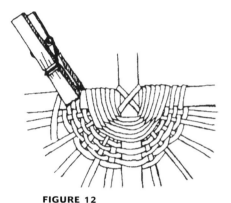

FIGURE 12

FIGURE 13

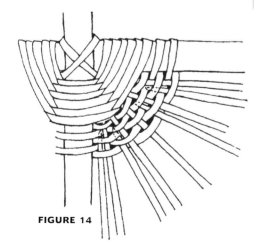

FIGURE 14

With the remainder of the weaver secured at the rim, bring the weaver behind the rim, over rib #1, under #2, over #3, etc., until you reach the other side (figure 11). Rewet the weaver anytime that it feels dry or stiff. Note: If the ribs pop out just put them back in and continue to weave. You must make the weavers fit in as closely as possible to the ear.

Weave five rows (figure 12). When a weaver runs out, add a new one (figure 13). Lay the new wet weaver on top of the old one. Weave with both the old and new weavers until the old one runs out, and then continue to weave with the new one.

Preparing and Inserting the Secondary Ribs

Again, from the #6 round reed, cut two of each of the following ribs: #1, 12 inches; #2, 14 inches; #4, 15 inches; #5, 13 inches.

Note: These measurements are approximate and may need slight adjustments.

The secondary ribs are inserted into the basket in the following places: #1 above #1; #2 above #2; #4 below #4; #5 below #5.

The secondary ribs are inserted beside a primary rib with the point reaching only under the first available weaver, not all the way into the ear (figure 14). Don't hesitate to add more if you need them. A good rule of thumb is that if you can get two fingers between any two ribs, you need to add another rib.

Finishing the Basket

Because of the shape of the egg basket, the rim and the bottom of the handle hoop will fill with weavers before the fullest areas do, leaving a football-shaped area unwoven (figure 15). As you weave, push the weaving on the rim and on the handle hoop outward toward the ears as much as you can. This will allow room for more weavers. When you can no longer squeeze in another weaver, turn around a rib and weave in the opposite direction. Note: For the sake of clarity, the finished figure shows more space between weaving than directed. The actual weaving should be tighter.

There are some ribbed baskets in which some filling in will be necessary. For example, on a full fanny egg basket or any ellipsoidal ribbed

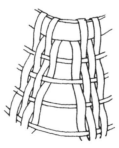

FIGURE 15

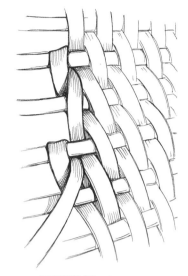

FIGURE 16

basket, the rims and bottom of the handle hoop will naturally fill with weavers more quickly than the other fuller parts of the basket, leaving an oval or wedge-shaped or crescent shaped area to be filled in. There are several ways of accomplishing this. The best one that I have seen was described by Tonny Stubblefield. The objective is to create a straight line of weaving from one side to the other. The unwoven area keeps the weaving line from being straight. The special "filling-in" turn-down is only done on the ribs where the row of weaving before was "under" (figure 18). Here is the special turndown. It is almost like a figure eight. The weaver comes back around to the inside of itself and crosses back to the outside. Again notice this is done on the rib where the row before was an "under" row. The turn-down will always be on every other rib. Once no more turn-downs can be made, the weaving continues as normal.

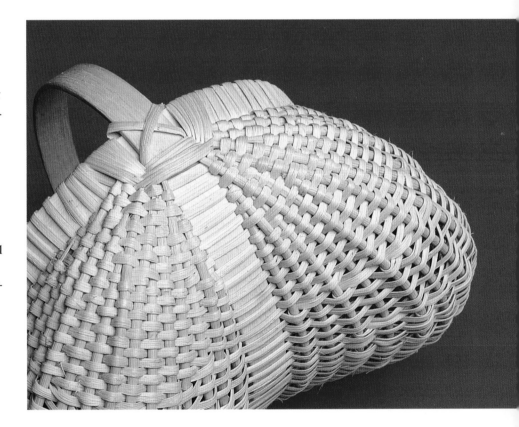

Materials

- ⅝-inch flat reed or ash (stakes)
- ¼-inch flat reed (weavers)
- Small square notched handle
- ⅜- or ½-inch flat-oval reed (rim)

Solid-Bottom Shaker Basket

SKILL LEVEL: **Moderate**

Originally inspired by a Shaker market basket, this one is smaller and has a stationary handle. The technique for making the solid bottom is unique and may be easier, compared with other techniques for solid bottoms that need to be filled in after the basket is finished.

DIMENSIONS
**APPROXIMATELY
7½ X 11 X 6½ INCHES**

BASKETMAKER
LYN SILER

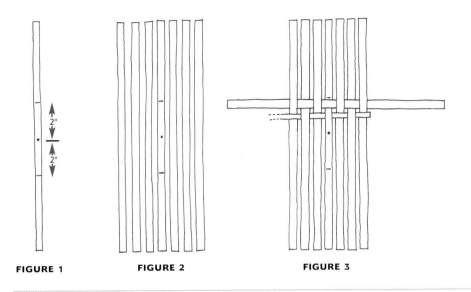

FIGURE 1   **FIGURE 2**   **FIGURE 3**

Note: The layout may look and feel strange because it's done just the opposite of most flat-bottomed baskets, with the longer stakes woven into the shorter ones.

Preparing the Materials

From the ⅝-inch flat reed, cut five stakes that are 21-inches long and seven stakes that are 18-inches long. Soak all the stakes.

Making the Base

Make a center mark on the wrong side of an 18-inch stake. Then make a mark 2 inches to the right of it and a second mark 2 inches to the left (figure 1). Lay it vertically on a flat surface. Lay the other six stakes with the marked one, three on each

side, all wrong side up (figure 2). The distance across the seven stakes should be approximately 7 inches.

Soak a long piece of ¼-inch flat reed. Begin the base by weaving one of the longer stakes in at the top 2-inch mark. Then beginning the ¼-inch flat, alternately weave across the vertical stakes (figure 3). Leave the ¼-inch flat reed lying out to the side—do not cut it. Be sure to leave a little tail sticking out at the beginning (it can be tucked in later).

Continue to alternately weave ⅝-inch stakes and ¼-inch flat rows (figure 4). The ¼-inch reed makes a 45° turn as it goes around the end of the stake, keeping the wrong side up (figure 5). Your base should measure approximately 4 x 7 inches.

Then, weave once around the perimeter of the base (figure 6). Upon reaching the starting point, pencil a dot on the stake immediately before the first one you wove around, to use as a reference point.

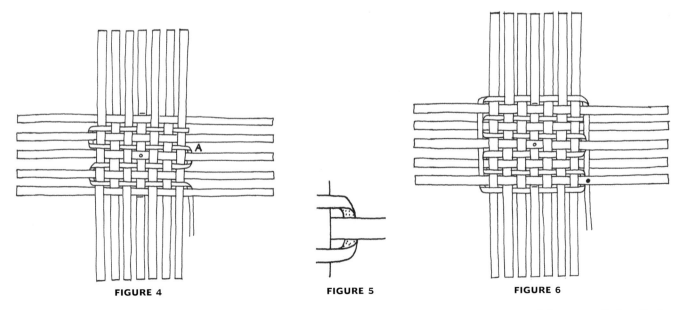

FIGURE 4   **FIGURE 5**   **FIGURE 6**

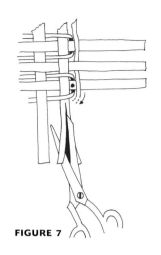

FIGURE 7

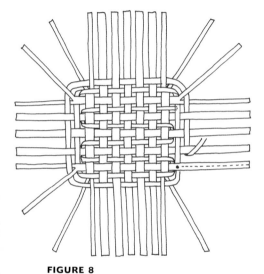

FIGURE 8

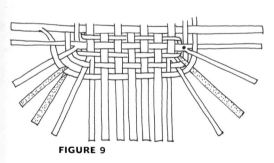

FIGURE 9

FIGURE 10

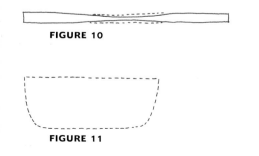

FIGURE 11

Cut the next stake after the dot in half (figure 7). Continue weaving in pattern, splitting all the corner stakes as you come to them (figure 8).

Adding the Corner Stakes

Return to the dotted stake and cut it in half, then add an odd stake. To add the odd stake, taper a piece of ⅝-inch flat reed for about 4 inches so it's no wider than ¼ inch when inserted. With this one stake inserted, this corner will have five stakes. The other corners will have six (the two you have already cut in half, creating four, and the two you are going to add as you weave around the next row).

Cut, soak, and mark a halfway point on three pieces of ⅝-inch flat reed, each 12-inches long. Taper an area in the center that is about 4-inches long, making it no wider than ¼ inch in the very center (figure 9). As you reach the corners, insert the added stakes by folding the tapered piece in half (with a twist to put the wrong side up) around the weaver (figure 10).

Forming the Sides

Continue weaving for five or six rows, turning the sides up as you weave. Do not upsett straight up-the sides are very gradually rounded upward. By the eighth or ninth row, the sides should be upright.

Add new weavers as necessary by the usual splicing method. Pay attention to the shape of your basket (figure 11).

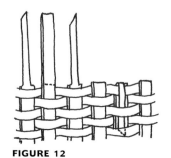

FIGURE 12

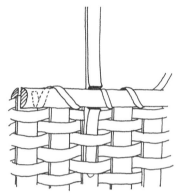

FIGURE 13

FIGURE 14

Finishing the Basket

Cut some of the width from the outside stakes; rewet them if necessary. Bend all the outside ones and tuck them into the weaving inside the basket (figure 12). Cut the inside stakes flush with the top of the basket. Insert the handle into the weaving with the center stake (figure 13).

Soak enough ⅜-inch flat-oval reed to reach around the inside and outside of the basket and overlap at least 3 inches. Scarf the ends of the flat-oval reed so they fit together smoothly. Place both pieces of the flat oval on the basket, fitting them in the handle notch; with a soaked piece of ¼-inch flat reed, begin lashing them together (figure 14). Lose the lasher between the two rim pieces at the beginning and the end. Lash only in one direction or in both, making X's, if you wish.

Flat-Bottom Egg Basket

SKILL LEVEL: **Advanced**

Another popular early American design is the Flat-Bottom Egg Basket. In constructing it, ribs were added, two at a time, from the ears outward as the basket was woven. This one features an unusual rim treatment.

DIMENSIONS
**APPROXIMATELY
8 INCHES IN DIAMETER**

BASKETMAKER
JUDY WOBBLETON

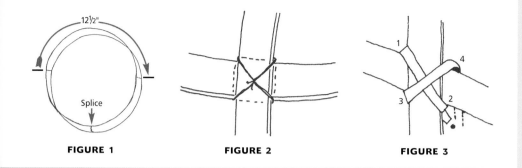

FIGURE 1   **FIGURE 2**   **FIGURE 3**

Materials

Two 8-inch hoops
(handle and rim)

Waxed string

$3/16$-inch flat reed
(weavers)

$1/4$-inch oval reed (ribs)

#5 or #6 round reed,
approximately
30 inches (lip)

Preparing the Hoops

On one hoop, mark off a $12\frac{1}{2}$-inch area to be the exposed handle, opposite the splice. Put your initials in the bottom, near the splice, as an identifying mark. Measure the circumference of the other hoop and divide it in half. Put a mark at the halfway mark and push the handle hoop over the rim hoop. The exposed handle mark should align with the halfway mark on the rim hoop (figure 1). Tie or nail the two hoops together (figure 2).

Making the Ear

Identify the wrong side of a long piece of $3/16$-inch flat reed. Soak and begin lashing, starting at the dot (figure 3). Make an X. Then begin the actual ear by bringing the weaver over the top of the handle hoop, up and around the right rim (6), down to (7), under the handle hoop, and up to the left rim (8) (figure 4). Repeat this procedure moving from one side to the other, keeping the wrong side of the weaver against the hoops, until you have five rows on both sides (count from the top of the rim). The finished ear should look like the illustration (figure 5).

Preparing the Ribs

From the $1/4$-inch oval reed, cut two of each of the following lengths and number the ribs as you cut them:

#1: 13 inches

#2: $13\frac{1}{2}$ inches

#3: 14 inches

#4: $13\frac{1}{2}$ inches

#5: $12\frac{1}{2}$ inches

#6: 12 inches

#7: 11 inches

#8: $9\frac{1}{2}$ inches

#9: 8 inches

#10: 6 inches

Taper all the ribs with a knife for at least 1 inch, making them pencil-point sharp at the ends (figure 6).

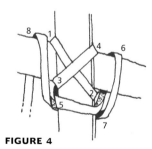

FIGURE 4

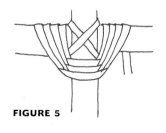

FIGURE 5

Inserting the Ribs and Weaving

Insert the #1 ribs into each opening beside the handle hoop, using the awl to open it sufficiently. Next insert rib #3 in the opening under the rim and force it downward. Then with the awl, make a hole in the center of the lashing and quickly insert the #2 rib. All three ribs inserted should resemble the illustration (figure 7).

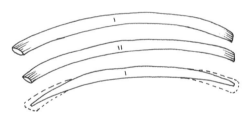

FIGURE 6

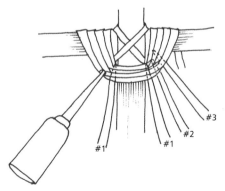

FIGURE 7

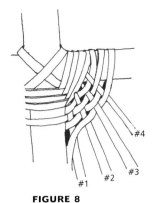

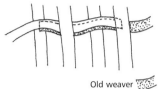

Old weaver

FIGURE 8

FIGURE 9

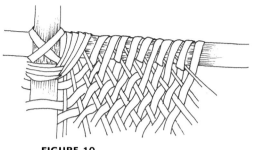

FIGURE 10

Note: There is no absolute rule for inserting the remaining ribs. You generally add a rib (one on each side) every other row, but whether you insert it after you have finished the fourth row (for instance), or at the beginning of the fourth row, or even after the fifth row is begun, is your decision. That decision must be made based on these factors: (1) keeping the overs and unders in correct order and (2) having the weaver go behind the hoop one round and in front of it the next. Sometimes depending on how the weaving is running, it is possible for the weaver to go behind the rim twice, in which case you need to reconsider the placement of the rib. Keep in mind that these rib measurements are the ones that have worked for me. They are not sacred and should be altered if necessary. The

bottom should be flat. From rib #4 outward, the lengths of the ribs begin to decrease.

Add the #4 rib (figure 8). When a weaver runs out, splice a new one (figure 9).

All ten ribs are eventually inserted, with an optional extra turn made around the rim (figure 10).

When all the ribs are in, fold a long soaked weaver around one end of the center unwoven area. Weave with one end of the weaver for a while, then the other. You will be working outward toward the ears. Add the weavers as usual (figure 11). Turn around the other rim and reverse, with both ends of the weaver. At the fullest part of the curve, you will stop weaving "outward" and return to the previously woven area to weave more. Eventually the two

areas will meet with very little, if any, filling-in to be done.

Making the Lip

To apply the lip, measure from one ear to the other. Cut a piece of round reed that length, plus 1/2 inch on each end to be pushed between the hoops. Taper the ends of the reed to paper thinness and push the ends between the rim and handle hoops (figure 12). Also push the end of a soaked piece of lashing between the hoops and begin lashing over the round reed, going under the rows of weaving around the rib (figure 13).

End the lashing at the other end the same way you began, pushing the other end between the two hoops on the other side. Lash the other side in the opposite direction.

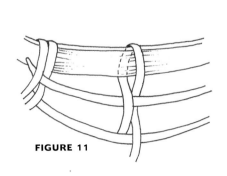

FIGURE 11

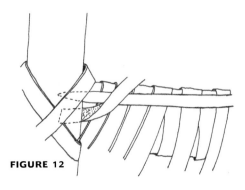

FIGURE 12

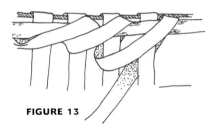

FIGURE 13

Feather Basket

SKILL LEVEL: **Moderate**

I n days gone by, this unusual square-to-round, lidded basket seems to have been used for gathering feathers. The top, which cannot be removed, could be raised and lowered quickly to keep feathers from blowing away—or even a chicken dinner from escaping.

DIMENSION
**APPROXIMATELY
12 X 12 X 18 INCHES**
BASKETMAKERS
**JIMMIE KENT, CAROLYN KEMP,
AND MARGARET BLYTHE**

Materials

- ⁷⁄₈-inch flat reed (stakes)
- ³⁄₈-inch flat reed (weavers)
- 12 x ⁷⁄₁₆-inch carnival hoop (shaping device)
- ¹⁄₂-inch flat-oval reed (rim)
- 12-inch U handle
- ³⁄₁₆-inch flat reed (lashing and weavers)
- #6 round reed, approximately 3 feet (rim)
- #4 round reed, approximately 8 feet (twining around lid)

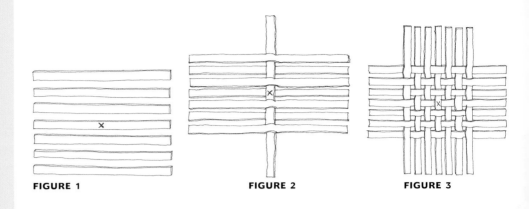

FIGURE 1   **FIGURE 2**   **FIGURE 3**

Cutting the Stakes and Weaving the Bottom

Cut 14 pieces of the ⁷⁄₈-inch flat reed, each 30-inches long. Mark the centers of two of these pieces with an X on the wrong side.

Soak all 14 pieces of reed for a minute or two in cool water. Place seven of the soaked stakes horizontally, wrong side up, making sure the fourth (or middle stake) has its center marked. The stakes should be approximately ¹⁄₄-inch apart (figure 1).

Once these seven stakes are in place, weave the other marked stake perpendicularly, over and under the other center. Be sure to match the two center marks (figure 2).

Now weave the other six stakes over and under, three on each side of the middle stake, making sure the weaving is alternating on each row. You have now formed the bottom of the basket. With a tape measure, measure from side to side at several points to be sure the bottom is square—it should be 8-inches square (figure 3).

Upsetting the Sides

To upsett the sides of the basket, bend and press each stake all the way over on itself to form a permanent crease at the base of the stake. You may want to use a flat ruler or piece of flat reed placed on the bottom of the stakes as a guide.

Press the stakes over the ruler in the direction of the woven bottom (figure 4). The stake will return itself to an approximate upright position. Continue all the way around.

Weaving the Sides

Soak one long strip of the 3/8-inch flat reed (weaver) for a couple of minutes. This basket does not have straight sides. Rather, they flare out gradually and the corners round, beginning with the very first row. It's important that you concentrate on rounding the corners, especially on the first and second rows of weaving. Once the form is established, the weaving will, for the most part, fall into place.

When you look at the woven bottom of the basket, notice that some of the stakes originate underneath the weaving and some originate on top. Begin weaving (with the wet weaver you soaked) by placing the end behind one of the stakes that originates on the top of the weaving. Weave with the right side of the reed on the outside of the basket. This way you're making the bottom stakes (the ones that originate from underneath) stand upright first. The next row of weaving will pick up the other stakes. Instead of trying to make the stakes stand upright, allow them to lean outward (as is their natural tendency), and do not pinch or square the corners. You may go back later and tighten if the weaving is too loose (figure 5).

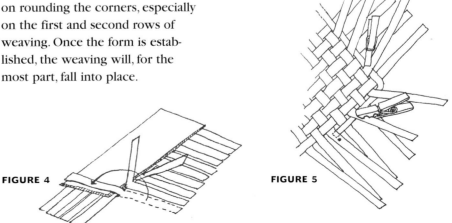

FIGURE 4   **FIGURE 5**

FIGURE 6

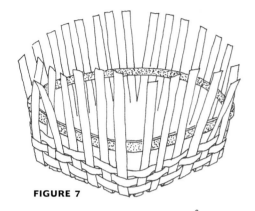

FIGURE 7

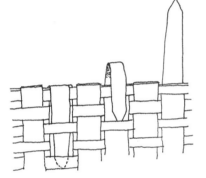

FIGURE 8

FIGURE 9

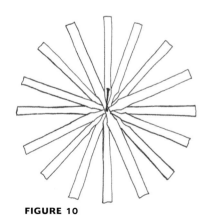

FIGURE 10

When you've woven over and under all the way around the basket, and are back to where you began, allow about 2 inches to overlap at the starting point and cut the weaver. Hide the ends of the weavers behind a stake. The end of a weaver need never show from the inside or the outside (figure 6).

Begin weaving the next row, and each row thereafter, in a different place to avoid a build-up.

When you've woven three rows, place a 12-inch hoop inside the stakes and clothespin it every 3 or 4 inches to the stakes. It should remain in the basket about 4 inches above the weaving until you're ready to finish off the rim. Move the hoop up a little as you weave; this will give you a guide to follow and will aid in the rounding process (figure 7). Weave to within 3 inches of the tops of the stakes.

Finishing the Tops of the Stakes

Note: You can leave the 12-inch hoop inside the basket and finish off the rim over the hoop if you desire. It certainly adds stability to the basket, but it's quite sturdy with only the $1/2$-inch flat-oval reed around the rim.

When you've finished weaving, you'll find that half your stakes are behind the last weaver and half are in front of it. Wet the top part of the stakes again. With scissors or wire cutters, cut off the inside stakes even with the last row of weaving. Then shape the outside stakes to a point. Bend the pointed stakes over and insert them into the weaving inside the basket, making sure they reach at least behind the third row of weaving, if not farther (figure 8).

Set the basket aside at this point and construct the lid. The handle is inserted only after the lid is made and fitted to the top of the basket. The handle is inserted through the lid, allowing the lid to be raised, but not removed.

Making the Lid: Cutting and Placing the Stakes

From the $7/8$-inch flat reed, cut seven strips, each 18-inches long. Mark the centers of all these pieces with a pencil on the wrong side.

With scissors, taper both sides of all seven strips for about 3 inches on each side of the center mark, so that it is about $3/8$ inch at the center (figure 9).

Place all seven of the strips, each on top of the other, until they look like spokes in a wheel. Space them as evenly as possible. These spokes may either be nailed down to a wooden surface, placed on a T-pin, or they can simply be held in place with one hand while you begin to weave with the other (figure 10).

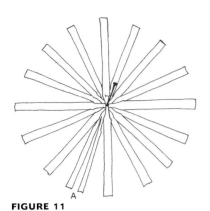

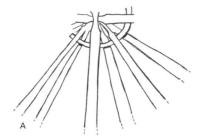

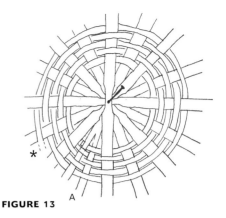

FIGURE 11

FIGURE 12

FIGURE 13

Beginning to Weave

With scissors, split any one of the 14 spokes in half. This split spoke will be referred to as A. You now have 15 spokes (figure 11).

Now take a ¼-inch or ³⁄₁₆-inch weaver that is approximately 4 feet in length. With scissors, begin cutting it in half lengthwise. For about 3 feet, the weaver will be about ⅛-inch wide. After approximately 3 feet, begin to taper the width, making the weaver wider and wider until it reaches its normal width. Coil the weaver and soak it for a couple of minutes.

Remove from water and insert the end of the ⅛-inch weaver between the two pieces of A and begin to weave over and under each spoke all the way around the circle of spokes (figure 12).

Note: You'll find that you must start the weaving about 2 inches out from the center. You want to be sure the first row is snug, but if you try to force this first row too close to the center, the second row will not fit. Weave five rows around and stop at the second spoke before A (figure 13).

Splitting the Spokes

When you have woven five or six rows, find the spoke immediately before A. With scissors, cut this spoke into three equal parts. Then cut all remaining spokes in half (figure 14). Then continue to weave over and under each new spoke, beginning with the spoke you cut into 3 equal parts.

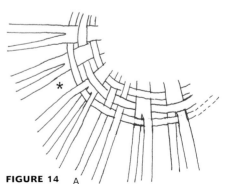

FIGURE 14

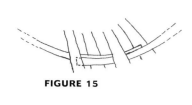

FIGURE 15

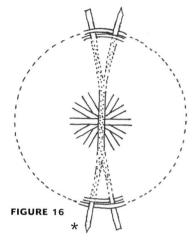

FIGURE 16

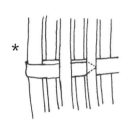

FIGURE 17

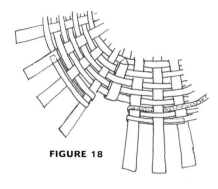

FIGURE 18

FIGURE 19

Note: As you weave this flat area, you'll need to spread the stakes apart, spacing them as evenly as you can. Make sure your woven area is staying round. If it isn't, use an awl to push areas in or pull them out to keep it round. You must also make every effort to keep the lid flat. There will be a natural tendency for the edges to curl up. Sometimes placing a heavy book on the woven area after about 6 inches will help to keep it flat. It doesn't seem to be too objectionable if the center rises a little, which often happens, as it prevents the edge from curling so much.

Splicing on a New Weaver

When you see that you have only 2 or 3 inches of the weaver remaining, it's time to splice on a new weaver. Lay a new 1/4-inch weaver on top of 2 inches of the old weaver you have left and hide the end under a spoke. Continue to weave with the two weavers together until the old one runs out. Then continue with the new one. Just don't exert a great deal of pressure on the new weaver until you have finished a complete revolution (figure 15).

Finishing the Top

Weave in this manner until the lid measures 11 1/2 inches or is within 1/2 inch of fitting your basket's top. You have two more rows to weave at this point, leaving a space for the handle to be inserted, so check the size closely. If the top of your basket, by some chance, is smaller or larger than 12 inches, you must adjust the lid size accordingly.

When your weaving is within 1/2 inch of the basket size, select one spoke that runs from one side to the other. (From the one original spoke, there are now four, since they were split.) Select the one spoke on each side that is on top of the weaving, taper the ends, and tuck them into the weaving on the wrong side. Eliminating this spoke from the weaving creates the space for the handle (figures 16 and 17).

Continue with the weaving until you reach the spoke you tucked under. Reverse directions around the spoke before it, weave back around to the other tucked in spoke. Reverse again. Return to the point at which you first reversed. Make the final turn, and cut the weaver so that the end hides behind a spoke (figure 18).

Begin a new weaver by wrapping it around the first spoke on the other side, leaving enough free to tuck under itself (figure 19). Weave two rows between this point and the other side, then cut and tuck the end under as before.

Finally, using the well-soaked #4 round reed (and beginning anywhere before the openings), fold it in half and twine all the way around the edge. When you reach the openings, make two twists and continue twining around each spoke. Tuck the ends into the weaving any way it is convenient (figure 20).

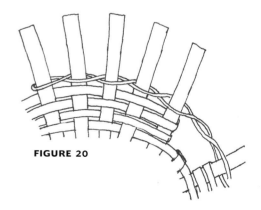

FIGURE 20

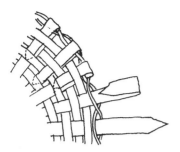

FIGURE 21

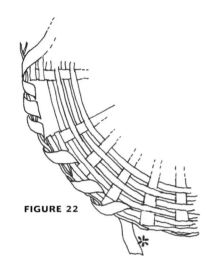

FIGURE 22

FIGURE 23. Weave ends together to finish lashing

Point all the spokes and tuck them into the weaving on the wrong side, inside of the lid (figure 21). With the $3/8$-inch flat reed, lash around the lid (figures 22 and 23).

Inserting the Handle

Insert the handle through the openings on the lid. Locate two center stakes on the basket, directly across from each other, (preferably the ones that were cut flush with the top of the basket), and insert the handle into the weaving on the inside (figure 24). The handle can be inserted into the weaving as far as it needs to give the desired height. Nail, glue, or staple it in place. A small tack through the handle and the top weaver works well. A lock handle also works and eliminates the need for nailing.

Applying the Rim

With all the outside stakes pushed down into the weaving and the handle in place, lift up the lid as far as it will go (hold in place with clothes-

pins if necessary) and wrap a piece of $1/2$-inch flat-oval reed all the way around the outside, overlapping the ends about 3 inches. Then wrap a piece of $1/2$-inch flat-oval reed all around the inside, overlapping the ends as before. Hold both pieces in place with the same clothespins.

Put a piece of #6 round reed between the two pieces of flat-oval reed, allowing the ends to overlap a little for the moment (figure 25). Be sure to bevel or thin the ends of the flat-oval reed so the overlapped area is the regular thickness of the reed.

Lashing the Rim

With a long strip of $3/16$-inch flat reed, begin to lash all the rim pieces together (figure 26). Use an awl, if necessary, to open the space for lashing. When you're within 1 inch of finishing, cut the piece of round reed so the ends butt against each other and finish by tucking the ends of the lashing weaver into the weaving discreetly.

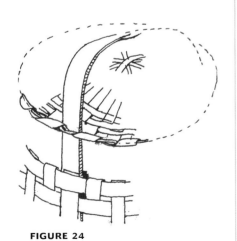

FIGURE 24

FIGURE 25

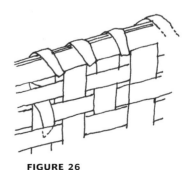

FIGURE 26

Amy's Basket

SKILL LEVEL: **Advanced**

I studied a very old version of this basket in the mountains of North Carolina. It was quite worn and had obviously seen a lot of service. My daughter commented that it had more character than any basket she had ever seen and that we should reproduce it. Hence, "Amy's Basket."

DIMENSIONS
**APPROXIMATELY
8 X 8 X 12 INCHES**

BASKETMAKER
JENNY ANTOLINE

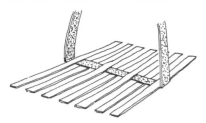

FIGURE 1

Preparing the Materials and Weaving the Bottom

From the 3/4-inch flat reed, cut 13 pieces that are 30-inches long. With the pencil, mark the center of all the pieces on the wrong (rough) side. Also, mark the halfway point on the inside of the bottom of the D handle. It will be about 4 to 4 1/2 inches.

Place all 13 pieces in cool water to soak for a few minutes. Remove them from the water and place three on the table horizontally, wrong side up, leaving 1/2 inch between them.

Next, place the D handle on top of the center marks, perpendicularly. Then lay four more strips across the D handle (horizontally), between and to the left and right of the original three pieces (figure 1).

Note: If all this is too difficult to hold with your hands, lay a heavy book on one end of the reed while you work on the other end.

Weave the other six pieces over and under the seven horizontal pieces, aligning the center marks with the center mark on the handle. Measure and true the base to 8-inches square (figure 2).

Upsetting and Weaving the Sides

To upsett the sides, bend each stake, vertical and horizontal, all the way over (to the inside) upon itself, forming a permanent crease at the base (figure 3).

Begin weaving around the basket with a piece of soaked 3/8-inch flat reed (figure 4). Make sure the wrong side of the weaver is against the stakes. Notice that the weaver wraps behind the stakes that originate from underneath the base. These stakes must stand up first. Weave over and under the stakes all the way around to the starting point. Use clothespins frequently to hold everything in place for the first two rows. Allow the two ends to overlap for at least two stakes. If the reed is extremely thick, shave some of the thickness off where the two ends overlap each other. Begin the next row and every subsequent row on a different side to avoid a build-up.

From the bottom up, our basket is woven with the following materials:

> 3 rows of 3/8-inch flat
>
> 3 rows of 3/16-inch flat oval
>
> 3 rows of 3/8-inch flat
>
> 3 rows of 3/16-inch flat oval
>
> 3 rows of 3/8-inch flat
>
> 3 rows of 3/16-inch flat oval
>
> 4 rows of 3/8-inch flat
> (last row covered by rim)

Materials

> 3/4-inch flat reed (stakes)
>
> 8 x 12-inch sharp top D handle*
>
> 3/16- or 1/4-inch flat-oval reed (weavers)
>
> 3/8-inch flat reed (weavers)
>
> 5/8-inch flat-oval reed (rim)
>
> #6 round reed (rim filler)
>
> 1/4-inch flat reed (lashing)

* The D handle is specially made to decrease in width from the bottom to the top, as do the sides of the basket. The handle will give you a guide by which to shape the sides. Use the measurements here as a guide, but by all means experiment with your own measurements and materials. Create your own heirloom. A regular D handle can be used. You control the shape by pulling tightly on the weaver as you proceed up the sides, thereby forming the handle to the shape you desire.

As you weave, you need to gradually tighten on the weaver and press in on the stakes, using the slant of the handle as a guide for how much to bring the sides in all the way around. Make a concentrated effort to round the corners gradually. It's

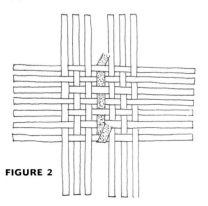

FIGURE 2

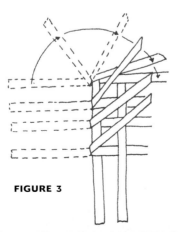

FIGURE 3

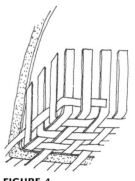

FIGURE 4

FIGURE 5

FIGURE 6

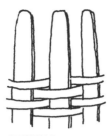

FIGURE 7

easy to pull in too much around the corners. You want the corners to slant at the same angle as the handle. Push down on the weavers after each row, packing them in as tightly as possible.

If you have any trouble making the sides decrease, place a large rubber band around the tops of the stakes while they're wet. Allow them enough time to dry and your stakes will be pre-formed for you (figure 5).

When you've woven about half the height of the basket, you'll find that because the sides are decreasing in diameter, the stakes will be pressed too closely together to weave between them. With a knife or scissors, taper the stakes until there is at least $1/4$-inch between them at all times. If you wish, you can point the ends of the stakes while you are tapering, since it must be done eventually anyway (figure 6).

Finishing the Stakes and Applying the Rim

When you've woven all 22 rows (or whatever number you choose to weave), you'll notice that some stakes are outside the last row of weaving and the alternate ones are on the inside. With scissors or a sharp knife, cut the inside stakes flush with the top row of weaving and taper or point the outside stakes (figure 7).

Rewet the stakes a little if they've dried out, and bend the pointed ones over and insert them into the weaving (inside the basket). They should hide behind a row of weaving.

After all the stakes are bent over and inserted, place a well-soaked piece of $3/8$-inch flat-oval reed around the outside of the basket, covering the top row of weaving. Allow the ends to overlap approximately 2 inches. This reed is normally very heavy and thick and both ends must be beveled or thinned where they will overlap. The overlapped area should be no thicker than the rest of the rim (figure 8). Hold this joint in place with clothespins.

Then, place another piece of $5/8$-inch flat-oval reed around the inside, flat against the top row of weaving. Bevel or thin the ends of this piece just as you did the other. Hold the two rim pieces in place with clothespins.

Place a piece of #6 round reed above the two rim strips. The ends of the round reed should be beveled in the same manner as the flat oval.

Begin a long, soaked $1/4$-inch weaver anywhere, preferably just past the joining point of the two pieces of the rim, and lash all the rim pieces together (figure 9). The weaver is inserted under the rim, wraps over the round reed three times, then goes under the rim again. Immed-

iately before and after, and while crossing the handle, you may find that you need more than three wraps around the #6 round reed. When you have wrapped the whole rim, tuck the ends behind a weaver and cut (figure 10).

To reshape the basket, soak it for a few minutes and mold it to the desired shape.

Note: There are other sizes of sharp top D handles available. Three are given below with the size reed used, the number of stakes needed, and the lengths they should be cut:

- 6 x 8-inch sharp top D: cut 13 pieces, 20-inches long from $1/2$-inch flat reed

- 7 x 10-inch sharp top D: cut 17 pieces, 23-inches long from $3/8$-inch flat reed

- 10 x 14-inch sharp top D: cut 17 pieces, 36-inches long from $3/4$-inch flat reed

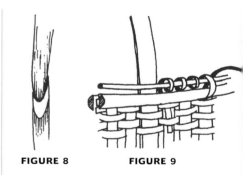

FIGURE 8   **FIGURE 9**

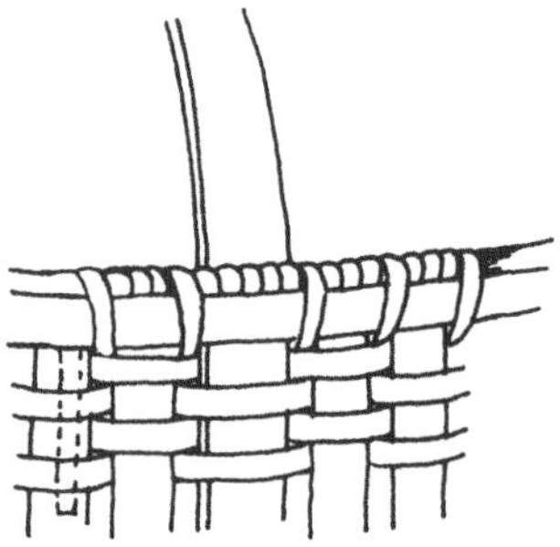

FIGURE 10

Utensil Basket

This plaited basket has a plain twill-weave base, and the sides are plaited diagonally or obliquely, creating an interesting herringbone design.

DIMENSIONS
APPROXIMATELY
5 X 5 X 8 INCHES

BASKETMAKER
CAROLYN KEMP

SKILL LEVEL
Moderate

DESIGNERS
**Lyn Siler and
Carolyn Kemp**

Materials

1/2-inch flat reed (weavers, stakes, and rim)

#1 round reed (twining around base)

#5 round reed (rim filler)

11/64-inch flat reed or 1/8-inch strip cut from the 1/2-inch flat reed (lashing)

Pattern Chart

U = Under, **O** = Over

TO THE RIGHT OF THE CENTER MARK
(reading from bottom to top)

Row 1, color: U2, O3, U3, O2

Row 2, natural: O1, U2, O2, U2, O2, U1

Row 3, natural: O2, U2, O1, U1, O2, U2

Row 4, natural: U1, O2, U2, O2, U2, O1

Row 5, natural: U2, O2, U1, O1, U2, O2

TO THE LEFT OF THE CENTER MARK

Row 1, color: O2, U3, O3, U2

Row 2, natural: U1, O2, U2, O2, U2, O1

Row 3, natural: U2, O2, U1, O1, U2, O2

Row 4, natural: O1, U2, O2, U2, O2, U1

Row 5, natural; O2, U2, O1, U1, O2, U2

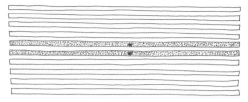

FIGURE 1

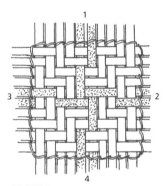

FIGURE 2

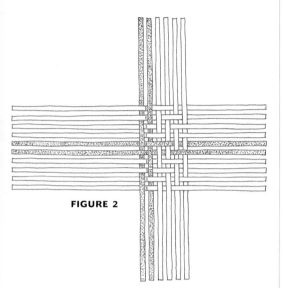

FIGURE 3

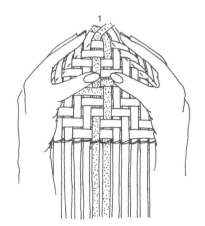

FIGURE 4. Bottom view

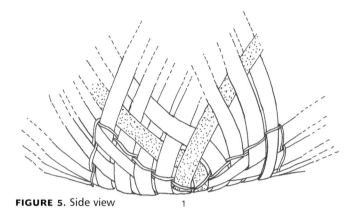

FIGURE 5. Side view

Cutting the Stakes and Weaving the Base

To weave the base, cut 20 pieces that are 34-inches long from ½-inch flat reed. Dye four strips in the color of your choice; rinse and wipe them well to avoid bleeding. Mark the centers of the four colored pieces on the wrong side. Lay two of them horizontally on a flat surface with four natural pieces on each side of them, and align the ends (figure 1).

Following the Pattern Chart on page 131, weave in the vertical stakes, beginning with the two other colored ones (one on each side of the horizontal center mark).

For clarity's sake, here's an example of how the base is woven (figure 2). However, the woven base should have a tighter weave. Measure and true the base to a 6-inch square. Soak the #1 round reed and twine all the way around the base, discreetly tucking the ends into the twining itself (figure 3).

Forming the Corners and Weaving the Sides

Make a mental note of the location of 1 in figure 3, as that point will become a corner. Lift the base and press on the two sides, forcing a corner to form at 1 (figure 4). The colored stakes will have a natural tendency to cross, but you may need to help them along. All the stakes on one side lean now, obliquely; weave them into the other side in an over 2, under 2 twill pattern (figure 5).

Note: Figure 4 is drawn looking down at the woven base and figure 5 is a side view once the sides are begun. Figure 6 is seen from the same angle as figure 5. Only three of the stakes have been woven (loosely) in figure 5, whereas all of them at corner 1 have been closely woven (figure 6).

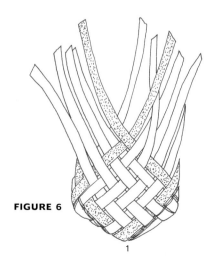

FIGURE 6

Repeat the folding and weaving process at the other three corners. Corners 1 and 4 are shown after being formed and woven (figure 7).

Once all four corners are formed, continue to diagonally weave all the stakes; they will fall into place. To create a stopping place, draw an imaginary line (draw it in pencil if it will help) across the line created when the two colored strips intersect at the top (figure 8). Cut the tops of all the stakes at the line (figure 9).

FIGURE 9

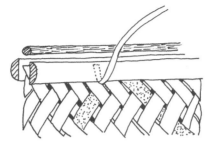

FIGURE 10

Finishing the Basket

Soak a piece of $1/2$-inch flat reed that is long enough to reach around the basket twice for an inside and outside rim. Also soak a piece of lashing material. Place the two rim pieces around the top of the basket, allowing 1-inch overlap, with the #5 round reed between (figure 10). Hold all the pieces with clothespins and begin lashing just past the splices. The lasher goes into every fourth space (figure 11). Be very sure to wrap under the lasher before going to the next space (figure 12). You may choose to lash into every other space, every third, or every fourth space, but you'll probably find the need to lash into the two consecutive spaces where the overlap is located, just to secure all the ends of the rim.

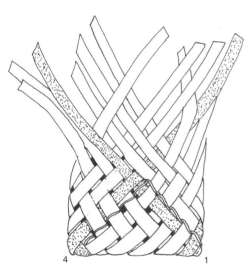

FIGURE 7

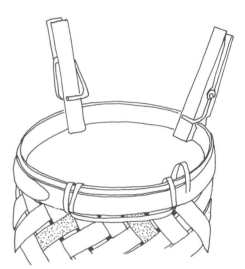

FIGURE 11

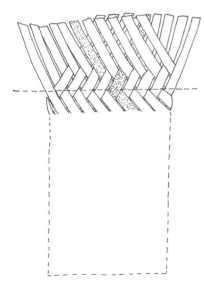

FIGURE 8

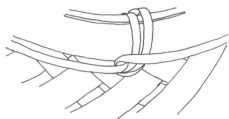

FIGURE 12

Gardening Tool Basket

SKILL LEVEL: **Advanced**   DESIGNER: **Dianne Kennedy**

Here is a sturdy basket design, extremely useful for carrying garden tools, or even basketmaking tools. The divider helps keep everything organized.

DIMENSIONS
**APPROXIMATELY
11 X 14 X 10 INCHES**

BASKETMAKER
DIANNE KENNEDY

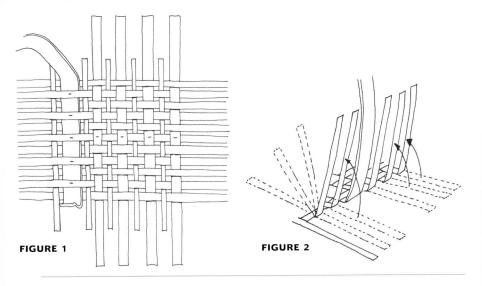

FIGURE 1

FIGURE 2

Materials

 ¾-inch flat reed (stakes)

14 x 10-inch high D handle

½-inch flat read (weavers and base fillers)

⅜-inch flat reed (divider)

½-inch flat-oval reed (rim)

#2 or #3 sea grass (rim filler)

³⁄16-inch flat reed (lashing)

Preliminary Steps

FROM THE ¾-INCH FLAT REED, CUT:

11 pieces, 24 inches long
8 pieces, 29 inches long
11 pieces, 18 inches long

FROM THE ½-INCH FLAT REED, CUT:

6 pieces, 20 inches long
8 pieces, 24 inches long

FROM THE ⅜-INCH FLAT REED, CUT:

1 piece, 20 inches long

Making the Base

Mark all the centers of all the pieces on the wrong (rough) side. Also, mark the center of the bottom of the handle.

Soak the pieces for several minutes until pliable.

Lay six of the 24-inch pieces of ¾-inch flat reed horizontally, wrong side up, aligning the center marks. Space them evenly so the measurement from side to side is 11 inches.

Lay the handle vertically on top of the six stakes. Lay the other five 24-inch pieces horizontally on top of the handle.

Using both the eight 24-inch pieces of ½-inch flat reed and the eight 29-inch pieces of ¾-inch flat reed, weave the base, alternating overs and unders. Begin by weaving a piece of ½-inch flat reed on each side of the handle and alternate sizes (½ and ¾ inch), ending with a piece of ¾-inch flat reed on both sides (figure 1).

Note: The first row on each side of the handle is woven in the same pattern as the handle. Pack the base pieces closely together so there are no holes. Measure and true the base to 11 x 14 inches.

Making the Divider

Upsett the stakes by bending them over upon themselves toward the center of the base (figure 2).

On the 20-inch piece of ⅜-inch flat reed (the divider bar), make a center mark. Lay the ⅜-inch piece on the base with the center mark aligned with the center mark on the handle.

Make marks on the ⅜-inch piece to correspond with the stakes that are woven perpendicular to the handle (figure 3).

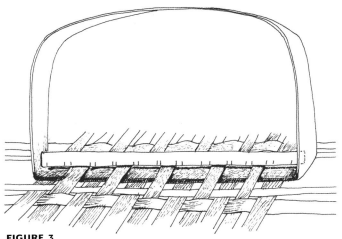

FIGURE 3

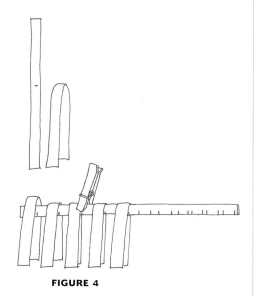

FIGURE 4

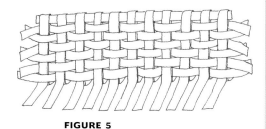

FIGURE 5

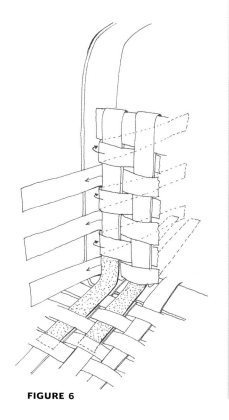

FIGURE 6

Soak the 11 pieces of $3/4$-inch flat reed that were cut 18 inches long (the divider stakes), then fold them in half, wrong sides together. Lay them over the $3/8$-inch piece (bar) on the marked spaces. Hold the stakes on the bar with clothespins (figure 4).

Using the six pieces of $1/2$-inch flat reed (20 inches long), weave over and under the divider stakes, aligning the center marks with the center stake. Leave the sides and ends extended freely (figure 5).

Push the ends of the stakes under the woven stakes in the base of the basket. Bend the ends of the divider weavers alternately right and left (figure 6). They will be woven in as the sides are woven.

Bend the stakes sharply at the base of the divider so they will lie flat in the base. If necessary, adjust the divider stakes to match the position of those in the basket.

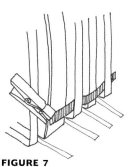

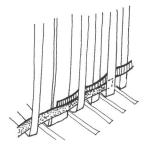

FIGURE 7

FIGURE 8

Finishing the Basket

Soak several long pieces of $1/2$-inch flat reed. Begin weaving around the basket in a plain over-under weave (figure 7). End a row, overlapping four stakes and cutting the weaver so it is hidden behind a stake (figure 8). Make sure the weavers are woven right-side out. Do not weave the $1/2$-inch filler pieces. Leave them lying flat until five or six rows are woven.

Weave the ends of the divider weavers in as you are weaving the rows (figure 9). Weave six start-stop rows.

If necessary, rewet the filler strips, bend them up and tuck them under several rows of weaving (figure 10).

Cut all the stakes on the inside of the top row of weaving flush with the top row.

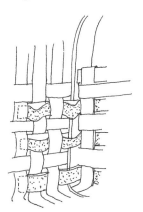

FIGURE 9

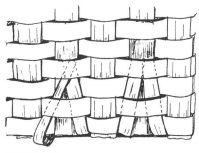

FIGURE 10

FIGURE 11

Point all the stakes on the outside of the basket, rewet them if necessary, bend them over to the inside of the basket, and tuck them behind the first available row of weaving (figure 11).

Soak two pieces of $1/2$-inch flat-oval reed. One of them should be long enough to reach around the outside of the basket. The other piece should reach around half the inside and the one side of the divider. Also soak a very long piece of $3/16$-inch flat reed for lashing and sea grass to fill the rim around the basket and the divider.

Place the soaked $1/2$-inch flat-oval reed around the top row of weaving on the outside of the basket, allowing the ends to overlap 2 to 3 inches. Mark the overlap and remove to shave the ends where they overlap. Bevel the overlapped area so it is no thicker than a single thickness of $1/2$-inch flat-oval reed. Replace it when the ends are beveled and hold it in place with clothespins.

Place another soaked piece of $1/2$-inch flat-oval reed around the inside rim of the basket, going around the inside wall of half the inside and one side of the divider

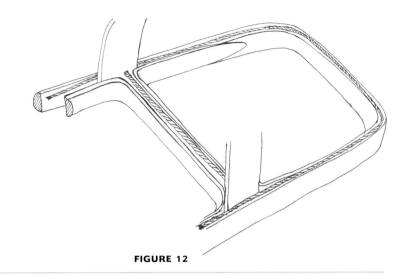

FIGURE 12

wall. Repeat on the other side of the basket inside (and the other side of the divider). Mark the overlap. Remove and plane the ends as before. Replace and hold all pieces in place with clothespins (figures 12 and 13).

Begin lashing on the divider wall at one end. Hook the end of the weaver over the wall, under the two rim pieces and lash in place, going over all the rim pieces and through each

space between stakes (figure 14). When the divider is lashed in place, continue lashing around the basket, ending where you began on the basket rim. End the lashing as you began, by hiding the ends between the rim pieces or inside the basket behind a weaver.

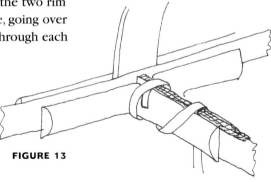

FIGURE 13

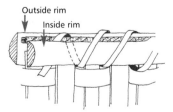

Outside rim

Inside rim

FIGURE 14

Hannah's Marriage Basket

SKILL LEVEL: **Advanced**   DESIGNERS: **Lyn Siler and Judy Wobbleton**

This is one of the most intriguing baskets I have ever seen. Its origin is obscure, although my prototype came from the mountains of North Carolina. There's definitely a Cherokee influence in the pattern design.

DIMENSIONS
APPROXIMATELY 3 X 12 X 9 INCHES

BASKETMAKERS
LYN SILER
JODY WOBBLETON

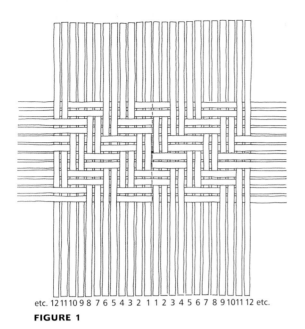

etc. 12 11 10 9 8 7 6 5 4 3 2 1 1 2 3 4 5 6 7 8 9 10 11 12 etc.

FIGURE 1

Preparing The Materials

From the ¼-inch flat reed cut 12 pieces, each 37-inches long and 48 pieces that are 27-inches long. Mark the centers on the wrong side of all the stakes. Soak all the pieces for a few minutes.

Lay the 12 longer stakes horizontally on a flat surface, wrong side up.

Weaving the Base

Begin weaving the base with the shorter stakes in the following manner, placing the center mark in the middle of the 12 horizontal stakes.

The following chart reads from bottom to top as you look at your base (figure 1):

Pattern Chart

U = Under, O = Over

LEFT SIDE OF CENTER

Rows 1–2: U4, O4, U4

Rows 3–4: U2, O4, U4, O2

Rows 5–6: O4, U4, O4

Rows 7–8: O2, U4, O4, U2

Rows 9–10: repeat rows 1-2

Rows 11–12: repeat rows 3-4

Rows 13–14: repeat rows 5-6

Rows 15–16: repeat rows 7-8

Rows 17–18: repeat rows 1-2

Rows 19–20: repeat rows 3-4

Rows 21–22: repeat rows 5-6

Rows 23–24: repeat rows 7-8

Materials

¼-inch flat reed (stakes and weavers)

⅜-inch flat-oval reed (rim)

#12 spline or a small strip of white oak (handle)

RIGHT SIDE OF CENTER

Rows 1–2: O2, U4, O4, U2

Rows 3–4: O4, U4, O4

Rows 5–6: U2, O4, U4, O2

Rows 7– 8: U4, O4, U4

Rows 9–10: repeat rows 1-2

Rows 11–12: repeat rows 3-4

Rows 13–14: repeat rows 5-6

Rows 15–16: repeat rows 7-8

Rows 17–18: repeat rows 1-2

Rows 19–20: repeat rows 3-4

Rows 21–22: repeat rows 5-6

Rows 23–24: repeat rows 7-8

Pack all the weaving tightly. Measure and true the base to 3 x 12 inches. Do not upsett the stakes. Soak a long ¼-inch weaver.

Weaving the Sides

As you look at the side nearest you (holding the stakes upright), find the four stakes to the left of the center mark that are coming from underneath the woven base. Begin by weaving around the last three stakes of that group and continue under the next three, over the next three, etc. (figure 2). Roll the stakes upward as you weave. On this and all subsequent rows, hide the end in the usual manner, overlapping the ends as many stakes you deem necessary to secure and hide them (figure 3).

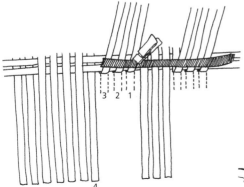

FIGURE 2

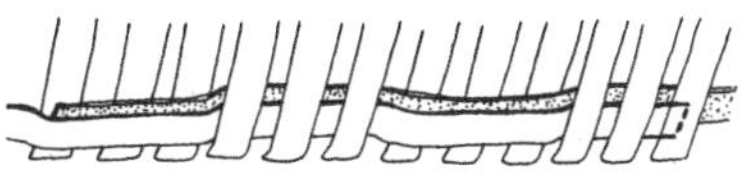

FIGURE 3

FIGURE 4

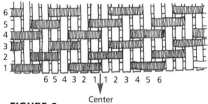

6
5
4
3
2
1

6 5 4 3 2 1 1 2 3 4 5 6

Center

FIGURE 5

29
28
27
26
25
24
23
22
21
20
19
18
17
16
15
14
13
12
11
10
9
8
7
6

8 9 10 11 12 13 14 15 16 17 18 19 20 21 22 23 24 25 26

Last row of twill weave   First row of pattern

FIGURE 6

The first six rows are a simple over 3, under 3 twill weave, stepping-up one stake each row. Remember to start every row on a different side or at a different spot to avoid a build-up from starting and stopping at the same spot (figure 4).

After weaving the six rows of plain twill, check your shape. Make sure you aren't pulling the sides in too much or allowing them to flare too much. You can either pinch the corners to square them or let them round, as does ours. Weave six rows of twill from the center mark (figure 5).

Row 7 begins the pattern rows (figure 6). Following are row-by-row directions for where to start each row:

Row 7: Locate the 9th stake from the left end (either side). Weave over stakes 9, 10, and 11 (O3). From that point, continue U1, O3, U5, O3, U1, O3, U5, etc.

Row 8: At any point there is a U1 (on the last row), begin by weaving over the U1 plus the two on each side of it (O5) and continue U3, O1, U3, O5, etc.

Row 9: At any point there is an O5, weave over the center three, under the next three and repeat O3, U3 around.

Note: Every third row will be O3, U3, O3, etc.

Row 10: Locate an O3 that is above an O5 on row 8. Begin O1 with the center one of the O3 and continue, U3, O5, U3, O1, etc.

Row 11: Find a spot you have an O1. Begin under that one plus the two on each side (U5) and continue O3, U1, O3, U5, etc.

Row 12: At a place you have a U5 begin under the center three and continue O3, U3, O3, etc.

Row 13: Find a U3 that is above a U5 (on row 11). Weave under the center one of the U3 and continue O3, U3, O3, U5, O3, U3, O3, U1, etc.

Row 14: Find the U1. Weave over it and the two on each side (O5); continue U3, O3, U3, O1, U3, O3, U3, O5, etc.

Row 15: Find an O5. Weave over the center three and continue U3, O3, U3, etc.

Row 16: Find an O3 that is directly above an O5. Weave over the center one and continue U3, O3, U3, O5, U3, O3, U3, O1, etc.

Row 17: Find an O1. Weave under that one plus the two on each side (U5). Continue O3, U3, O3, U1, O3, U3, O3, U5, etc.

Row 18: Find an U5. Weave under the center three and continue O3, U3, O3, etc.

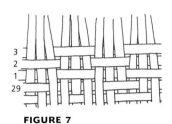

FIGURE 7

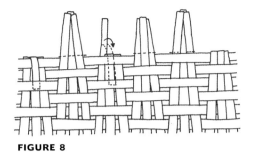

FIGURE 8

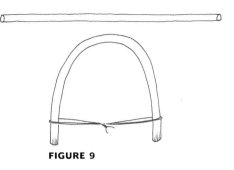

FIGURE 9

From here the pattern repeats itself. I found that the simplest process is to make light pencil marks on the row you want to repeat and follow exactly what is done there.

Following is a chart of which rows are repeated and their order:

Row 19: repeat row 17

Row 20: repeat row 16

Row 21: repeat row 15

Row 22: repeat row 14

Row 23: repeat row 13

Row 24: repeat row 12

Row 25: repeat row 11

Row 26: repeat row 10

Row 27: repeat row 9

Row 28: repeat row 8

Row 29: repeat row 7

After weaving row 29, begin an O3, U3 starting at a spot there was a U1; go over that one and one on each side (O3). This is not a twill O3, U3, but a regular plain weave. You must begin on this first row of the plain weave to pull the three stakes together so they can be treated as one (figure 7).

Finishing the Basket

Weave seven rows in plain weave. When they're done, cut two of the three stakes in a group, leaving the outside one. Point it if necessary and tuck it into the weaving inside the basket (figure 8).

Make the handle by soaking a 16-inch piece of spline (if that is what you have chosen to use) until it is pliable. Bend it in the shape you want and tie it as until it dries (figure 9). Notch it with a knife, tapering the ends to paper thickness (figure 10). Insert the handle into the basket, centering it as much as possible (figure 11).

Next soak two pieces of ${}^3/_8$-inch flat-oval reed long enough to reach around the basket twice. Scarf or bevel the ends and allow them to overlap about 2 inches. Apply the rim and hold it in place with a clothespin (figure 12). Scarf the ends (figure 13). Lash the two flat-oval rim pieces on with a $^1/_4$-inch flat reed, losing the end between the two rim pieces.

Although the directions here reproduce the basket as authentically as possible, the basket would also make a wonderful tote, simply requiring handles on each side or two swing handles attached by ears or loops.

FIGURE 10

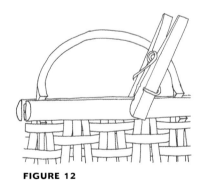

FIGURE 12

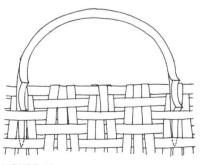

FIGURE 11

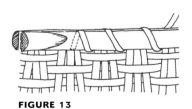

FIGURE 13

Hannah's Marriage Basket 141

Double-Lidded Picnic Basket

SKILL LEVEL: **Advanced**

There are several means of attaching a lid to any ribbed basket. The technique used here is unique in that a woven bar is used instead of one or two dowels.

DIMENSIONS
**APPROXIMATELY
20 X 12 X 20 INCHES**

BASKETMAKER
JIMMIE KENT

Materials

Two 12 x 20-inch oval
hoops (frame)

#10 round reed
(lid frame)

¼-inch flat or flat-oval
reed (weavers)

⅜-inch oval or #7
round reed (ribs)

³/16- or ¹¹/64-inch flat reed
(handle trim)

Positioning the Hoops and Constructing the Bar for the Lid

Place the two 12 x 20-inch oval hoops together (figure 1). Hold them in place temporarily with clothespins or tie with waxed string. Adjust the position of the hoops, while measuring with a tape measure from one side to the other, until the distance is equal on all four sides. Make a pencil mark on both hoops, on all four sides, at the intersecting points (figure 2).

Separate the hoops and prepare the #10 round reed for the bar. Since the two oval hoops are the same, you may use either for the exposed handle.

Cut a piece of #10 round reed 30-inches long, or the length required to form the bar. Shave about half the thickness off the reed from approximately 4 inches on one end with a knife or shaper. Shave half the thickness from the opposite side of the other end of the reed. Note: The two ends will overlap and should be about the same thickness as the whole #10 round reed when spliced together. Scoop out a 1-inch area approximately 13 inches from one end and 16 inches from the other

end (figure 3). This area wraps around the handle and should be thinned to about half its thickness.

Soak the shaped #10 round reed thoroughly (at least 30 minutes). Fit the bar around the handle hoop, just above the pencil mark you made across the rim hoop (figure 4). Hold the bar in place with clips, string, or nails,

Weaving the Bar

Soak the longest ¼-inch flat or flat-oval reed you can find. When it's pliable, begin by pushing the end between the two pieces of the bar where they are spliced, about 1½ inches from the handle. Wrap around the two pieces of the splice moving toward the handle (figure 5). When you reach the handle, begin to weave, figure-eight style, around the two sides of the bar. Fit the first row as close as possible to the handle (figure 6). When you have woven to the other handle, hide the end by pushing it back into the weaving or down behind the bar as it wraps around the hoop (on the outside). Take care to weave the bar with even tension so the width of the bar will remain consistent. If time allows, let the bar dry before starting to weave.

Note: If your weaver isn't long enough to weave all the way across, add a new one by weaving with both the old one and a new soaked one together for about an inch, then continue with the new one alone. Cut the old one if need be, so the end hides inside the bar or under the new weaver.

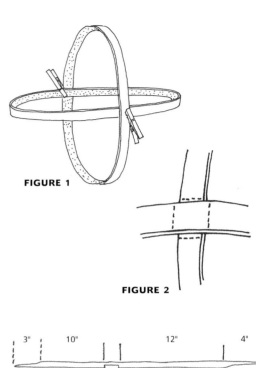

FIGURE 1

FIGURE 2

FIGURE 3

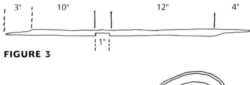

FIGURE 4

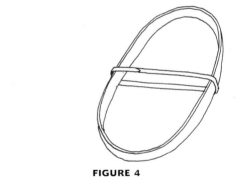

FIGURE 5

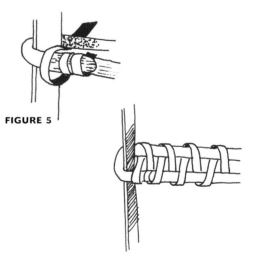

FIGURE 6

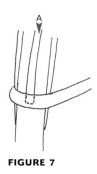

FIGURE 7

Decorating the Handle

Any decoration may be used or the handle may be left plain. If you feel the handle needs more width, consider using a piece of #7 reed on both sides of the handle hoop and do a simple over-under weave or add the wheat braid as illustrated in the following step:

Cut two pieces of #7 round reed 2 inches longer than the exposed handle. For about an inch (on all sides), shave the ends on two sides until they are about the thickness of flat reed. Push two of the pieces down between the bar and the handle hoop, one on each side of the handle (figure 7).

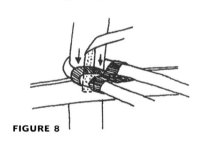

FIGURE 8

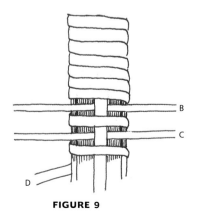

FIGURE 9

Cuts

1) From ³/16-inch flat reed, cut and soak a piece (A) approximately 5 inches longer than the handle.

2) From ³/16-inch flat reed, cut and soak two strips (B and C) that are three times as long as the exposed handle. Mark a halfway point on the wrong or rougher side.

3) Locate and soak a very long piece of ¹/4-inch flat or flat-oval reed (D).

Push one end of the ³/16-inch flat reed (A) between the bar and the rim hoop to secure.

Push one end of the long weaver (D) between the two hoops on the inside (figure 8). Begin with (D) wrapping around the handle solidly, over (A), seven or eight times. Wrap around both the handle and the two pieces of #7 round reed.

Insert strip (B) under (A), aligning the halfway mark under (A), wrong side up. Make one complete revolution around the handle—with (D) going over (A).

Insert strip (C) under (A), again aligning the center mark directly under (A), flat side up. Make another wrap with (D). At this point, your handle should look like the illustration (figure 9).

Note: The above procedure will be easier if you'll remember that following every movement with (B) and (C), the weaver (D) makes one complete turn around the handle.

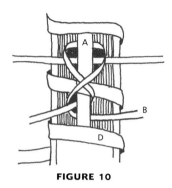

FIGURE 10

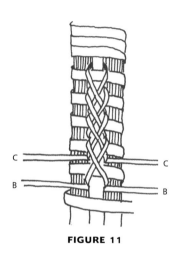

FIGURE 11

Braiding

Bring the left side of (B) down and under (A), entering from the right and coming out on the left (figure 10). Next, bring the right side down, entering from the left, move under (A) and under the left side of (B), bringing it out on the right side. Pull both ends of (B), tightening the figure eight. With (D), make one complete turn around the handle, over (A). Repeat the procedure with (C). Be sure to tighten and wrap with (D) after each figure eight. You'll have five braid crosses, with (C) to be braided next (figure 11).

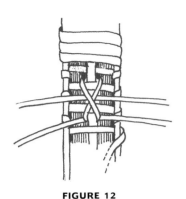

FIGURE 12

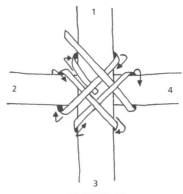

FIGURE 13

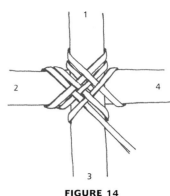

FIGURE 14

Alternative Weaving of the Handle

This is basically the same handle treatment. The only difference is that instead of wrapping all the way around the handle and the round reed, you weave over one round reed, under the handle, over and around the other round reed, over the handle this time, under the round reed, etc. (figure 12).

Making the Braided God's Eye

Note: The God's Eye is made right over the bar and the handle wrapping.

Start the weaver on top of the hoops, with the tail on top pointing between the rims 3 and 4 (figure 13). The weaver moves behind 1 and diagonally to 2, under itself, and diagonally to 3. Then it goes behind 3, under itself and diagonally to 4, behind 4, under itself and diagonally to 1.

At this point, the procedure changes somewhat (figure 14). The weaver will now go under itself on 1, diagonally to 2 and underneath the outermost on 2, behind 2, under itself and the outermost weaver on 3, etc. It will be necessary to use the awl to lift the second weaver up enough

for the end of the weaver to slip under it. It might also be helpful to point the end of the weaver. The weaving moves from one hoop to the next, counter clockwise, always going under itself and the outermost weaver on the next hoop.

Continue weaving in this manner until you've made seven revolutions (or more if you like), counting from the back of the hoops, with the weaver ending on 4 at the top of the right rim. Now you're ready to begin weaving the basket. Do not cut the weaver. Secure it at the rim with a clothespin and begin with another soaked weaver to repeat the procedure on the other side of the basket until you've finished the God's Eye (figure 15).

Note: Figures show God's Eye loosely woven for clarity.

Weaving the Basket

Note: I've made this basket using both of the suggested materials (#7 round reed and 3/8-inch oval-oval reed) and have found the oval reed to produce a sturdier basket.

From the #7 round reed (or oval reed) cut and number two each of the following lengths:

PRIMARY RIBS

#1: 29 inches

#2: 31 inches

#3: 34 inches

#4: 36 inches

#5: 29 inches

SECONDARY RIBS

#6: 28 inches (inserted below #1)

#7: 34 inches (inserted below #3)

#8: 31 inches (inserted below #4)

#9: 25 1/2 inches (inserted below #5)

With a sharp knife, shaver, or pencil sharpener, point all the rib ends (figure 16).

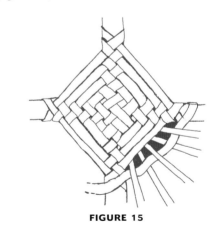

FIGURE 15

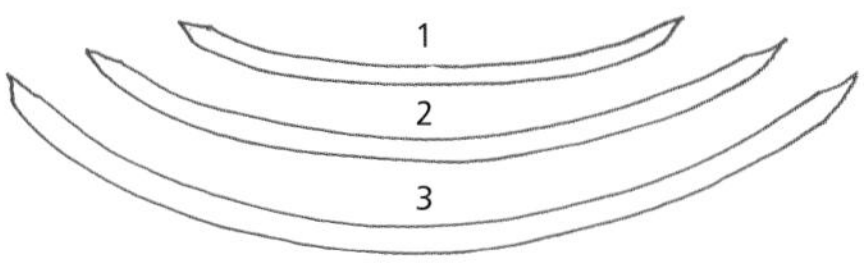

FIGURE 16

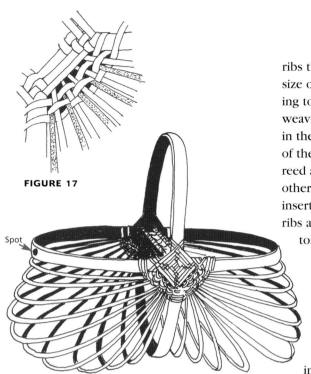

FIGURE 17

Spot

FIGURE 18

Begin by placing the ribs in the God's Eye; they actually just lie inside the ear. Although figure 15 shows all five primary ribs inserted when the weaving begins, you may find it much easier to begin with ribs #1, #3, and #5, weave a couple of rows and then add #2 and #4. Then weave five or six rows with the weaver left over from the God's Eye, before adding the secondary ribs in the places indicated in the length chart (figure 17). The weave is a simple over-under, turning around the handle to reverse the weave. Rewet the weaver any time that it feels dry or stiff. Push each row of weaving as snugly as possible against the previous row. The illustration shows the weaving loose only for clarity.

After adding the secondary ribs and weaving several rows, you will find that there are still spaces between ribs that are wider than 1 inch. The size of the spaces will vary according to the tension you've used while weaving. You should add more ribs in these spaces. Estimate the length of the additional ribs by holding the reed around from one side to the other, allowing enough extra to insert into the weaving. Be sure the ribs are in keeping with the skeleton already formed (figure 18).

Splicing a New Weaver

When you have 2 or 3 inches of weaver left, it is time to join a new soaked weaver. This joining should not take place at the rim, so backtrack if necessary. Overlap the new weaver on top of the old one (figure 19). You'll be weaving with two pieces of reed for two or three ribs. Hide the ends if possible.

Finishing the Basket

Weave approximately the same number of rows on each side to keep the basket balanced. When

you've woven (on both sides) for 5 or 6 inches from the ears, begin a new weaver in the middle of the unwoven area that remains. The place for this weaver to begin is marked with a dot in figure 18.

Fold a long soaked weaver in half over the rim (figure 20). Use clothespins frequently to keep the ribs evenly spaced. You're now weaving with one end of the weaver at a time, in two directions-one end towards the left and one end towards the right. When this weaving covers about 5 or 6 inches of the rim, stop weaving here and return to the original weaving on either side. When the two areas meet, you should fill in the triangular unwoven space in the following manner. When you can no longer squeeze another weaver in around the rim, do one of the following:

1) Turn around the first rib, reversing direction just as you did around the rim (figure 21), or

2) Cut the weaver inside the basket and begin a new one going in the opposite direction (See Figure 22).

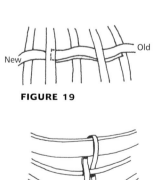

New   Old

FIGURE 19

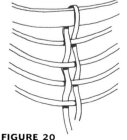

FIGURE 20

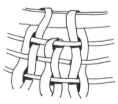

FIGURE 21

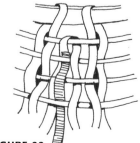

FIGURE 22

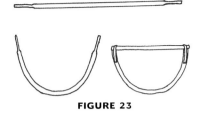

FIGURE 23

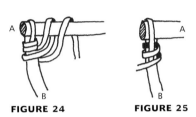

FIGURE 24   **FIGURE 25**

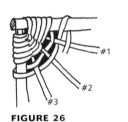

FIGURE 26

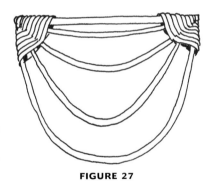

FIGURE 27

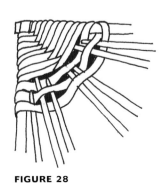

FIGURE 28

Making and Attaching the Lid

Measure, as accurately as possible, the distance from inside one God's Eye to the other (across the basket at the bar). Cut a piece of #10 round reed or a $1/4$-inch diameter dowel (A) the length of your measurement. Next, measure from inside one ear all the way around the rim to the outer ear. Be sure the lid will fit on top of the rim and inside the ear. Cut a piece (B) 6-inches longer than the measurement (figure 23).

For 3 inches on each end, shave away at least half the thickness of the reed. Soak the #10 round reed and tie it, as it forms the shape of the rim on which it is to fit. Fold the thinned ends around the straight piece of #10 round reed while it is wet, and hold it in place with cable clips or clothespins. When the frame is dry, soak a long piece of $1/4$-inch flat reed and begin weaving the lid ears (figures 24 and 25).

Insert the weaver and wrap it as tightly as you can around the splice two times. Next, begin a 2-point lashing, around bar A and then around B, forming a V-shaped ear. You should have five or six wraps on each side. Repeat the procedure on the other side of the lid. Do not cut the weaver.

From the #7 round reed, cut two each of the following ribs:

#1: 15 inches

#2: $17 1/2$ inches

#3: 20 inches

Begin with three primary ribs. Rib #1 is inserted into the opening in the ear closest to the straight side, rib #3 into the opening at the bottom, and rib #2 into the center of the openings. You must create an opening with the awl. Weave over and under, just as you wove the basket, for three or four rows (figure 26). Double-check the approximate placement of the first three ribs (figure 27).

Add four more ribs (figure 28). It should be easy for you to eyeball the lengths of these ribs-you want the space between the ribs, at their fullest point, to be no wider than 1 inch. Add more ribs, if needed, after 2 or 3 inches of weaving. Weave some on each side of the lid to keep the weaving balanced and the lid in shape. Again, you may want to begin a weaver in the middle of the unwoven area after about 4 inches of weaving from the ear. The two areas to be filled in will be on the sides (figure 29). Fill them in with the same techniques you used on the basket.

The lid can be attached to the bar with a piece of soaked reed pushed through the lid and around the bar and tied underneath. A strong piece of waxed string, leather, or wire can also be used to join the two.

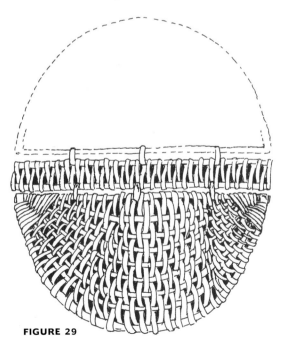

FIGURE 29

Fishing Creel

SKILL LEVEL: **Advanced**   DESIGNERS: **Lyn Siler and Carolyn Kemp**

Sometimes called an Adirondack creel and often called the Curragh Creel, this fishing basket probably had its origins in English willow. It is "kidney" shaped to fit on the fisherman's side.

DIMENSIONS
**APPROXIMATELY
6 X 12 X 7 INCHES**

BASKETMAKERS
**LYN SILER AND
CAROLYN KEMP**

20½"

7½"

FIGURE 1

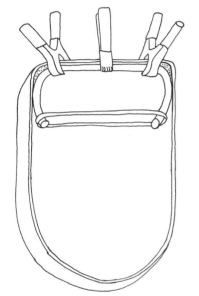

FIGURE 2

Base Front

Center

FIGURE 3

Materials

#10 round reed

#5 round reed

#4 round reed

³/16-inch flat or flat-oval reed

4 feet of cloth belting material or a 1-inch wide strip of leather

Making the Basket

Begin by cutting a piece of #10 round reed 20½-inches long. Mark the center at 10¼ inches (figure 1). It should be preformed to the shape of the basket before you begin. You may find something that works better, but we found a 10-inch D handle was the perfect mold. Place the well- soaked #10 round reed inside the handle, using cable clips to hold it in place (figure 2). Tie the ends or use a very heavy rubber band to pull them into shape. Also, cut two pieces of the #10 round reed, 7½-inches long, to be used as the back corner posts.

When the frame is dry and pre-formed, cut 16 pieces, each 36-inches long and 20 pieces, that are 16-inches long from the #5 round reed. From the center mark on the formed frame, make marks at 1-inch intervals. You should have eight marks across the front and five on each end (figure 3).

With a sharp knife, split the #10 round reed frame in half (length-wise) so you can push the #5 spokes through. Cut all the way around, leaving approximately 1½ inches unsplit on each end.

Note: Keep the rubber band on the ends of the frame while you weave so it doesn't lose its shape.

Push the 36-inch spokes through the split frame at the marked spots (from front to back) in pairs, leaving 12 inches on the front and 24 inches on the back, which will become the base and the back of the basket. Use clothespins to hold the spokes in place (figure 4). Do not put the side spokes in yet.

With a soaked piece of ³/16-inch flat reed, lash the spokes in place by beginning at one end and wrapping around itself to hold it in place (figure 5). Continue lashing across the front. Cut any remaining weaver and end the lashing by tucking it in between the two split pieces (figure 6).

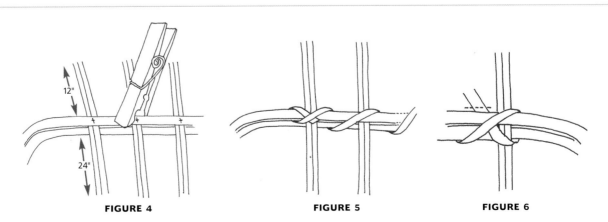

12"

24"

FIGURE 4   **FIGURE 5**   **FIGURE 6**

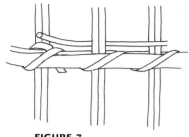

FIGURE 7

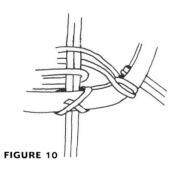

FIGURE 8

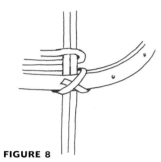

FIGURE 9

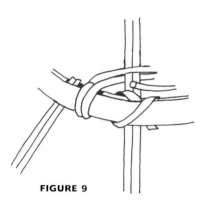

FIGURE 10

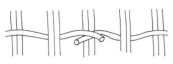

FIGURE 11. Splicing

Soak a long piece of #4 round reed and begin weaving across the back to front spokes in a simple wicker weave (figure 7). Turn the last spokes around, reversing directions (figure 8). Begin making an extra turn around the rim at the corners and insert the 16-inch spokes on the ends at the marked spots. Insert one spoke on each end with an extra turn made around the rim (figures 9 and 10).

Any time a weaver runs out, splice on a new one (figure 11).

Continue weaving back and forth across the base, inserting new stakes at the marks and wrapping an extra turn around the rim between rows.

Because of the fullness on the ends of the base, a few extra turns are necessary to fill in. Simply turn around at the marked spokes, reversing directions for a short row.

End the weaving on the base at B. Add another piece into the weaving and with the two pieces, twine across the back (figure 12). Tuck the ends into the weaving.

Note: Do some shaping by pushing the weaving toward the front (in the center back). The back should be slightly curved as in the figure.

Use a very small nail or tack to secure the two 7½-inch posts to the ends of the existing frame. Be sure you realize that they're standing up while the frame is flat and has been woven for the base.

Turn the base over so you are now working from the outside of the basket. Begin a three-rod wale by starting three separate weavers, each behind three consecutive spokes and bring each weaver, farthest one to the left first, over the two stakes to the right, behind the next and out to the front (figure 13). Begin at post B. Rewet the spokes at this point. Work the three-rod wale all the way around the base, back to A. As you round post C, start to roll the spokes upward, following the shaping you did while twining. Continue to B. Using post D or point B as your starting point, work two more rows of three-rod wale all the way around the basket, upsetting the spokes as you weave.

Note: If any spoke breaks, replace it by pushing a new one into the weaving.

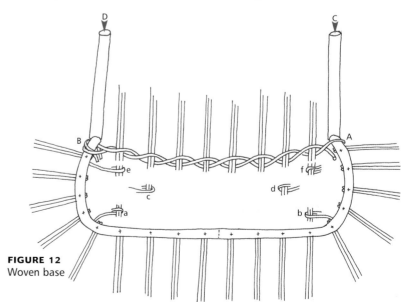

FIGURE 12
Woven base

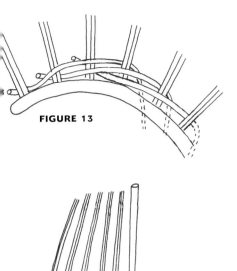

FIGURE 13

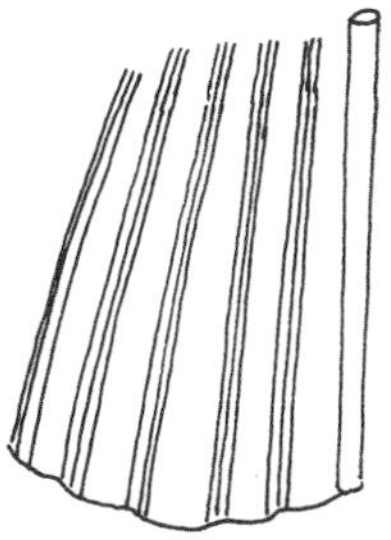

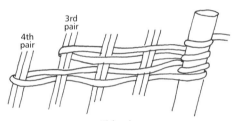

FIGURE 14. Side view

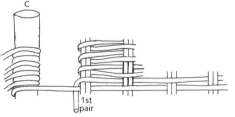

FIGURE 15. Side view

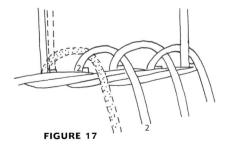

FIGURE 16. Back view

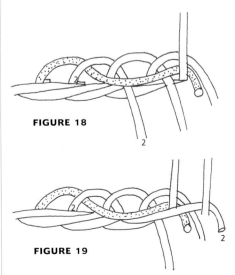

FIGURE 17

FIGURE 18

FIGURE 19

When you round post D the third time, end one of the weavers by pushing the end into the weaving beside a spoke. Continue weaving a chase-weave with the two weavers (over 1, under 1 with the weaver and under 1, over 1 with the chaser) all the way around the basket for about 5 inches.

Note: You must control the shape of this basket by your weaving tension and by doing some molding with your other hand, i.e., push in on the back as you weave while you loosen up on the sides and front. After about 3 inches of weaving, you must bring all the spokes in very gradually-the front and two sides lean inward, while the back remains fairly straight (figure 14). At 5 inches, the front is as high as it will be.

Weaving one side at a time, increasing the height on the two sides by turning and reversing to post C two times, making an extra wrap around post C (figure 15). Start a new weaver on the other side and increase to D.

Now turn your attention to the back. Tuck a new weaver in behind the first pair of spokes (figure 16). Weave back and forth, reversing directions at the 1st and 8th pair of spokes for eight rows. This creates an opening for the straps. End the weavers.

Now, starting three weavers on the back, work one row of three-rod wale all the way around the basket. End the three rods by cutting them on the inside of the basket.

Of each pair of spokes still standing, cut one off flush with the top row. Do a closed border by the following means: (1) Bring each spoke behind the one to its right, to the outside, (2) Take them all back to the inside going over the next two and (3) Bring all of them back to the outside going behind the next (4th) spoke. Cut smoothly on the outside (figures 17, 18, and 19).

Making the Lid

Using strong clothespins or cable clips, secure a piece of #10 round reed to the top of the basket, allowing it to lie on the rim. Let the ends overlap 1 to 2 inches. Leave it to dry so the lid will be formed to the shape of the basket. It should be about 29-inches long.

Scarf the ends so they lie smoothly and are the same thickness as the rest of the #10 reed when overlapped. You may need to cut a wedge from the reed to make the sharp corners on the back.

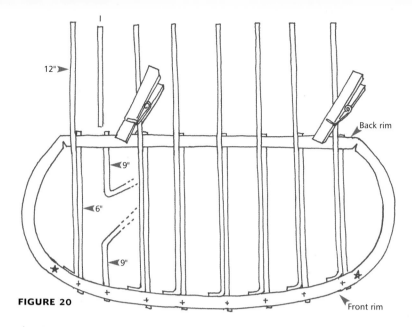

FIGURE 20

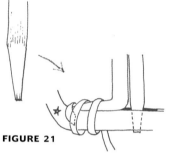

FIGURE 21

Cut the rim in half, lengthwise, from ★ to ★ on the front (figure 20) and across the back, leaving about an inch on each end unsplit. Note: You need not try to split the back where the two ends overlap; just thin the end on that spoke so it will lie in the scarfed area. Mark the places for the spokes to be placed, eight spots that are about 1-inch apart.

From the #5 round reed, cut seven pieces, 6-inches long; seven pieces, 12-inches long; and three pieces, 9-inches long. There are no side (or end) pieces, only front-to-back spokes. There are two openings in the lid—a small one in the center front and a larger fish hole to the left of the center.

Shave only one end of all the 12-inch spokes and two of the three 9-inch

spokes for about $\frac{1}{2}$ inch, making them little more than paper thin for the last $\frac{1}{4}$ inch (figure 21). Shave both ends of all the 6-inch spokes in the same manner. Spoke I is the only one that need not be tapered at all.

Soak a long piece of $\frac{3}{16}$-inch flat reed for wrapping the rim and begin on the left at the *. Wrap solidly. When you reach the spot marked for the first spokes to be inserted, lay the tapered end, bent to the left, of a 12-inch spoke on the rim and

wrap over it. Immediately, push one end of a 6-inch spoke through the rim, flush against the long one, and continue wrapping. The next marked spot requires only a single 9-inch spoke pushed through the rim. Each pair of the remaining spokes should be treated as the first two, i.e., the long one bent with the wrapping over it and the short one pushed through the rim. End the wrapping as you did on the base.

Insert the other end of the 6-inch spokes through the back rim, and insert the other shaved 9-inch spoke opposite the first one.

Spoke 1 will be inserted later into the weaving when it is done, beside the existing spoke. Cut the ends of the inserted spokes flush with the rim. Try to ignore the long ends of the 9-inch spokes (singles) while you are weaving; they'll be woven into the lid as you come to them. Wrap solidly, the whole back rim, with another soaked $\frac{3}{16}$-inch flat reed. Begin weaving the lid with a soaked #4 round reed weaver (figure 22).

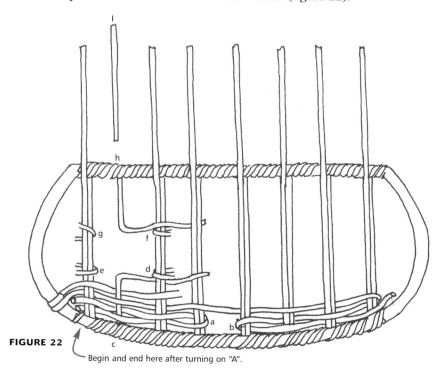

FIGURE 22

Begin and end here after turning on "A".

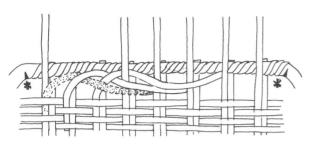

FIGURE 23

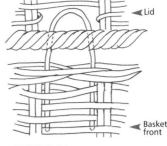

FIGURE 24

FIGURE 25

Start on the inside (left) and turn around point A, the fourth spoke from the left, and end where you began. The ends can be left longer and tucked into the weaving later. Start next on the right side, turn around B, the fourth spoke from the right and return. Keep on weaving now across the whole top, to point D or E (depending on the direction from which you approach it). Bend the end of the single spoke C to the right and weave it into the lid, joining another weaver wherever it happens to end. At points D and E, the weaving reverses, leaving a fish hole. Make an extra turn around the first and third spokes throughout this whole area up to points F and G. Spoke H weaves into the lid as did C. When you have woven to within ¼ inch of the back rim, end the weaver on the right side.

Make a closed border by the following means: (1) Insert spoke I into the weaving beside H. (2) Beginning with the far left long spoke, bend it,

and each subsequent one, to the right, going under 1, over 2 and ending behind the fourth spoke. Continue with each remaining spoke (figure 23). Clip the ends on the inside so they lie smoothly.

Attach the lid to the basket by pushing a piece of soaked reed through the weaving around the back rim of the lid and through the weaving around the back rim of the basket. The spots for attachment are designated by an asterisk (*) in figure 23. Twist or tie the reed so it won't pull out. The ends can be worked into the weaving to make it more secure.

Push a piece of small round reed or wire into the basket (center) so it will extend up through the center hole in the lid (figure 24).

Making the Latch

From the #10 round reed, cut a piece 2¾-inches long. Taper one end on one side, for about 1 inch to approximately half its thickness at

the end (figure 25). Then on the opposite side from the taper, hollow out an opening, as in the figure, about 1½-inches long. A good way to start the opening is to use a small drill bit, just to get the hole started. From there you should be able to hollow it out with your knife. If the end splits off, use a tiny nail and some glue to hold the two pieces together at the end.

Attach it to the lid by running a small piece of round reed (or wire) through the opening in the latch and through the lid (hiding the ends in the weaving), making sure the latch will reach through the holder you put in the basket that sticks up through the hole in the lid. Another piece of round reed wraps over the latch and down into the lid just to hold the latch in place better (figure 26).

Attach the strap by taking it through the two holes on the back and joining the ends on the inside (figure 27).

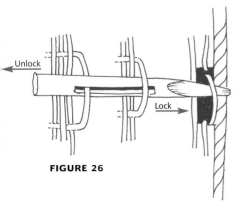

FIGURE 26

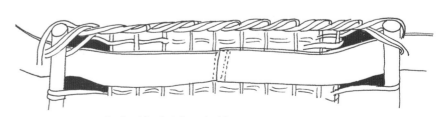

FIGURE 27. Back of basket from inside

Key
Basket

SKILL LEVEL: **Advanced**

A number of different shapes and sizes of
the traditional Key Basket can be found.
Originally made to hang on a wall to hold keys,
there are many other things it could hold as well.
It can be made vertically oval, horizontally oval, or round.

DIMENSIONS
**APPROXIMATELY
8 X 12 INCHES**

BASKETMAKERS
**CAROLYN KEMP AND
GERTIE YOUNGBLOOD**

Materials

8-inch Key D (frame)

8 x 12-inch oval hoop (frame)

#6 round reed (ribs)

1/4- or 3/16-inch flat reed (weavers)

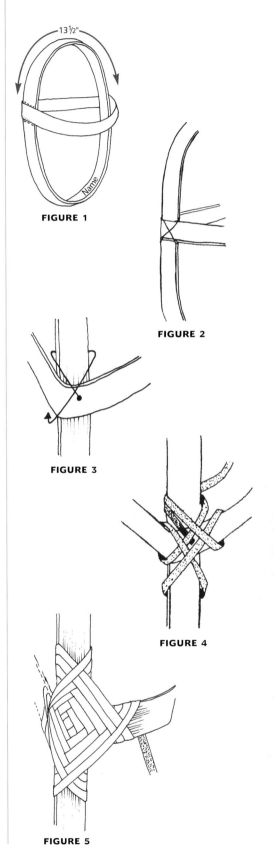

FIGURE 1

FIGURE 2

FIGURE 3

FIGURE 4

FIGURE 5

If you choose to experiment with your own shapes and sizes, simply decide what you'll use for a handle hoop and a rim (some type of D frame). Then construct the ears as shown in the following directions, and sight the ribs by holding the round reed from one ear to the other, one at a time, until the shape looks right to you. Generally, the #1 rib should protrude from the key frame about 1 inch in the front. The #2 rib is 2 to 3-inches longer than #1. The #3 rib is 1 1/2 inches to 2-inches longer than #2. The #4 rib is 1 1/2 to 2-inches longer than #3. And the #5 rib should lie almost even with the bottom of the handle hoop. The back is easy to sight because it is flat and the five primary ribs are about 2-inches apart. As with any basket, use your imagination to alter any of the measurements given here, if the shape doesn't appeal to you.

Securing the Hoop and Frame

Slide the frame over the 8 x 12-inch oval, but not quite halfway. The shorter part of the hoop will be the handle and the longer part the basket. With a flexible tape, measure the handle; it should be about 13 1/2 inches (figure 1).

On the oval hoop, place pencil marks above and below the key frame. At this point, either tie the two pieces together or nail them with a small nail or tack (figure 2).

Note: It's helpful to place your initial in the inside of the handle hoop on the area that will become the bottom of the basket, so you won't forget which part is the handle and which is the basket.

Making the God's Eye

Soak a long piece of 1/4-inch flat reed (or 3/16 inch) until the reed is pliable.

Begin the God's Eye by bringing the weaver around the handle hoop, diagonally down to the left rim, etc., until you've completed one revolution (figure 3 and 4). Continue wrapping in this manner for five more revolutions. Do not cut the weaver until you've finished the God's Eye (figure 5).

Note: If your weaver runs out before you finish the God's Eye, splice a new one on by tucking a new end under the weaving inside the God's Eye and wrapping over the old end, cutting it at a point so it will lie flat and be inconspicuous.

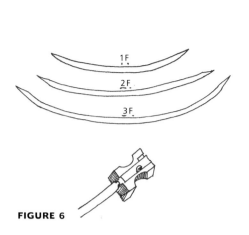

FIGURE 6

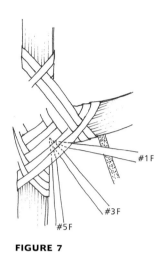

FIGURE 7

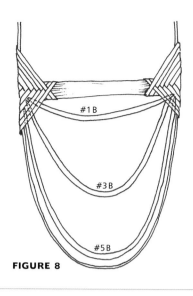

FIGURE 8

Cutting and Inserting the Primary Ribs

You must cut front and back ribs for this basket. As you cut the front ribs, number them with a pencil 1F, 2F, 3F, etc., and 1B, 2B, 3B, etc., for the back. Mark them near the center since you must sharpen the ends and do not want to lose your number in the sharpening (figure 6).

CUT ONE EACH OF THE FOLLOWING FRONT RIBS:

1F: 12^{1}/$_{2}$ inches

2F: 15^{1}/$_{2}$ inches

3F: 17 inches

4F: 19 inches

5F: 18^{1}/$_{4}$ inches

CUT ONE EACH OF THE FOLLOWING BACK RIBS:

1B: 7^{1}/$_{2}$ inches

2B: 9^{1}/$_{2}$ inches

3B: 12 inches

4B: 15 inches

5B: 16^{1}/$_{2}$ inches

Sharpen all the ends. The point should begin to taper about ^{3}/$_{4}$ inch from the end of the reed and eventually become as sharp as a pencil point.

Insert ribs 1F, 3F, and 5F in the front, pushing the ends into the pocket formed by the God's Eye, and ribs 1B, 3B, and 5B in the back, using the same pocket (figures 7 and 8).

Rewet the weavers that were left from making the God's Eye and begin to weave by going over the first rib, under the second, etc., and treating the hoop as another rib and turning to reverse direction around the rims (figure 9). Weave three rows on both sides. Stop and insert ribs 2F and 4F in the front. Rib 2F goes under 1F and 4F goes under 3F. Add the 2B and 4B ribs in the back in the same places (figure 10).

With the new ribs in place, begin weaving again for two more rows, for a total of five rows, until you achieve the basic skeleton of the basket (figure 11).

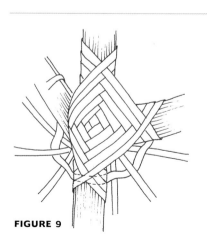

FIGURE 9

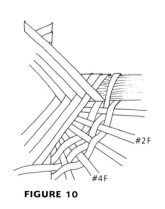

FIGURE 10

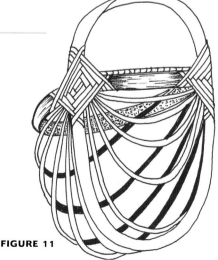

FIGURE 11

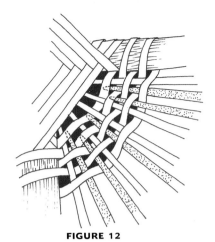

FIGURE 12

FIGURE 13

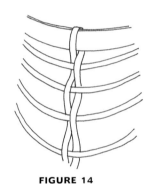

FIGURE 14

Cutting and Inserting the Secondary Ribs

Cut the following secondary ribs, again from the #6 round reed:

SECONDARY FRONT RIBS

S1: $11^1/2$ inches, inserted below 1F

S2: $12^1/2$ inches, inserted above 2F

S3: $16^1/2$ inches, inserted below 3F

S4: $17^1/2$ inches, inserted below 4F

S5: $17^1/4$ inches, inserted above 5F

SECONDARY BACK RIBS

S6: 7 inches, inserted below 1B

S7: 9 inches, inserted below 2B

S8: 11 inches, inserted below 3B

S9: $13^1/2$ inches, inserted below 4B

Sharpen them all and insert into the weaving (figure 12). Remember that every person weaves differently, which can affect the placement of secondary ribs. Alter any of the lengths or placements of the ribs you deem necessary.

Finishing the Basket

Rewet the weaver and resume weaving, going over and under each rib. To add a new weaver, simply soak a new one, slide one end under a rib (over the old weaver) and continue weaving with both of them until the old one runs out (figure 13).

Continue weaving on both sides of the basket for approximately ten rows. Do not weave all of one side, then all the other. Instead, weave three or four rows on one side, then the same on the other; this helps keep the basket balanced.

At some point, after about 12 rows, the curve will become very obvious and the weavers may begin to curl instead of lying flat. It is time to move to the center of the unwoven area and fill in.

Fold a long, soaked weaver in half and begin to weave with both ends (figure 14). Turn around the rib on

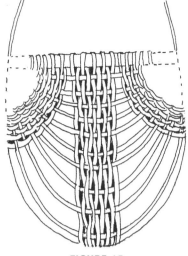

FIGURE 15

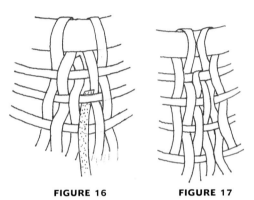

FIGURE 16　　　**FIGURE 17**

the back and continue weaving outward in both directions (figure 15). The filling in will be done on each side when the two woven areas meet. Fill in by one of the following methods: When you can no longer squeeze in another weaver, either (1) turn around the first available rib and reverse directions (figure 16), or (2) cut the weaver inside the basket when there is no more room at the rim and start a new one on top of an existing weaver (figure 17).

BASKETMAKER: **GERTIE YOUNGBLOOD**

Materials

- #3 round reed (approximately ½ lb. for weavers)
- #2 round reed (8 pieces, approximately 6 feet long for weavers)
- #4 round reed (4 pieces, approximately 36 inches long for weavers)
- #3 round reed, dyed (weavers)
- #5 round reed (spokes)

Southwest Urn

SKILL LEVEL: **Advanced**   DESIGNER: **Genie Jackson**

This basket teaches several round-reed techniques and produces a pleasing urn-shaped vessel that could be used to hold flowers or perhaps even some rolled towels.

DIMENSIONS
**APPROXIMATELY
9 X 9 INCHES**

BASKETMAKER
GENIE JACKSON

Preliminary Step

Using the #3 round reed, dye four long pieces in four of your favorite colors.

Weaving the Base

From the #5 round reed, cut eight pieces that are 7 inches long. Mark the center of each piece. Also from the #5 round reed, cut 28 pieces that are 22 inches long. Soak the 7-inch spokes and the #2 round pieces until they're pliable. Split four of the 7-inch spokes through the center with an awl for about 1 inch or $\frac{1}{2}$ inch on each side of the center mark (figure 1). Insert the other four 7-inch spokes through all the split ones and center them so there are four spokes each way forming a cross (figure 2).

Pinch and fold a long piece of the #2 round reed about 2 feet from one end. Mentally (or physically) letter the groups of spokes A through D.

Loop the fold around group A, with the short weaver (1) behind A (figure 3). To reverse twine, weaver 1 moves over the next group of spokes, crossing over weaver 2. Weaver 2 falls into place behind the next group (B). Continue this movement, turning the base in a counterclockwise direction while weaving in a clockwise direction, each time bringing the "behind" weaver over the next group (figures 4 and 5). Be sure to check the completed revolution (figure 6).

Continue these movements, turning the cross after every stroke so the spokes being covered are always on the right. This section of the base is completed when there are four rows of weaving showing on all groups of spokes. End the short weaver in the angle between A and B.

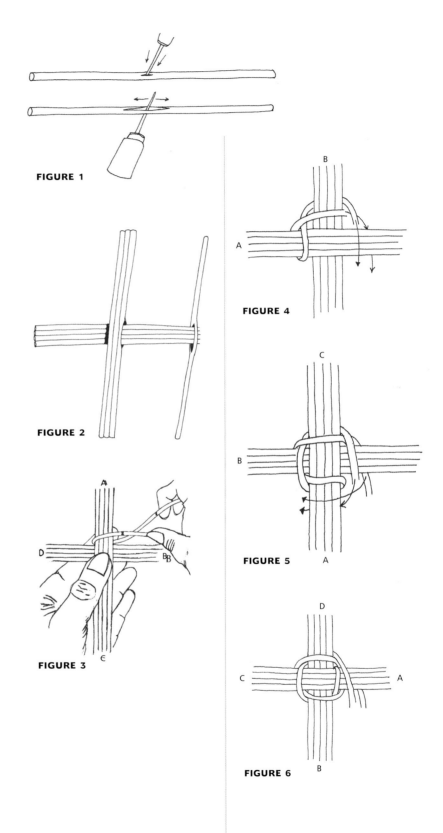

FIGURE 1

FIGURE 2

FIGURE 3

FIGURE 4

FIGURE 5

FIGURE 6

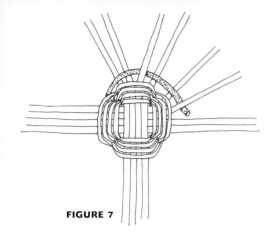

FIGURE 7

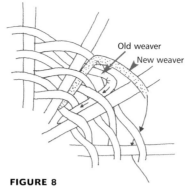

Old weaver
New weaver

FIGURE 8

FIGURE 9

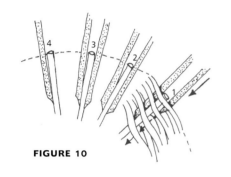

FIGURE 10

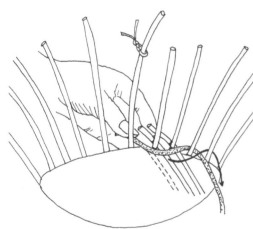

FIGURE 11

With the long weaver, continue to weave, separating the spokes in Japanese weave, over two spokes and behind one with the single weaver (figure 7). Separate the spokes evenly and keep the rounds close together. To add a new weaver, allow the old weaver to end under a spoke and tuck in to the left of that spoke. Tuck the new weaver to the right of the previous spoke and carry it over the tuck of the old weaver, then behind the next spoke as you continue with the Japanese weave (figure 8).

The base should be slightly domed (figure 9). To create that effect, push up on the base with the palm of your hand or hold the edge of the base in your palm and push up with your fingers (see photo on page 162).

Continue to Japanese weave until the base measures 5 inches across. End the weaver by tucking it beside a spoke.

Bi-Spoking and Upsetting the Sides

Soak the 22-inch long side spokes and point them on one side of one end.

Insert the pointed end of the spokes, one on each side of three consecutive spokes for about 1 inch into the weaving. Insert only one new spoke to the left of every fourth spoke (figure 10). At the same time you're inserting new spokes, trim the base spokes as near to the Japanese weave as possible. The domed side (or the side covered by over twos) is the inside of the basket. An awl will help to open up the space into which the spoke is inserted.

To separate the side spokes equidistantly, one row of three-rod arrow is needed. Three-rod arrow consists of one row of triple weave (three-rod wale), a step up, and one row of reverse triple weave. Cut three pieces of #3 round reed, each measuring at least twice the circumference of the base, and place one end behind three consecutive spokes. Mark the first of the three spokes, as it is the first spoke of the arrow.

Three-Rod Wale

Triple weave, or three-rod wale, for one round by bringing the farthest left weaver in front of two spokes, then behind the third and out. Continue to do this, always picking up the left weaver, until the weaver comes out to the left of the marked spoke (figure 11).

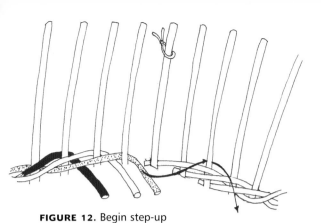

FIGURE 12. Begin step-up

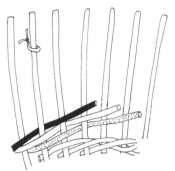

FIGURE 13. Complete step-up

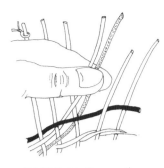

FIGURE 14. Reverse three-rod wale to start arrow

Step-Up

Now using the weaver on the right, weave in front of two spokes, to the right, behind one and out (figure 12). Take the next (middle) weaver to the right in front of two spokes, behind one and out. Take the remaining weaver to the right in front of two spokes, behind one and out. The step-up is complete (figure 13).

Reverse Three-Rod Wale

To form the second half of the arrow, start the triple weave again with the weaver on the left. Weave in front of two spokes, but make the weaver go under the other two weavers, behind one spoke and out (figure 14).

Continue in this manner, always using the left weaver, until the weaver comes out on the left of the marked spoke.

To end the three-rod arrow, the first (left) weaver passes in front of two spokes, goes under the top two weavers and ends behind spoke one, to be cut later (figure 15).

The second weaver moves in front of two spokes, under the remaining weaver to the right and also under

the top weaver in place, ending behind spoke two.

The third weaver passes in front of two spokes and the two weavers which are the first and second stoke of the second row of the arrow and ends behind spoke three. Cut the ends short and at an angle, making them conform to the shape of the base when the basket is dry.

Before upsetting the sides, soak the basket base, side spokes and some #4 round reed. With needle nose pliers, pinch the side spokes close to the weaving of the arrow. A four-rod coil is used to upsett the base. With side spokes pointing upward, insert four weavers of #4 round reed behind four consecutive spokes. Mark the #1 spoke. Remember you are now working on the outside of the basket-hold the base with the underside towards you. To do a four-rod coil, you will take each farthest left weaver in front of three spokes, behind one spoke, and out to the front (figure 16). Guide the direction of the spokes as you weave so they turn evenly and are the same distance apart. Weave one row of the four-rod coil, always moving the weaver on the left. End the weavers behind the spokes where they started. Lock the coil by lifting (in order

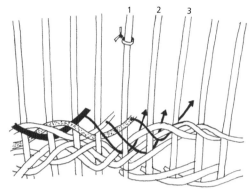

FIGURE 15. Ending three-rod arrow, first step

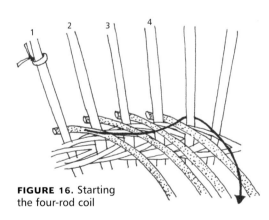

FIGURE 16. Starting the four-rod coil

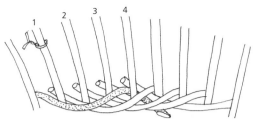

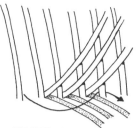

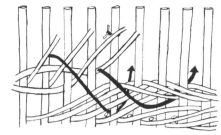

FIGURE 17. Locking the four-rod coil

FIGURE 18

FIGURE 19. Lock-in rod reverse

from right to left) the ends of the weavers, D, C, B and A, and slip the final ends between them and the spoke. The final end of D goes under the beginning of D. Cut the ends at an angle when dry, close to the weaving (figure 17).

Weaving the Sides

Triple weave the sides with the natural #3 round reed for about 5¹/₂ inches. Allow the sides to flare a little. By the time 5 inches of weaving is done, the diameter of the basket should be about 9 inches. End the weavers behind the spokes where they started, and cut at an angle when dry.

Using the four different colors of the #3 round reed, weave three rows of four-rod arrow, with each row consisting of:

1) One row of four-rod wale (explained previously in figure 16 on page 161)

2) A step-up, which is the same as a three-rod wale step-up, just done with four weavers instead of three (as shown in figures 12 and 13 on page 161)

3) A row of four-rod reverse wale. Four-rod reverse wale is done exactly like four-rod wale, except that the farthest left weaver must move under the three weavers to the right of it, behind the fourth spoke and out to the front (figure 18). Work a lock-in to end the first arrow. The first weaver passes in front of and under the other three weavers and ends behind the starting spoke (figure 19). The second weaver passes in front and under the other two weavers and also under the weaving already in place, ending behind spoke two. The third and fourth weavers end in the same manner.

Do not cut off any weavers, as you'll continue to make two more sets of

arrows. Start your next row of a four-rod coil by bringing your weaver back to the outside of basket behind the original starting four spokes. Complete two more sets of four-rod arrows. At the end of the final set the weavers will be cut off short. Avoid adding new weavers during this step-up at the start of each new row, as it could easily cause mistakes. Rewet the tops of the spokes and triple weave (three-rod wale) with #3 natural round reed for eight rows, or about 1¹/₂ inches. As you weave this section, push inward on the spokes and pull gently on the weavers to obtain the urn shape. End the weavers behind the same spokes as they started and cut them at an angle when dry.

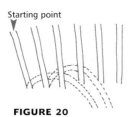

Starting point

FIGURE 20

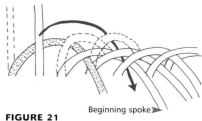

Beginning spoke ▶

FIGURE 21

Making the Border

Soak the spokes thoroughly before weaving the border. With needle nose pliers, pinch the spokes just above the list row of weaving. Take any spoke behind the two spokes to the right and to the outside (figure 20).

When you have returned to the starting point, two spokes will remain. Pull up the beginning spoke a little and push the far left remaining spoke under it. Then pull up the second woven spoke so the last spoke can be pushed through (figure 21).

Next move each spoke over two spokes to the right and insert it to the inside of the basket, going under the loop formed by the first row of the border (figure 22).

The last two rows are worked on the inside of the basket. Hold three spokes out, bring the left spoke over the right two, and drop it down next to the side of the basket (figure 23).

Each row is ended when you have two spokes remaining. To find where to tuck the far left spoke, push up on the beginning spoke. Again, bring the far left spoke to the right and tuck into the loop formed by pushing up the beginning spoke. Now push up the second spoke and tuck the remaining spoke into the loop formed nearest the basket edge (figure 24).

Repeat this row, taking each spoke over two spokes to the right and ending just as before. Be sure to keep the spokes wet while working the border. Cut the spokes to approximately $1/2$ inch when border is complete.

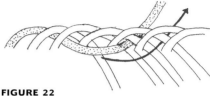

FIGURE 22

FIGURE 23

FIGURE 24

One-Two-Three Twill

SKILL LEVEL
Advanced

DESIGNER
Sosse Baker

S osse Baker's shaping technique for this extraordinary basket is wonderfully simple (at least when she does it!), requiring only some practice. The total number of stakes must be a number divisible by seven plus four.

DIMENSIONS
**APPROXIMATELY
9 X 13 INCHES**

BASKETMAKER
SOSSE BAKER

Materials

- ¼-inch flat or flat-oval reed or 7mm flat-oval reed (stakes)
- ¹¹/₆₄-inch flat-oval reed (weavers)
- ½-inch half round (rim)
- #15 round reed (handle) or a purchased handle

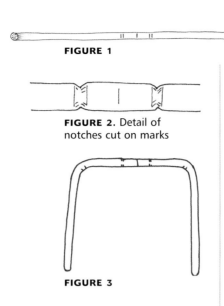

FIGURE 1

FIGURE 2. Detail of notches cut on marks

FIGURE 3

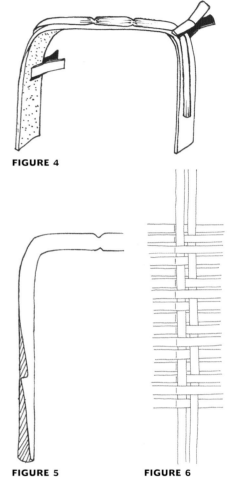

FIGURE 4

FIGURE 5   FIGURE 6

FIGURE 7

Preliminary Step

To form the handle, soak a piece of #15 round reed for an hour (or until it bends easily). Choose the shape you want your handle to take. Locate or construct a form—pegs driven into a board or a round or square hoop. The example here uses a square hoop. Make a center mark on the reed. Next, mark 1 and 2 inches to the right and left of the center mark. Mark a center on the hoop. Aligning the center marks, bend the round reed around the hoop and hold in place with heavy-duty clamps until it dries. Remove when dry (with a knife or trimming plane and sand paper), carve the handle on the marks and sand until smooth. Notch the handles approximately 3 inches from the ends, cutting through half the thickness of the reed at the notch and tapering the thickness until it becomes very thin at the end (figures 1 through 5).

From the ¼-inch flat reed (or whatever material you are using for stakes), cut 32 pieces, each 28 inches long. Dye them the color of your choice. Mark the centers on the smooth side and soak them until they're pliable.

Making the Base

Lay 16 pieces of stake material horizontally, aligning the center marks, right (smooth) side up. Weave one of the other 16 pieces vertically just to the right of the center mark, going under 2, over 2, etc., ending with over 2 (figure 6).

Weave six more pieces to the right and eight pieces to the left of the center mark in a 2/2 twill pattern (figure 7). All these are woven right side up. Measure and true the base to approximately 4¾ x 4¾ inches.

Weaving the Sides

Soak a long piece of ¹¹/₆₄-inch flat-oval reed. Begin weaving, with the end going over 2, under 2 (figure 8). Weave with the base on a flat surface for several rows. As you weave keep the right side of the weaver up. Do not allow it to turn at the corners. Weave the first row of over 2, under 2, as closely and snugly as possible.

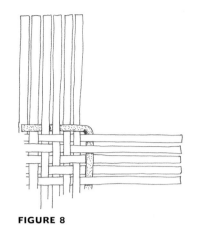

FIGURE 8

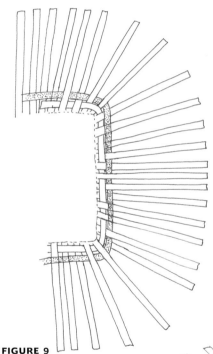

FIGURE 9

With one revolution of over 2, under 2 complete, begin the pattern weave, weaving over 3, under 1, over 1, under 2, repeating all the way up the sides of the basket (figure 9). The weave is continuous, not one row at a time.

From the very first row, spread the stakes from the center stake outward toward the corners. By the fourth or fifth row, the corners should be completely filled in with spokes. You must hold the spokes in place with one hand and weave with the other as you round the corners. Use clothespins if necessary. The pieces will stay in place after several rows of forced placing. After the fifth row, lift the base, place your thumbs on the inside of the basket and press down on the corners, bending the sides of the basket (figure 10). You are creating the cat-head shape on the bottom of the basket (figure 11). Replace the basket on a flat surface and continue weaving for two or three more rows, repeating the shaping procedure as needed.

Note: Everyone must find his or her own shaping method. You may find you want to lift the basket sooner. Experiment to see what works best for you.

Lift the base, holding it with the ends of stakes pointed away from you, and continue weaving around the basket. The sides will begin to stand up. You must control and create the shape you want. The longer the base remains on a flat surface, the fuller the sides will be. The sooner it is held with stakes pointing away from you, the straighter the sides will be.

Ideally, the shape should have a diameter of approximately 10 inches at the fullest point and approximately 8 or 9 inches at the neck (figure 12). Naturally, to bring the sides in, increase the tension on the weaver and press inward on the stakes, being careful not to tighten too quickly.

FIGURE 11. Profile of base

FIGURE 10

FIGURE 12

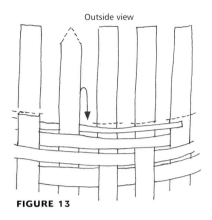

Outside view   Inside view

FIGURE 13

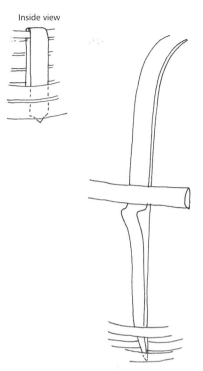

FIGURE 14

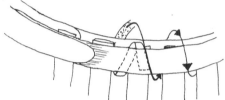

FIGURE 15

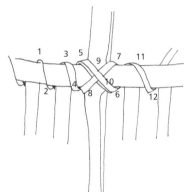

FIGURE 16

Finishing the Basket

When the weaving is within $2\frac{1}{2}$ inches of the ends of the stakes, taper the weaver for several inches, making it $\frac{1}{8}$ inch at its narrowest. Cut the stakes on the inside of the basket flush with the top row. Rewet and point the remaining stakes; bend them over the top row and tuck them under the first available row of weaving on the inside of the basket (figure 13). Insert the handle on the outside of the basket, pushing the ends only under two or three rows of weaving so the notch falls on the top row (figure 14). Cut two pieces of $\frac{1}{2}$-inch half-round reed, each long enough to reach around the top of the basket and overlap at least 2 inches.

Place the rim pieces around the top of the basket, covering two rows of weaving. Mark in pencil on both ends where the ends overlap. Remove from basket. With a knife or trimming plane, bevel the area of overlap from both ends so the overlapped area is no thicker than a single thickness of $\frac{1}{2}$-inch half-round reed.

Replace the rim on the basket, placing the overlapped areas near, but not on top of, each other. Hold it in place with clothespins. Soak a long piece of natural $\frac{3}{16}$-inch flat oval until it is pliable. Lash the rim pieces in place, hooking the end over the basket wall just past the overlapped areas (figure 15). The lasher goes under the inside rim, over the wall and behind a weaver on the outside of the basket. With the long end, lash around the rim, going in every space between stakes. Create an X pattern on the handle, if you wish (figure 16). The lasher is moving from outside to inside around the rim. When the handle is reached, the X is made by going diagonally to 6, up behind the rim to 7, diagonally across to 8, up behind the rim on the left of the handle to 9, and over the first stroke of the X from 9 to 10, where regular lashing resumes. Repeat on the other side of the handle. End the lashing as it began, or tuck the end discreetly under a weaver on the inside of the basket.

Double Chief's Daughter Urn

SKILL LEVEL: **Advanced**

The woven pattern of this "floor" basket is of Cherokee origin. Don't be intimidated by its size; bigger doesn't necessarily mean more difficult to make.

DIMENSIONS
**APPROXIMATELY
10 X 10 X 15 INCHES**

BASKETMAKER
JUDY WOBBLETON

Materials

$\frac{1}{4}$-inch flat reed (stakes and weavers)

#0 round reed (locking row)

$\frac{3}{8}$-inch flat-oval reed (rim)

Preliminary Step

Dye approximately $\frac{1}{3}$ hank of $\frac{1}{4}$-inch flat reed rust, or the color of your choice. Also dye two long pieces dark brown or black.

Weaving the Base

From the natural $\frac{1}{4}$-inch flat reed cut 72 pieces, each 50 inches long. Mark the centers of all the pieces on the wrong side. Soak all the pieces until they're pliable.

Lay 36 pieces horizontally in front of you, wrong side up, aligning the center marks. Use a spoke weight or heavy book to hold them in place.

Weave two pieces vertically through the horizontal pieces just to the right of the center marks (figure 1). Beginning at the bottom, weave over 4, under 4, etc., with two pieces. Place the center mark of the vertical piece in the center of the 36 horizontal pieces.

Continue to weave with two pieces in the following pattern (row 1 is already woven):

Row 2: U2, O4, U4, O4, etc., ending with O2

Row 3: U4, O4, U4, etc.

Row 4: O2, U4, O4, U4, etc.

Repeat these four rows until 18 pieces are woven in to the right of the center mark.

Next, weave the other 18 pieces to the left of the center mark, again repeating the following 4-row pattern:

Row 1: O2, U4, O4, U4, etc.

Row 2: U4, O4, U4, O4, etc.

Row 3: U2, O4, U4, O4, etc.

Row 4: O4, U4, O4, U4, etc.

Row 5: repeat Row 1.

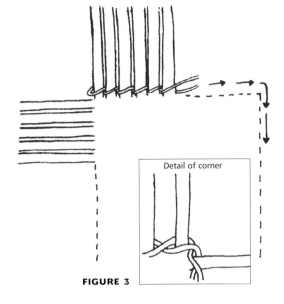

Detail of corner

FIGURE 3

Here are four rows woven to the right of the center mark and four rows woven to the left (figure 2).

Measure and true the base to 10 x 10 inches. Mark the corners of the base when it's trued in case any slipping occurs.

All rows should fit flush against each other as snugly as possible. Pack and repack, as some shrinking will occur when the reed dries.

The next step is optional. If you foresee a need for a locking row, twine around the base with #0 round reed to hold everything in place while you begin weaving up the sides. Fold a soaked piece of #0 round reed in half, loop the fold around any set of two stakes and twine around the base (figure 3). End the twining by tucking the end under itself where it began.

The twining can be removed later if you wish (after the sides are well on their way up).

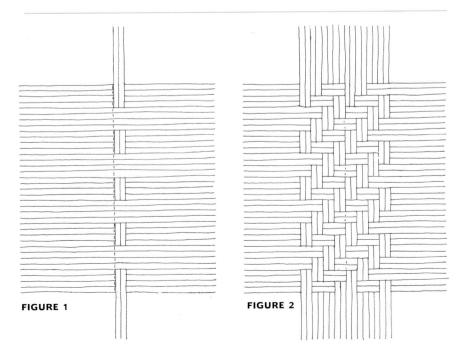

FIGURE 1   **FIGURE 2**

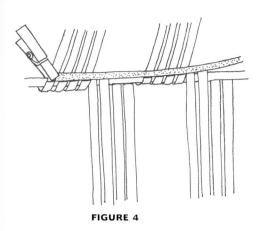

FIGURE 4

FIGURE 8

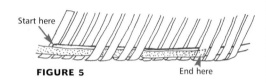

Start here

End here

FIGURE 5

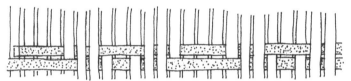

FIGURE 9

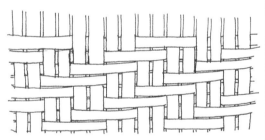

FIGURE 6

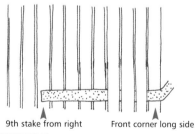

9th stake from right Front corner long side

FIGURE 7

Weaving the Sides

Note: From the bottom of the basket, the order of color and natural woven up the sides is as follows:

Row 1–6: natural

Row 7–33: rust

Row 34–41: natural

Row 42: black

Row 43: rust

Row 44: black

Row 45–53: natural

Starting anywhere with a soaked $1/4$-inch flat reed, weave over 4, under 4 around the basket (figure 4). Be sure the right side of the weaver is on the outside. Cut the weaver after it has overlapped the beginning, and hide the end behind the fourth group of stakes (figure 5).

Weave six rows in this same manner, making the over 4 move over two stakes each row (figure 6).

When six rows are done, soak several pieces of rust $1/4$-inch reed. To locate a starting place, count from the right corner (any side) to the ninth stake. Place the end of the weaver over the ninth, tenth, eleventh, twelfth and thirteenth stakes (figure 7). Go under the next 3, over 1, under 3, etc., following the graph (figure 8). Then begin the second row (figure 9). Be sure to start each row on a different side from the row before. Continue following the graph through row 33. Pack each row down tightly against the previous row.

Weaving the Neck

Row 34 (natural) is over 3, under 3. Locate an over 5 on the last pattern row. Take the weaver under the center 3, over the next 3, under the next 3, etc.

Row 35 (natural) is also over 3, under 3, but opposite the row before (not twilled), as are the rest of the rows. On this row, begin to pull the three stakes you're weaving over (or under) together, treating them as one (figure 10). They must be pushed together to allow space for the weaver to fit in.

Also, after Row 35, start to pull tightly on the weavers to restrict the diameter of the neck. The diameter should decrease about 2 inches by time the eight natural rows are done.

Next, weave in a black weaver, still pulling tightly on the weaver. The next row is a rust weaver and then another black one (figure 11).

Now you must make the stakes flare outward. If you want, try to control the flare by weaving from the inside of the basket and pressing outward on the stakes. If you have trouble getting them to flare, soak the ends of the stakes and turn the basket upside down, making the stakes spread out drastically. Place some heavy object on the bottom (now on top) so the stakes are pressed outward as far as possible—far more exaggerated than you eventually want them

(figure 12). They will invariably pull in some as you weave.

Weave over 1 (treating three stakes as one), under 1 until you are within 2 inches of the ends of the stakes.

Finishing

When you're within 2 inches of the ends of the stakes, cut off the stakes on the outside of the basket flush with the top row of weaving. One of the three stakes on the inside of the basket gets tucked into the weaving on the outside of the basket and the other two in the group are cut flush with the top row of weaving (figure 13).

Soak a long piece of ³⁄₈-inch flat-oval reed. Measure around the top rim of the basket. Allowing enough for a 3-inch overlap, cut and bevel the ends for 3 inches so the thickness of the overlap is no thicker than a single thickness of ³⁄₈-inch flat oval. Place one piece around the rim on the inside and one on the outside, covering just the last row of weaving and holding them in place with clothespins. Place the overlapped areas near, but not on top of each other. Begin lashing just past the two overlaps (figure 14). Hook the lasher over the basket wall going under the inside rim, then lash around the rim pieces, taking the lasher in each space between every three stakes. End the lasher as you began or hide it behind the top row of weaving.

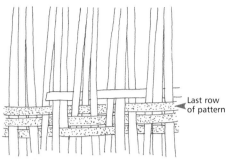

FIGURE 10

Last row of pattern

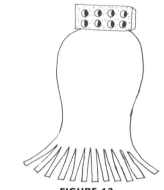

FIGURE 11

First row of pattern

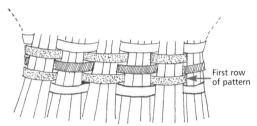

FIGURE 12

FIGURE 13

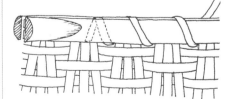

FIGURE 14

Herb Basket

SKILL LEVEL: **Advanced**

In the old days, this basket was filled with gathered herbs, but today it's used mostly to carry pies. It's a kitchen classic that's well worth the time it takes to make.

DIMENSIONS
**APPROXIMATELY
10 X 10 INCHES**

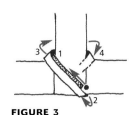

FIGURE 3

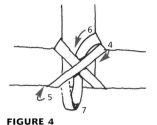

FIGURE 4

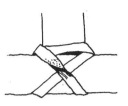

FIGURE 5. Back view

Materials

Herb frame
(short D handle*)

10-inch hoop (frame)

#6 round reed (rib)

$^3/_{16}$-inch or $^1/_4$-inch flat
reed (weavers)

$^3/_8$-inch flat reed, 1 to 2
yards (bow-knot ear)

∗ The handle is very similar
to a D handle. It is usually
found in 6, 8, 10, and 12-inch
diameters and is several inches
shorter than a D handle. The
hoop is the same diameter
as the handle. The basket is
very shallow, of course, but
a 1- to 2-inch wide handle
works best. It's somewhat
different from other ribbed
baskets because you only
weave the bottom.

Securing the Hoop and Handle

Place the hoop inside the handle.
Tie the hoop in place with twine or
waxed thread. Measure (with a flexible tape measure) from one side of
the hoop to the other (on both
sides) to make sure the distance is
the same. Make adjustments, if necessary, by sliding the hoop. Mark on
each side of the handle so you'll
know if the hoop moves (figure 1).
Nail the two pieces together with a
small nail or tack. The string can be
removed after nailing (figure 2).

Place two strips of $^3/_8$-inch flat reed
(each about 18 inches long) in
warm water to soak while reading
through the next step.

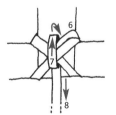

FIGURE 6

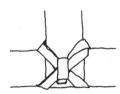

FIGURE 7

Constructing the Bow-Knot Ear

Using a piece of soaked $^3/_8$-inch flat
reed, place the wrong side against
the handle and begin at the dot.
The wrong side of the reed is
the rougher, hairy side. Construct
the ear, referring to the illustrations
(figures 3 through 7) and the following pattern:

From the dot, move up to 1 and
down inside to 2, up to 3, covering
end of weaver, behind handle to 4
(figure 3). Go down to 5 (figure 4),
up to 6, twisting the weaver (on the
inside) to put the wrong side on
top (figure 5). Go down through the
X you made to 7, up in front and
down through the X again (figure 6).
Pull the end of the weaver tightly
and cut it at the bottom of the rim
and your ear is finished (figure 7).

Inserting the Primary Ribs

There are six primary ribs in the
bottom and three on each side of
the handle base. You must make
holes in the $^3/_8$-inch flat reed for
all these ribs (figure 8).

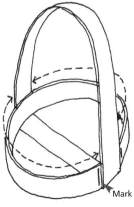

Mark

FIGURE 1

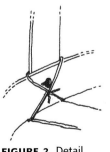

FIGURE 2. Detail
of inside view

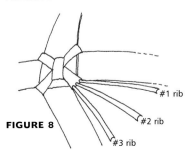

#1 rib

#2 rib

FIGURE 8

#3 rib

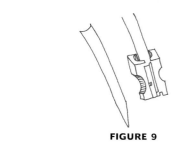

FIGURE 9

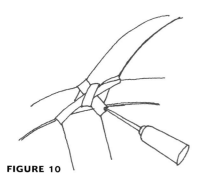

FIGURE 10

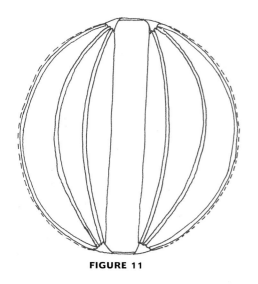

FIGURE 11

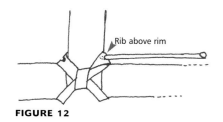

Rib above rim

FIGURE 12

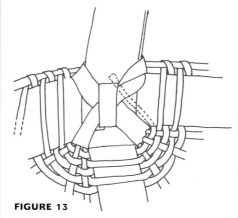

FIGURE 13

Using a pencil sharpener, point one end of a piece of #6 round reed, using #5 for smaller baskets (figure 9). With the awl, make a hole in the $^{3}/_{8}$-inch reed near the rim (figure 10). Insert the sharp point into the hole you made and hold the rib around the edge of the rim, sliding your fingers around the two pieces together all the way to the other ear, to be sure the rib is exactly parallel with the rim.

Allow $^{1}/_{4}$ inch for sharpening. Mark, cut, sharpen, and insert into the ear. Repeat the procedure for the other side of the basket.

The second rib is easy to sight. It is about 3-inches shorter than the first. Make a hole in one ear, sharpen one end of round reed again, and insert and hold the reed around to the other side, sighting it to be about 3 inches from the first one. Repeat the procedure used on the first two ribs.

Then cut a third rib about 2 inches shorter than the second. Insert on both sides. Double-check the spacing of all six primary ribs (figure 11).

Also, most people like to put a rib above the rim of the basket to give it more depth; two may be added if you prefer. Use the same procedure to measure this rib. This rib is inserted also into the $^{3}/_{8}$-inch flat reed, with the aid of the awl, above the rim (figure 12).

Beginning to Weave

A very narrow $^{3}/_{16}$-inch weaver is necessary for weaving this basket. If you don't have a $^{3}/_{16}$-inch weaver, then use scissors and split a long strip of $^{1}/_{4}$-inch flat in half to use for at least the first five rows. As you move toward the fullest part of the basket, you can change to a larger weaver. The old herb baskets were woven entirely with weavers usually no wider than $^{1}/_{8}$ inch. The weaving will be nicer and tighter if you have the patience to weave the entire basket with $^{1}/_{8}$ inch.

Begin by tucking the end of the weaver behind the ear anywhere it will stay securely. Bring it over the first rib, under the second, over the third, under the handle base, over the third rib on the other side, etc. Continue all the way to the rib above the rim. Go around the top rib and reverse directions. Continue weaving in the opposite direction, this row weaving over the unders, and under the overs. Continue for five or six rows. Be sure to count each row separately, but not from the rim (figure 13).

Splicing a New Weaver

When you have 2 or 3 inches of the weaver remaining, you need to splice on a new one. Simply lay a new, wet weaver on top of the old one, hiding the ends under a rib (figure 14). Weave with both until the old one runs out. Continue with the new one. You never want to add a new weaver on the rim. If you foresee this happening, backtrack a few ribs to avoid it.

Adding the Secondary Ribs

On a 10-inch herb basket, you'll need to add six more ribs, three on each side. You can also easily sight these ribs, holding a piece of round reed from one side, curving to the other side, and making sure the ends will reach only into the weaver, not into the ear. The ends of the secondary ribs need only to be hidden under the first available weaver. Each secondary rib will be placed underneath the corresponding primary rib, in the same space with the primary rib (figure 15).

Note: An 8-inch basket will need only four secondary ribs and a 6-inch basket may need only the three primary ribs. Use our rule of thumb for adding secondary ribs: If you have more than 1 inch between any two ribs, at their fullest point, you need to add more.

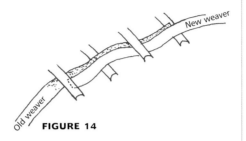

FIGURE 14

Finishing the Basket

Continue weaving from one side of the basket to the other, on both ends, until the handle base fills in. Push the weaving outward, toward the ears, and squeeze weavers in across the base until you can no longer get another one in. When it's absolutely full, turn around the nearest rib, reversing the direction of the weaving. You're now working with only one side at a time.

Continue to weave to the rim and back to the first available rib, reversing around that rib, until the V-shaped area fills in (figure 16).

To begin weaving the second unfilled side, simply hide the end of a weaver under a rib or the handle base and begin a new row (figure 17). Remember to rewet the weaver anytime it feels dry. When the entire bottom is filled-in, clip any hairs or splinters, and stain your completed basket if you desire.

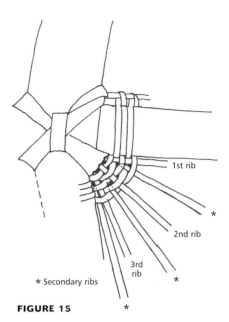

FIGURE 15

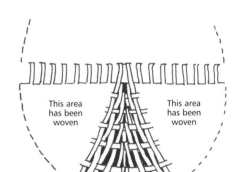

FIGURE 16. Filling-in

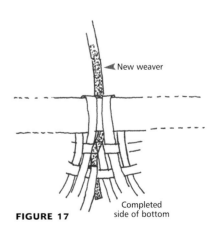

FIGURE 17

Beaded Swirls Basket

SKILL LEVEL: **Advanced**   DESIGNER: **Judy K. Wilson**

Materials

- 3 or 7 ply waxed linen thread
- 8/0 or 11/0 variegated Japanese beads
- 7½ x 3-inch piece of cardboard

Beaded Swirls was an experiment to create something strikingly beautiful and yet simple, using only one bead and one or two threads of waxed linen. While twining is not difficult, working with tiny beads and thread can be.

DIMENSIONS
**APPROXIMATELY
2³⁄₈ X 4 INCHES**

BASKETMAKER
JUDY K. WILSON

Getting Started

Draw an arrow at one end of the cardboard and face the arrow pointing towards you. Always start and end the thread at the arrow. There are 18 spokes; wrap the waxed linen around the cardboard 18 times (figure 1). Only cut at the arrow end. Pinch the center of the spokes together and lay aside. Repeat, making a second set of spokes and also lay them aside.

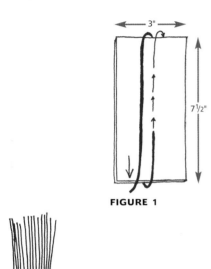

FIGURE 1

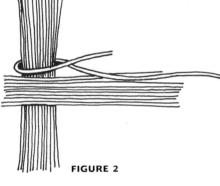

FIGURE 2

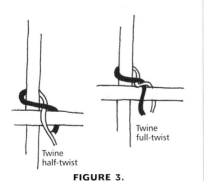

Twine
half-twist

Twine
full-twist

FIGURE 3.

Beginning the Basket

For the weavers, cut off about 4 yards of waxed linen at a time. Place the ends together, thus doubling it, and lay the looped end near you. Find the dead center of each of the groups of spokes and cross them at that point, with one group at 12:00/6:00 and the other group at 3:00/9:00. Pick up the looped end of the weaver and place the loop over the 12:00 group of spokes (figure 2).

Begin to twine around each of the groups, but use a full twist and twine around each group. A twine is a half twist; full twist is two half twists or two twines (figure 3). When you reach the point where you began, stop and place a slipknot in the first spoke on the left of the 12:00 group. The knot will signal that you've made one complete revolution (figure 4).

Check to make sure that your spokes are as high on one side as they are on the other by pulling them upward together. The center point can drift slightly. Even out any spokes that are shorter than others by gently sliding them. As you twine, keep the weaver snug, but not extremely tight. Work to keep the spokes straight within the center square.

When you reach home, begin to divide and twine around eight spokes at a time, creating a small circle around the square. Here you have 18 spokes in each group. Out of the first group, you'll have two groups of eight each, then you will have two left over. Simply pick up six from the next group and continue picking up eight spokes (figure 5). Each group will have leftover spokes: 1st group, two spokes; 2nd group, four spokes;

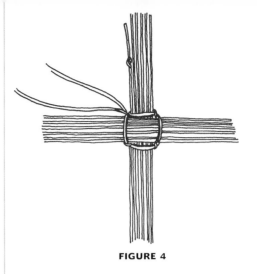

FIGURE 4

FIGURE 5

3rd group, six spokes; and 4th group, eight spokes to make the last group, giving you nine groups of spokes with eight spokes in each one.

As you weave, keep a gentle soft touch, yet pull out all the slack. Each row will require a bit more of the weaver used, as each row is slightly larger than the row before. Keep this is mind as you weave and allow a little more weaver. Keep the bottom basically flat. Twine a total of four rows and stop at home.

At home, you will be dividing the spokes from eight's to four's with the same two weavers. Gently pull the two groups apart as you are twining to help the rows touch each other. Twine a total of seven rows over four spokes each.

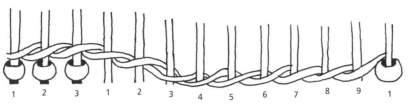

FIGURE 6

At home, with the same two weavers, divide the spokes into pairs. Again, gently help the spokes apart so that the rows touch as much as possible. Your basket should be almost flat at this point. It can have a slight curve to the bottom, but it must be very slight or you will come in too quickly. Twine six rows over pairs in this way and stop at home.

At home, you will still be weaving over pairs as before, but you'll now gently turn the sides up. The sides need to go up (sides are actually turned downward to go up) but not straight up. Gently lean the spoke outwards as you weave. This should be a gentle lean as you want the basket sides to go up but still outward. Twine a total of nine rows over pairs (including the six previous rows) and stop at home.

At home, divide all the pairs of spokes into ones and stop at home. Also, here, you need to have a fairly long weaver on your basket (about 50 to 60 inches each). You can add weavers, but it must be between (centered) beads so that the end of the weaver is well caught. Beads do not hold the end of a weaver in place well at all.

Note the puckers in the basket. The puckers are caused by the beads themselves and the correct weaving. It is not something that you do to the basket. Do not try to help the puckers. Work to keep the weaving even and smooth, the rows touching each other and the puckers will happen for you, without extra effort.

Adding Beads

FIRST ROW:

At home, you'll begin to place the beads. Add one bead to each of the next three spokes. Nip the ends of the spokes off at an angle and re-twist, if you're having trouble getting the bead to go on. Then twine over the beads, plus nine empty spokes (figure 6). When you're twining, your rows must touch the previous row. When you're coming down off a bead, by the third spoke after the third bead, the rows should touch. Do not force the thread down by packing. Turn the basket so that you can weave it down instead. Do not pack at all. Follow the contour of the basket with your weaving.

Count carefully as it is easy to make a mistake. The first row must be correct for the basket to be correct. There are 72 spokes, six swirls of beads, each using a total of 12 spokes (three beaded and nine empty). Divide them beforehand into six groups, if you must, but make it correct.

After you've placed the first set of beads and twined the nine empty spokes, then add beads again until you have completed the row.

SECOND ROW:

Now you'll bump the beads one spoke forward, per row, to make the swirl. You'll notice the uphill and downhill undulation of the weave in the second and third rows (figure 7). Follow this pattern and continue to gently weave outward. Continue doing this until you have eight rows of beads. The basket needs to still go out and up at the same time. It's easiest to do this on top of your leg. The basket should look like a very shallow bowl with a wide lip. Once you complete eight rows, lean the spokes inward as you twine and continue adding beads, keeping consistent thread tension. Don't tighten up if you see the sides are going in. Once you have 16 or 17 rows of beads, the basket will have come in as far as it probably can. Make sure each row has the same number of beads on it.

Now you're ready to do the little chimney part of the basket. Stand the spokes straight up as you weave, even slightly outward (never inward here) and continue twining to make the chimney section. Twine 15 rows going straight up and stop at home. Cut both weavers 1 inch past the weaving and cross the left one over the right one to the inside of the basket.

Finishing the Top

Start approximately 1 inch to the left of where the last row of weaving ends. Pick up any spoke (call it spoke #1) and work to the right. Take spoke #1 in front of spoke #2. Hold, pinch gently with your fingers, go behind spoke #3, then between spokes #3 and #4, back to the outside of the basket (towards you), and hold.

Now pick up spoke #2, go in front of spoke #3 (towards you), behind spoke #4, between #4 and #5 to the outside of the basket. Repeat with the next spokes in line until you are down to two spokes only (figure 8).

Take the spoke on the left, come in front of the spoke on the right. With an awl, open up a hole under the very first spoke you bent over. Go through that hole to the outside of the basket. Hold the last spoke and with the needle or awl, open up the same hole a little more, and go through it in the opposite direction (toward the inside of the basket) for the exact spot. Open up the hole, place the spoke through the hole from the inside to the outside of the basket. Gently pull on the spokes you just worked with to make the top rim look even and smooth (figure 9).

Now place two beads on each of the spokes, one at a time. You'll have to experiment with where the knot

goes. It is about ³/₄ inch out from the basket. Snip off the ends past the knot as you place the beads. Tie the knots loosely at first until you are sure where you want them. Place two beads on each spoke, knot it and cut off the ends. Cut off any ends of weavers flush with the basket inside and out. Straighten up the beaded spoke ends.

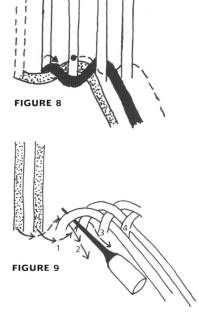

FIGURE 8

FIGURE 9

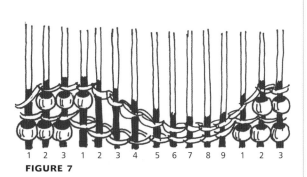

1 2 3 1 2 3 4 5 6 7 8 9 1 2 3

FIGURE 7

Swirling Star Bowl

SKILL LEVEL: **Advanced**
BASKETMAKER: **Joan Moore**

M̲ake this lovely southwestern bowl to match your color scheme. Shown on page 183 are other color variations. Make either or, better yet, make both.

DIMENSIONS
**APPROXIMATELY
15 X 4 INCHES**

BASKETMAKER
JOAN MOORE

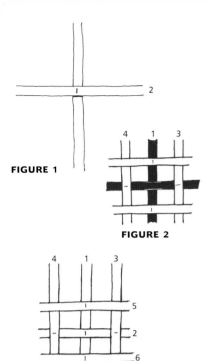

FIGURE 1

FIGURE 2

FIGURE 3

FIGURE 4

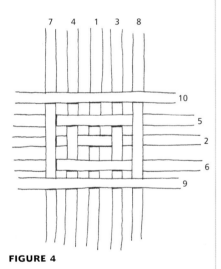

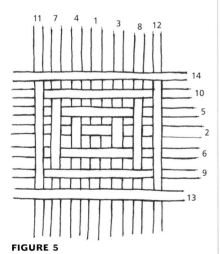

FIGURE 5

Materials

- ¼-inch or 7mm flat-oval or heavy ¼-inch flat reed (spokes)
- ¼-inch or 7mm flat-oval lightweight reed (weavers)
- ³/₁₆-inch flat reed (rim)
- ½- or ⅜-inch flat-oval reed (rim)
- Fine cane (lashing)
- #5 or #6 round reed (rim filler)

Preliminary Step

Cut 38 spokes that are each 26-inches long. Dye 16 of them a light color, 16 a dark color, and six a medium color (or use any three colors of your choice). Mark the centers on the rough or flat side. Soak all the pieces before beginning to weave the base.

Weaving the Base

The base is woven with the wrong (flat) side up. The first 16 spokes are the lightest color. Beginning at the center of the base with a light spoke, place one vertically. Lay the second piece of lightweight perpendicular to the first, aligning the center marks (figure 1).

Note: Or you could start with one dark vertical piece and one dark horizontal piece and then return to the regular pattern (figure 2).

Lay the third, fourth, fifth, and sixth pieces (figure 3). Spokes 1 and 2 are center spokes. Align the center marks on other spokes with the 2 center spokes. Continuing to use the light color, lay the seventh, eighth, ninth, and tenth pieces (figure 4). Lay the eleventh, twelfth, thirteenth, and fourteenth pieces (figure 5).

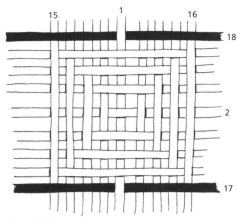

FIGURE 6

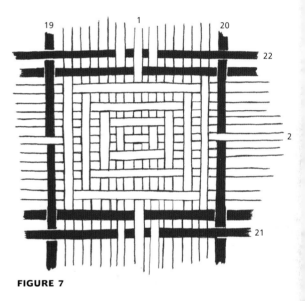

FIGURE 7

Lay the last two light pieces (fifteenth and sixteenth) vertically, one on each side of the center. Until now, the pieces have simply been laid on top of the others. From now on, newly added spokes will be woven under and over existing spokes. Changing to the dark spokes, the seventeenth and eighteenth spokes are woven under spoke 1 and over the others (figure 6).

Dark spoke 19 is woven under the center spoke, as is spoke 20. Dark spokes 21 and 22 are woven under the center 3 spokes and over the others (figure 7).

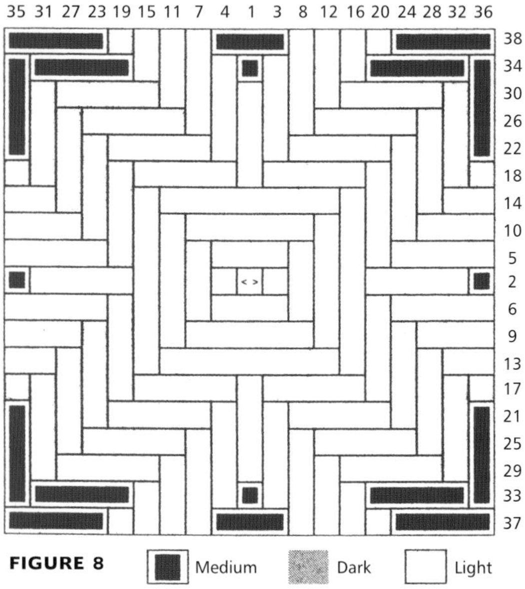

38
34
30
26
22
18
14
10
5
2
6
9
13
17
21
25
29
33
37

FIGURE 8 ■ Medium ▨ Dark □ Light

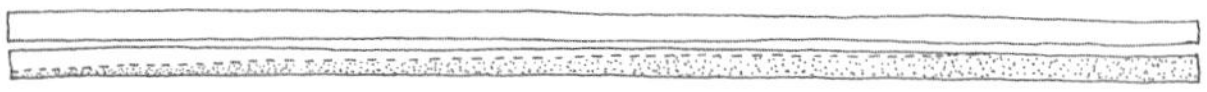

FIGURE 9. ¼" cut in half, then tapered

Spokes 23–32 are dark (figure 8) and woven in the following pattern:

Row 23: under center 3, over the others

Row 24: under center 3, over the others

Row 25: under center 5, over the others

Row 26: under center 5, over the others

Row 27: under center 5, over the others

Row 28: under center 5, over the others

Row 29: under center 7, over the others

Row 30: under center 7, over the others

Row 31: under center 7, over the others

Row 32: under center 7, over the others

Rows 33–38 are woven with the medium color in the following pattern:

Row 33: over center 1, under 4 on each side, over others

Row 34: over center 1, under 4 on each side, over others

Row 35: over center 1, under 4 on each side, over others

Row 36: over center 1, under 4 on each side, over others

Row 37: over center 3, under 4 on each side, over others

Row 38: over center 3, under 4 on each side, over others

Tighten the spokes so there's no space between them. The base should measure approximately 4½ x 5 inches.

Weaving the Sides

Turn the base over, with the flat-oval side of the reed up now.

Soak a long, flexible piece of natural ¼-inch flat-oval reed for

several minutes until it's pliable. Cut it in half lengthwise, making it ⅛ inch. Taper the end of one of the split pieces for 1 to 2 inches (figure 9). Begin weaving on one side by going over 3, under 2, etc. If you're right-handed, weave to the left for now, so when you hold the basket, you'll be working from the outside, weaving from left to right. (If you're left-handed, weave to the right for the moment.)

Leave a tail sticking out when you begin. As the weaver goes around once and returns to the starting point, go over the tail to secure it when you begin the second round. Weave over 3, under 3 in a continuous weave; when the end of a row is reached, continue around the basket again-the over 3 steps over 1 spoke automatically (figure 10).

Note: In order for the swirl pattern to be most effective, you must keep the spokes relatively close together-no farther than ¼-inch apart.

Weave the first three rows around with the base flat on a table. Do not attempt to make the sides stand yet. As you weave the first several rows, make the spokes move towards their respective corners, creating a sunburst with the corners filled with spokes (figure 11).

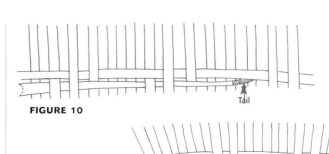

FIGURE 10

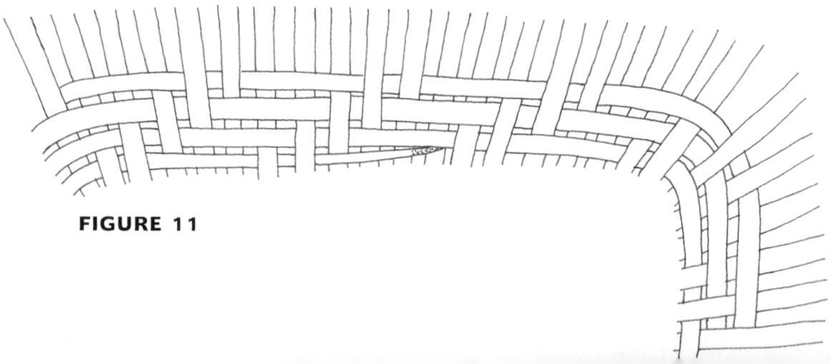

Tail

FIGURE 11

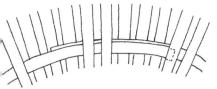

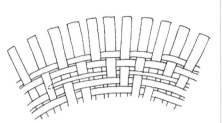

FIGURE 12. Splicing a new weaver

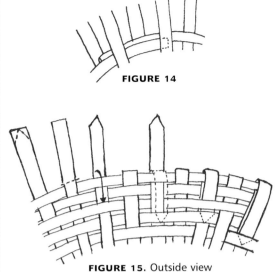

FIGURE 14

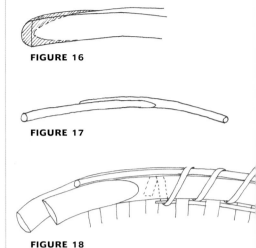

FIGURE 16

FIGURE 17

FIGURE 13. Taper ending and two of start-stop

FIGURE 15. Outside view

FIGURE 18

After three rows of weaving around the base and forcing the spokes to move and fill in the corners, the sides may start to stand a little on their own. You may lift the base and hold it with the spokes pointed away from you, and weave from the outside of the basket. If you find the sides going up too fast, put the basket back on the table and weave from the inside. Just the presence of your hands inside the basket will make the sides lean out. Add on a new weaver when necessary (figure 12). If needed, shave some of the oval side from the overlapped area.

Continue weaving around the basket until there are approximately 2½ inches of the spokes remaining. Taper the end again to ⅛-inch wide and end the weaving directly above the starting spot (figure 13).

Weave two rows of start-stop weaving with the ³⁄₁₆-inch flat or flat-oval reed. Begin a soaked weaver on top of a spoke, weave around the basket going over one spoke, under the next, etc. End the row by going over the beginning to the fourth spoke. Cut the weaver behind the fourth spoke (figure 14). Start and stop the next row in a different place.

Point the spokes on the inside of the basket, rewet them if they're dry, bend them over the top row of weaving, and tuck them into the weaving on the outside of the basket flush with the top row of weaving. Cut the spokes that are on the outside of the basket flush with the top row of weaving (figure 15).

Applying the Rim

Measure around the top of the basket and add 3 to 4 inches for overlapping. Cut the pieces of ½-inch flat-oval reed according to the measurements. Mark off the areas of overlap and shave both ends with a knife or plane, until they're no thicker than a single thickness of ½-inch flat-oval reed (figure 16).

Place the ½-inch flat oval around the top of the basket, covering the top two rows of ³⁄₁₆-inch flat reed with the overlapped areas near, but not on top of, each other. Lay a piece of #6 round reed between the two rim pieces with the ends beveled for several inches like the rim (figure 17). Begin lashing just past the two areas of overlap by hiding the end of the lasher under the rim. Hook the end over the basket wall. Bring the lasher around the rim pieces and through each space under the rim between the spokes (figure 18). End the lasher as it began or discreetly secure the end behind a weaver on the outside of the basket.

Swirling Star Bowl 183

SKILL LEVEL
Advanced

DESIGNER
Judith Olney

Undulating Twill Basket

Shaping is really important here. If your basket shape ends up different from the one pictured here, you have just created an "original." Patterns can turn out quite interesting, so let your creative urge run wild.

DIMENSIONS
**APPROXIMATELY
12 X 12 INCHES**

BASKETMAKER
JUDITH OLNEY

Materials

- $1/4$-inch flat reed (stakes)
- $3/16$-inch flat-oval reed, cut in half lengthwise (weavers)
- $11/64$-inch flat oval reed (weavers)
- $1/4$-inch or 7mm flat-oval reed (weavers)
- $1/2$-inch half-round reed (rim)
- $11/64$-inch flat reed or common cane, used reed side out (lashing)

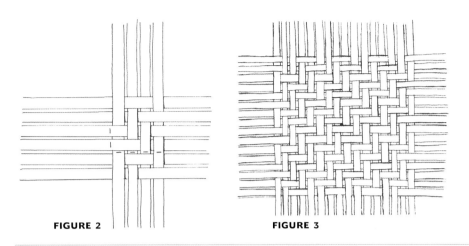

FIGURE 2

FIGURE 3

Preliminary Step

Dye the weavers the color of your choice. Before dying them, taper all the wider pieces down to a width of $3/16$-inch cut in half.

The weaving pattern on the sides of the basket is a continuous weave of over 3, under 2. You can make any size basket you want, but consider that the total number of stakes must be divisible by 5 plus 1 (or plus 4). For example, making a square base that's 16 stakes by 16 stakes gives a total number of 64, which is divisible by 5 (plus 4). Another manageable size to consider is a 19 x 19: 76 total, which is divisible by 5 (75 plus 1).

The stakes must stay relatively close together ($1/4$ inch) so the weaving pattern is provided a background. From the $1/4$-inch flat reed, cut 32 pieces, each 32-inches long. Mark the centers of all the pieces on the wrong side. Soak all the pieces until they're pliable.

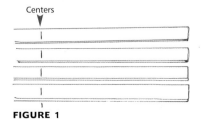

Centers

FIGURE 1

Weaving the Base

The base is a 2/2 twill (over 2, under 2). Lay four stakes horizontally with the centers aligned (figure 1). Number them 1 to 4 (mentally or physically), with number 1 closest to you. Placing the center marks above the #4 horizontal stake, weave the next four stakes vertically, to the right of the center marks on the horizontal pieces in the following pattern:

1) under 1 and 2, over 3 and 4

2) under 2 and 3, over 1 and 4

3) under 3 and 4, over 1 and 2

4) under 1 and 4, over 2 and 3

Weave the first 4 rows of the pattern to the right of the center marks. Repeat the pattern until half the vertical stakes are in place to the right of the center marks. Two stakes are woven to the left of the center marks. Row 1 on the left is a repeat of row 4 on the right, and row 2 is a repeat of row 3, etc. The

stakes to the left are simply in a reverse pattern of the ones to the right (figure 2). Finished, there should be eight pieces to the right of the center and eight to the left.

Now, weave the remaining horizontal pieces, four more below the center marks and eight above. If you still have problems with the twill pattern, turn the base $1/4$ turn. Repeat the weaving pattern of the four now vertical stakes (1 to 4) to the right and reversed (4 to 1) to the left until the base is finished (figure 3).

Framing the Base

The first row of weaving is a start-stop row using an $11/64$- or $3/16$-inch flat reed cut in half. The important thing about this row is that the weaver must move from outside to inside or inside to outside at the corners. The weaving pattern on this row only is over 2, under 2. The rest of the basket is over 3, under 2. Try starting at several different places, anticipating the corners. If 2/2 doesn't work, go over 1, under 1 or over 2, under 1 at the corners—whatever you have to do to make the transition from outside to inside or vise versa at the corners (figure 4). Do not allow the weaver to flip over at the corner. Rather, make it go about $1/8$-inch beyond the edge of the last stake and bend the weaver back on itself, making a crease before turning the corner. Refer to the illustration to see how to end the first row (figure 5).

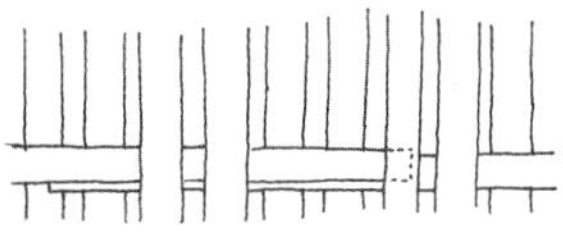

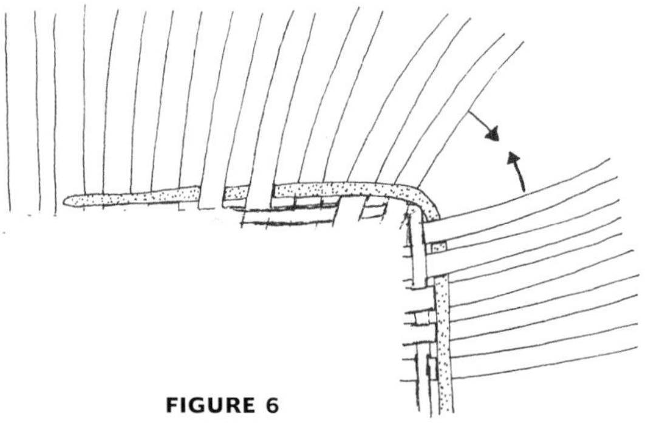

Weaving the Sides

Turn the base over so the right side is up. You're now weaving on the outside of the basket and will continue to for the entire basket. Begin with $11/64$-inch flat-oval reed that has been tapered, starting on the side opposite you. Weave over 3, under 2, etc., the rest of the basket. As you weave, work the stakes toward the corner in order to fill the corners and achieve a sunburst of stakes (figure 6). All the corners should be filled by the sixth row around (figure 7).

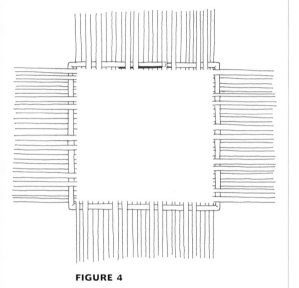

FIGURE 4

FIGURE 5

FIGURE 6

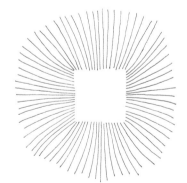

FIGURE 7. Sunburst. Not an exact count of spokes

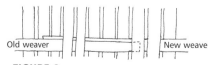

Old weaver   New weaver

FIGURE 8

Leave the base lying flat as you weave around for at least eight rows. After the eight rows, lift the basket and hold it with the stakes pointing away from you and continue to weave from the outside. The sides will begin to go up immediately almost on their own, so be careful they don't go up too fast.

As you weave around the basket, the over 3 moves over 1 stake each row, making the pattern spiral up the basket sides. When you need to add a weaver, change to a different width (with the end tapered to match the size you were using). Add another piece, starting the new one behind a stake before the old one runs out (figure 8). Weave with both of them for several stakes and continue with the new one, ending the old one behind a stake. Consult the pattern options below to decide which widths to use and in what order.

Reversing the Pattern

To reverse the weaving direction, you must make an intentional mistake in the same place in each row, which will cause the weaving pattern to shift visually (but you will continue to weave in the same direction). For instance, if you're weaving right-handed (to the right around the basket) and the weaving pattern is moving to the right, when you make the mistake, you will continue to weave right-handed around the basket, but the weaving pattern will begin to move to the left. On a 16 x 16 stake basket, the mistake is over 2, under 1. When you've woven as far as you want in one direction, and there's enough weaver remaining to go around the basket two times, taper the weaver so it's almost thread like.

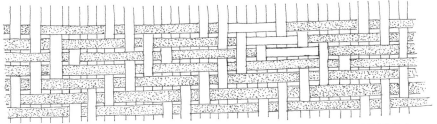

FIGURE 9

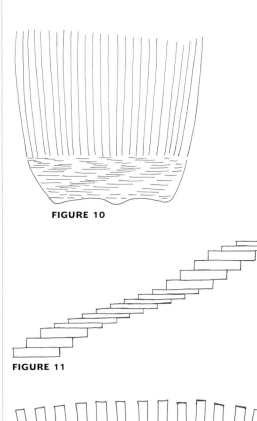

FIGURE 10

FIGURE 11

FIGURE 12. Inside view

Near the end of the second round, make the mistake, which will reverse the pattern. Add a new weaver that's tapered just as thin as the other one was for at least two more rows. This way the point of the pattern, formed when it reversed, looks more defined because of the very skinny weaver. The weaving pattern is shown moving to the right, then the mistake row and two more rows with the pattern reversed, showing the mistake still being made (figure 9). Notice that the mistake is technically in the same place every row, but the same place moves over one stake every row. If you have trouble knowing when to make the mistake, put a string or twist tie around the first stake in the over 2 the first time you do it and move it every row to help you spot the correct place.

Note: On a 19 x 19 stake basket, the mistake is either over 4, under 3 or under 4, over 3. Use whichever works for you.

Weave, making the mistake with the pattern reversed as far as you want. When you want to make the pattern reverse to the right again, do not make the mistake any more. Simply return to the regular over 3, under 2 pattern instead of making the mistake.

The shape of the basket is coming together (figure 10). You may reverse as many times as you want, but the undulation shows more clearly with larger areas moving in one direction. The undulation is achieved by changing from a wide weaver (7mm perhaps) to a very thin one ($^{11}/_{64}$ inch, cut in half) for several rows (figure 11). Remember to taper the wider weaver to the size of the smaller one when changing widths.

If you want the neck of the basket to decrease in diameter as the example does, push in on the stakes when you want to decrease and apply a little extra tension on the weaver.

When you are within 2 inches of the ends of the stakes, taper the weaver the width it was when you began weaving and stop directly above the starting place (figure 12).

Rimming the Basket

Soak a piece of $^1/_2$-inch half-round reed that is long enough to reach around the rim once and overlap 2 to 3 inches. Place it on the basket and mark the area of overlap. Remove it from the basket and, with a knife or plane, shave half the thickness from the top of one piece and half from the bottom of the

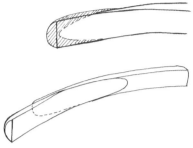

FIGURE 13

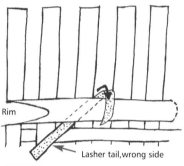

Rim

Lasher tail, wrong side

FIGURE 14

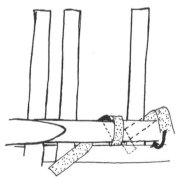

FIGURE 15. Outside view

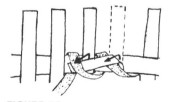

FIGURE 16

other, so when they're overlapped, the thickness will be equal to that of a single thickness of half-round reed (figure 13). Dampen the ends of the stakes and a lasher. Taper one end of the lasher for about 6 inches and place the lasher behind a stake, with the wrong side of the stake and lasher touching. Leave about 1 inch of lasher sticking out to the left, and angle the lasher from lower left to upper right behind the stake. The lasher comes to the outside of the basket between the stake it is behind and the next stake on the right. Place the rim piece against the outside of the stakes just at the top of the weaving. The beveled end of the rim should be placed just to the left of the stake that has the lasher behind it (figure 14).

Take the lasher over the top of the rim, around and under the bottom, back to the inside of the basket through the same space between stakes (figure 15). Pull down on the lasher inside the basket to seat the rim firmly at the top of the weaving. Bend the stake the lasher went behind down to the right over against the inside of the basket.

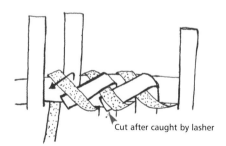

Cut after caught by lasher

FIGURE 17. Inside view

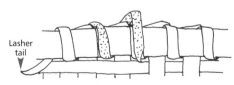

Lasher tail

FIGURE 18. Outside view

Bring the lasher up to the next right space between stakes, catching the bent stake as you do so (figure 16). After the stake has been folded over and caught by the lasher, it can be cut (figure 17).

Continue this process until you reach the start. The folded over stakes should lie flat against the inside of the basket. Pull very hard on the lasher. It should bind the bent-over stakes to the rim as tightly as possible. At the point where the ends of the rim must overlap, you'll only have one stake left standing. Thin about 6 inches of the lasher nearest the basket to prevent lumps as the end of the lashing overlaps the beginning. Pull on the starting end to tighten the beginning of the lashing. Trace the beginning of the lashing, duplicating each wrap exactly. You'll have to raise the bent-over stakes to feed the end of the lashing under them (figure 18).

After you have duplicated three or four wraps around the rim, cut the lasher as it emerges from under a folded-over stake. Trim the beginning of the lasher.

Acknowledgments

I am grateful to the many basket makers who have shared their talents and ideas with me, and for their inspiration and guidance. A very special thank you to my partner, Carolyn Kemp; to Judy Wobbleton, Dianne Kennedy, Judy K. Wilson, Suzanne Moore, Jim and Jimmie Kent, and Tonny Stubblefield for their generosity of time and talents. Thanks to Suzanne Moore, at North Carolina Basketworks, who provided the materials on page 9, and many thanks to all the other people who contributed to this book. Your help has been invaluable to me.

Glossary

AGING. The process that occurs when a basket turns dark from natural environmental elements.

ARROW. Two rows of weaving that form an arrow pattern. Consists of one row of regular weave, a step-up, a reverse weave, and ending.

ASH SPLINTS. Strips of ash that are thinned enough to use for stakes or weavers.

AWL. A tool resembling an ice pick used for opening spaces and making holes in reed.

BAR STITCH. A coiling stitch made by going into the same hole a second time. A perpendicular stitch.

BASE. The bottom of a basket; woven mat.

BEVEL. To cut a square edge to a sloping edge; scarf.

BINDER CANE. Cane that is wider than regular strand cane; used recently to lash basket rims in place.

BI-SPOKES. Extra or added spokes, inserted beside the original ones.

BOW-KNOT EAR. A four-point lashing ear, wrapped only once and "tied" in front.

BRAIDED GOD'S EYE. A four-point lashing like the regular God's Eye except it is interwoven and appears braided to the eye; a woven God's Eye.

BRAIDED HANDLE. Any of several different methods of interweaving the reed around the handle; specifically, the wheat braid.

BRAKE. A short piece of reed woven alternately above the beginning of a weaver to hold it in place.

BUTT. To bring the ends of any two pieces together, flush against each other.

CANE. The outer peel of rattan, used in weaving as an embellishment and on chair bottoms.

CHAIN PAIRING. The same as pairing or twined arrows.

CHASE WEAVE. A method of weaving with two weavers at once. Continuous weaving over an even number of stakes. The weaver moves first, and the chaser (the other weaver) follows alternately.

COIL. One row of waling that ends with a step-up and a lock.

COILING. A weaving technique using an inner core that is wrapped solidly with a smaller thread.

CONTINUOUS WEAVE. Weaving done over an odd number of weave stakes.

D HANDLE. A basket handle that continues across the bottom of the basket and that, turned on its side, resembles the letter D.

DIAGONAL WEAVE. A method of weaving in which the weave elements interweave with themselves. Also called diagonal plaiting and oblique weaving.

DIAMOND STITCH. A coiling stitch that has first a row of overcast stitch to the right and then a row of overcast stitch to the left, forming a diamond design.

DOUBLE-BOTTOM. A method of construction in which one base is woven and a second (woven) one is placed on top of the first.

DYEING. Coloring reed with any number of natural or commercial dyes.

EAR. Weaving or lashing done at the intersecting point of the rim and handle that holds the two pieces securely. Lashing into which the ribs are inserted. Loops that join a swing handle to the basket.

EMBELLISHMENT. Any decorative treatment done to the handle or body of a basket that is not essential to its construction.

FANNY. The twin, gizzard-shaped bottom of an egg basket; buttocks.

FILLING IN. On some ribbed baskets a wedge-shaped area remains unwoven when the rim is full; it must be filled in by some type of back-and-forth weaving; also called packing.

FIVE-POINT LASHING. A lashing (ear) done around any five intersecting pieces.

FRAME. The support (usually wood) around which the basket is woven.

FRENCH RANDING. A strong diagonal randing pattern that uses short rods (weavers) which are begun at the base one at a time.

GOD'S EYE. A four-point lashing; ear.

GRAPEVINE. A vine used for weaving baskets and handles.

HAIRS. The splinters from the reed that usually occur from overuse, to be clipped or singed when the basket is finished.

HANDLE. The part of the basket by which it is carried.

HONEYSUCKLE. A wild vine used for weaving baskets, smaller than grapevine.

HOOP. Ring or piece of wood shaped into a circle; machine or handmade, present in ribbed baskets.

INDIAN WEAVE. A method of continuous weaving over an even number of stakes/spokes, adjusted each round by weaving over two spokes so the alternate over/under pattern resumes.

JAPANESE WEAVE. Weaving over two spokes and under one.

KINKING. Making a permanent bend to a piece of willow.

LASHER. The piece of reed that wraps around and secures all the rim pieces together.

LASHING. The act of wrapping all the rim pieces or wrapping the ear; the pieces of reed used to wrap are also referred to as lashing.

LOOP. An ear that holds the swing handle and pushes down into the basket.

LOSING A LASHER. A means of hiding the end of the reed in the rim or in the weaving.

MAT. The woven base of a flat basket.

NOTCH. The indented space on a push-in handle made to fit under the rim and prevent the handle from pulling out.

OAK SPLINTS. Strips of oak wood thinned enough to use as stakes or weavers; also called splits.

OBLIQUE WEAVE. Diagonal plaiting or weaving.

OSIER. Any of various willows that have tough, flexible twigs or branches which are used for wicker work.

OVERCAST STITCH. A coiling stitch taking the needle around the bundle of pine needles from front to back.

PACKING. Pushing each row snugly down beside the previously woven row. A method of building up or filling-in an area by turning one spoke sooner each row.

PAIRING. Twining.

PLAIN WEAVE. Over-one, under-one weave; randing.

PLAITED. Woven.

PRE-FORM. Shaped or formed before being used.

RANDING. A simple over-under weaving with a single weaver and an odd number of stakes.

RAPPING IRON. An iron tool used for rapping or beating the rows of willow work so it will stay in place.

RATTAN. A climbing palm (vine) from which reed is made.

REED. The inner core of rattan that has been cut into either flat, round, flat oval, half round, or oval shapes; used for baskets and furniture.

RIB. The round or oval pieces that extend from one side of the basket to the other and form the basic skeleton.

RIM. The pieces, inside and outside, that fit over the top row of weaving to form an edge and give stability to the sides.

RIM FILLER. A piece of round reed, sea grass or other suitable material that goes between and on top of the two rim pieces.

SCARF. A joint in which the ends of any two pieces are cut so they overlap each other and join firmly.

SCARFING. To join by cutting the two end pieces, usually beveled or on a slant, so they fit together smoothly.

SEA GRASS. A twisted rope of grass suitable for weaving.

SHAPER. An instrument used for shaving away wood; a small rasp.

SIGHT. To look at a basket frame and determine the rib lengths to give the desired shape; to eyeball.

SLATH. The part of the basket in which 4 or more elements are interwoven to start the basket base.

SLEWING. A wickerwork weave done with two or more paired weavers in a randing pattern.

SLYPE. A long, mitered (pointed) cut.

SPIRAL. The result of twill weaving (under two, over two) continuously over an odd number of spokes. A gradually widening curve winding away from a base to create a design.

SPLICE. The place where two pieces of wood, having been scarfed, overlap.

SPLINE. A wedge-shaped reed made primarily for use with pressed cane; also used to make loops and handles in baskets.

SPOKE. The elements, usually round reed, which form the rigid framework of a basket.

STAINING. A term that has come to mean coloring reed to give it an aged look.

STAKE. Pieces of the woven mat (base) which are upsett and become the upright elements.

STEPPING-UP. A term used in twill weaving meaning to start the next row one stake to the right (or left, as the case may be) of the starting point on the previous row.

STROKE. A movement of the weaver.

SWING HANDLE. A handle attached to a basket by means of a loop or protruding ear that allows it to swing freely from side to side.

THREE-POINT LASHING. The wrapping used to cover the intersecting point of any three elements.

THREE-ROD WALE. Inserting three weavers, each behind three consecutive stakes, with all three weaving, one at a time, over two and under one.

TRUE. To measure the woven base, making sure all sides are the correct length, adjusting if necessary and marking corners.

TUCKING IN. When the basket is woven, the outside stakes are pointed, bent over and tucked into the weaving on the inside of the basket; also called down staking.

TWILL. A method of weaving in which the weaver passes over and under the stakes two or more at a time.

TWINING. A method of weaving in which two weavers are used alternately in a twisting pattern in front of one spoke and behind one spoke.

UPSETT OR UPSTAKE. To bend the stakes up and over upon themselves (toward the base), creating a crease at the base of the stake.

WALE. A method of weaving in which the left weaver is always moved over the weavers and spokes to the right, behind one and out to the front.

WARP. The stationary, usually more rigid, element in weaving.

WEAVER. The fiber, often reed, used as the weft that moves over and under the stakes, spokes or ribs (warp).

WEFT. The more flexible weaving element that is interlaced around the warp.

WHEAT STITCH. A coiling stitch that is a combination of the overcast stitch and the bar stitch.

WICKER. From the Swedish vikker, meaning "willow" or "osier." Generally refers to any round, shoot-like material used for basket making.

WICKERWORK. A basketry technique that employs round, vertical stakes or spokes, and round weavers which are woven perpendicular to the spokes.

WILLOW. An osier which yields its long, slender branches for use in basket weaving.

WISTERIA. A climbing vine that is particularly flexible and used for basket weaving and for making basket handles.

Contributing Designers

Sosse Baker

Sosse has become known for her double-weave reproductions, concentrating mainly on the intricate patterns of the Chitimacha Native Americans. Her exceptional work can be found in many galleries, including her own in Chester, Connecticut.

Bonnie Gale

Known for her extraordinary willow work, Bonnie is originally from England. She has been a professional willow basketmaker for the past twenty years and is proprietor of English Basketry Willows and founder of the American Willow Growers Network. Her website is www.msu.edu/user/shermanh/galab.

Genie Jackson

Genie has been making baskets since 1982 and teaching since 1984. She is particularly well known for her favorite techniques—wooden handles and braided round-reed borders. She divides her time between Florida and Michigan.

Dianne Kennedy

Dianne owns Bungalowe Baskets in Asheville, North Carolina, and specializes in plaited-cloth handles and space-dyed reed. An active member of the North Carolina Basketmakers Association and other professional organizations, she teaches workshops around the country. Her website is www.bungalowebasics.com.

Jimmie Kent

Miss Jimmie has been making baskets for many, many years and, as her husband Mr. Jim will tell you, she is the happiest when sharing her knowledge with others. She is president of the North Carolina Basketmakers Association.

Dianne Masi

Dianne lives in North Carolina near the ocean, where she collects many of her basket "starts." After working in many mediums, she feels at home with pine-needle and gourd art.

Joan Moore

A veteran basketmaker, Joan has given the basketmaking world many wonderful designs over the years. Always the innovator, Joan was an early student of Grace Kabel. She lives and works in Highland, Michigan.

Judith Olney

Judith is from Rowley, Massachusetts, and her work is widely known as most creative and inspired. Best known for her unusual basketry shapes and techniques, she has shared her love of basketmaking with thousands around the world.

Joel Simpson

Joel is an aerospace engineer with as big a need for creating with his hands as for working from a desk. He also designs and builds furniture, buildings, and boats in Virginia.

Kathy Tessler

Kathy is a self-taught basket artist from Saginaw, Michigan. She has become best known for her double-wall technique. She teaches workshops around the country and is president of the Association of Michigan Basketmakers. Her work is inspirational to basketmakers everywhere.

Judy K. Wilson

Judy is a self-taught basket genius. First known for her uniquely beautiful polychrome egg baskets, she is now quite well known for her work with intricately twined and coiled patterns in waxed linen and silk. Visit her website at www.judywilson.com.

Judy Wobbleton

Judy began weaving as a hobby, with no thought that it would take her on a 22-year journey of designing, teaching, and weaving baskets. She is co-founder of the North Carolina Basketmakers with Lyn Siler.

Metric Conversion Chart

INCHES	METRIC (MM/CM)	INCHES	METRIC (MM/CM)	INCHES	METRIC (MM/CM)	INCHES	METRIC (MM/CM)	INCHES	METRIC (MM/CM)	INCHES	METRIC (MM/CM)
1/4	6 mm	1	2.5 cm	8 1/2	21.6 cm	16	40.6 cm	23 1/2	59.7 cm	31	78.7 cm
1/8	3 mm	1 1/2	3.8 cm	9	22.9 cm	16 1/2	41.9 cm	24	61 cm	31 1/2	80 cm
3/16	5 mm	2	5 cm	9 1/2	24.1 cm	17	43.2 cm	24 1/2	62.2 cm	32	81.3 cm
1/4	6 mm	2 1/2	6.4 cm	10	25.4 cm	17 1/2	44.5 cm	25	63.5 cm	32 1/2	82.6 cm
5/16	8 mm	3	7.6 cm	10 1/2	26.7 cm	18	45.7 cm	25 1/2	64.8 cm	33	83.8 cm
3/8	9.5 mm	3 1/2	8.9 cm	11	27.9 cm	18 1/2	47 cm	26	66 cm	33 1/2	85 cm
7/16	1.1 cm	4	10.2 cm	11 1/2	29.2 cm	19	48.3 cm	26 1/2	67.3 cm	34	86.4 cm
1/2	1.3 cm	4 1/2	11.4 cm	12	30.5 cm	19 1/2	49.5 cm	27	68.6 cm	34 1/2	87.6 cm
9/16	1.4 cm	5	12.7 cm	12 1/2	31.8 cm	20	50.8 cm	27 1/2	69.9 cm	35	88.9 cm
5/8	1.6 cm	5 1/2	14 cm	13	33 cm	20 1/2	52 cm	28	71.1 cm	35 1/2	90.2 cm
11/16	1.7 cm	6	15.2 cm	13 1/2	34.3 cm	21	53.3	28 1/2	72.4 cm	36	91.4 cm
3/4	1.9 cm	6 1/2	16.5 cm	14	35.6 cm	21 1/2	54.6	29	73.7 cm	36 1/2	92.7 cm
13/16	2.1 cm	7	17.8 cm	14 1/2	36.8 cm	22	55 cm	29 1/2	74.9 cm	37	94.0 cm
7/8	2.2 cm	7 1/2	19 cm	15	38.1 cm	22 1/2	57.2 cm	30	76.2 cm	37 1/2	95.3 cm
15/16	2.4 cm	8	20.3 cm	15 1/2	39.4 cm	23	58.4 cm	30 1/2	77.5 cm	38	96.5 cm

Index